The Art of Classroom Inquiry
A HANDBOOK FOR TEACHER-RESEARCHERS

REVISED EDITION

The Art of Classroom Inquiry
A HANDBOOK FOR TEACHER-RESEARCHERS

Ruth Shagoury Hubbard & Brenda Miller Power

HEINEMANN • PORTSMOUTH, NH

HEINEMANN
A division of Reed Elsevier Inc.
361 Hanover Street
Portsmouth, NH 03801–3912
www.heinemann.com

Offices and agents throughout the world

The authors and publisher wish to thank those who have generously given permission to reprint borrowed material:

Figure 4–7 from "Unofficial Literacy in a Sixth-Grade Classroom" by Ruth Hubbard. *Language Arts* 65 (2). Copyright © 1988 by the National Council of Teachers of English. Reprinted by permission.

Figure 4–11 Created by Jill Ostrow.

Excerpt by Bill Talbot from "Writing for Learning in School: Is It Possible?" by Bill Talbot. *Language Arts* 67 (1). Copyright © 1990 by the National Council of Teachers of English. Reprinted by permission.

Excerpt by Lyn Wilkinson from "When Teaching's as Exciting as Christmas!" by Lyn Wilkinson. *Language Arts* 66 (7). Copyright © 1989 by the National Council of Teachers of English. Reprinted by permission.

Library of Congress Cataloging-in-Publication Data
Hubbard, Ruth, 1950–
    The art of classroom inquiry : a handbook for teacher-researchers / Ruth Shagoury
    Hubbard, Brenda Miller Power.—New ed.
        p.   cm.
    Includes bibliographical references and index.
    ISBN 0-325-00543-5
    1. Education—Research—United States—Handbooks, manuals, etc.   2. Teaching—
United States—Case Studies.   I. Power, Brenda Miller.   II. Title.
LB1028.25.U6H83 2003
370'.7'2—dc21   2003006323

Editor: Leigh Peake
Production: Elizabeth Valway
Interior design: Jenny Jensen Greenleaf
Cover design: Jenny Jensen Greenleaf
Composition: Publishers' Design and Production Services, Inc.
Manufacturing: Steve Bernier

Printed in the United States of America on acid-free paper
07   **RRD** 10 9 8 7

For the people who first taught us
that learning comes from taking risks:

Charles and Helen Shagoury
and
Patrick and Dolores Miller

Contents

Preface to the Revised Edition

Ten years ago we published the first edition of *The Art of Classroom Inquiry*. The book grew out of work early in our careers with novice teacher-researchers. There were many books and articles praising teacher research, but few at that time showed teachers how to begin. We created a modest handbook that we hoped would be that starting point for new teacher-researchers. We have been gratified over the years by teachers' positive response to our book.

While you will notice a number of changes within this revised edition, we hope you will recognize that the philosophy and structure remain the same. We wanted to keep most of the core examples and strategies that have weathered the last decade well, as well as the compact and narrow scope of the original text.

We find ourselves dismayed with some new editions of books we've treasured over the years that are expanded or so greatly changed as to become wholly new texts. These books bring to mind gracefully aging actresses who go into a panic over a few wrinkles. Plastic surgery renders them unrecognizable—with looks more suited to a witness protection program than to a new film role. We didn't want to make the same mistake with our book. The newest references aren't always the best references, and we knew that many aspects of the original text resonate with readers and needed to be preserved.

At the same time, the field of teacher research has grown and flourished during the past ten years. With this growth has come new insight, many wonderful new voices, and subtle changes in the teacher-researcher movement, which we've tried to represent here. Perhaps the biggest change in the last decade is the emergence of strong communities of teacher researchers. When we wrote the first edition, many teacher-researchers toiled alone, with little support from administrators and the larger education community. Now teacher research is often supported by administrators, and many school leaders undertake field-based projects of their own. Preservice teacher education programs across the country help intern teachers learn to be teacher-researchers right from the start. Foundations, universities, and service organizations support research through grant programs, awards, and acknowledgment of teacher research as a viable and vibrant new tradition.

But we can't publish a new edition of *The Art of Classroom Inquiry* without acknowledging the tough times teachers face if they are of a mind to question their teaching, curricula, or accepted practices in education. We write these words in the midst of the testing and standards movement. Some may say that the fact that teacher research isn't necessarily "reliable or replicable" renders it irrelevant. We believe teacher research matters more than ever because it gives teachers a touchstone for their beliefs, a firm foundation for practices, and a haven to return to whenever they wonder if their questions matter.

We hope this revised edition conveys the passion many teachers feel about their research. We believe every educational research methodology has value, as well as the potential to inform and inspire the work of students and teachers. But teacher research is personal. The investment we make in it shapes and colors all the stories from our classrooms, and the stories we take in from other teacher-researchers. As Jeanne Henry (1995) writes:

> In traditional qualitative research, only those with no emotional investment in the events being observed can describe them "objectively," which is meant to mean "accurately." But someone this detached tells only part of the story. I have done research in other teachers' classrooms and have found myself going home, notes in hand, thinking, "Damn, he really balled that lesson up. Bet he doesn't sleep a wink tonight." So what attracts me to teacher research is that I do care about my students and my teaching, and I think that emotional stake is part of the story my research needs to tell. My lack of detachment as a teacher-researcher does not allow me to separate the knowledge of a failed technique from the pain of that failure. When I am up all night, readers of my research are going to hear about it. And when it looks like I am doing something right, well, tee hee hee. And one

thing an outside researcher cannot do that I will is show you how I corrected the mistakes I saw myself make with that first class. (109–10)

Here is the revised edition, filled with the stories of these up-all-night teacher-researchers—warts and all. We are thankful to the hundreds of teachers over the past decade who have chosen to invest time, wisdom, and passion into their research. They have been our teachers as well as our research informants. Any improvements from the first edition belong to them.

Introduction

If we knew what it was we were doing, it would not be called research, would it?
—Albert Einstein

Teachers throughout the world are developing professionally by becoming teacher-researchers, a wonderful new breed of artists-in-residence. Using our own classrooms as laboratories and our students as collaborators, we are changing the way we work with students as we look at our classrooms systematically through research.

Over the past twenty years, a wealth of materials has been published about teacher research. Teachers have presented their findings in major journals and argued eloquently about the value of teacher research; however, most of these accounts lack specific information about how teachers become researchers. This book evolved from our work with hundreds of teacher-researchers as we explored the research craft. We struggled together to figure out the kinds of interviews that work best in different research studies; how to collect data in the midst of wholehearted teaching; and how to cull information from hundreds of pages of material for a brief, publishable article. This handbook describes the process of doing classroom research and provides many effective research techniques.

If you are already aware of the power of teacher research, this handbook may help you begin to see yourself as a teacher-researcher. But we hope it will do more than that. We hope the techniques and research activities that follow will enlist you as a member of the growing worldwide network of teacher-researchers.

Although many of us have been conducting informal classroom research as part of our teaching for years, we often do not think of ourselves as researchers. Julie Ford shares her changing notions of the definition of researcher:

> When I think of research, I think of the big *R* type with long hours in the library, notes that could fill a novel, and a bibliography several pages long. I think of tension and stress lurking in the shadows. Feeling as I do about *Research*, the thought of conducting it in my classroom didn't curl my toes. But as I read the research [relating to classroom-based research], I felt as though a door was beginning to open. My definition of research took a turn, and that familiar twinge of anxiety didn't come rushing forward.
>
> I began to think of "wonderings" I had regarding my students and my teaching. I pondered ways of pursuing these wonderings, feeling I was capable of doing some groundwork studies. I could look at my own initial research, related to my own very familiar environment. I didn't need to read for hours about studies conducted by *Researchers* elsewhere and then connect the findings to my room. My students and I could participate together, learning about our own classroom.

When Julie and other teachers like us read the research accounts of our fellow teachers, we realize that our wonderings are worth pursuing. By becoming researchers, we hope to find strategies to develop more principled classroom practice. But where to begin? And how to get past the internal critics who lurk in the back of our minds repeating, "Who are we to assume we have the ability to become researchers or to answer our own questions about teaching through research?"

Our answer is a resounding, "Who better to do this?" We teacher-researchers bring to our work an important element that outside researchers lack—a sense of place, a sense of history in the schools in which we work. Because of our presence over time at our research sites, we teachers bring a depth of awareness to our data that outside researchers cannot begin to match. We know our schools, our students, our colleagues, and our learning agendas. Our research is grounded in this rich resource base.

And while we expect our research to move us to a better understanding of our students and to better practice, we don't expect the research to shift the ground beneath us. Glenda Bissex (1996), one of the founders of the modern teacher-research movement, remembers vividly how disappointed some teacher-researchers were when she met with them about their findings at the time they first considered what they had learned from teacher research. It was only after continued reflection that they saw the full impact on their professional lives:

> I remember getting together with my first group of Case Study students—teachers who were doing research in their own classrooms—at the end of winter, after they'd been gathering data for months. As we went around the table where we sat and each spoke, there was an accumulating disappointment that they had not arrived at any monumental conclusions and a relief to find that others had the same experience. . . . I don't know that any of the dozens of teacher-researchers I've worked with have felt they came up with earth-shattering conclusions. I also can't think of one who felt that she or he hadn't learned something from doing the study. If they learned less than they sought to learn, they also learned more; for they learned how to observe; they learned "why" they were teaching the way they were; they learned to reinterpret some events through seeing them from their students' points of view; and they learned, among other things, that they could trust their own powers of learning. (182–83)

As teacher-researcher Peggy Groves reflects: "The difference between my recent classroom research and my usual classroom practices is that for my research I kept notes about what I did, I looked more closely at what happened, I asked myself harder questions, and I wrote about it all. These differences took a lot of time, but I think I'm a better teacher for it. And maybe even a better writer."

We began collecting materials for this book almost twenty years ago, when we realized there were far more research findings published than accounts of the process of becoming a teacher-researcher. For example, when we read an account of a teacher-researcher successfully analyzing her reading group procedures, we may find it hard to imagine her as a beginning researcher. The fluid narrative may include some awkward questions about her teaching practices, but it rarely includes questions about research methods. The novice researcher may have little sense of how the teacher-researcher got from there to here—from the struggle to find and frame a research question to a clear and thoughtful presentation of her findings.

In our work as teacher-researchers, we have learned that this struggle is a natural one. You will see the line between teaching and research blur often as you read many examples of teachers doing research in this handbook because teaching and research have many of the same skills at their core. Some of these skills were described by Charles Kettering in writing about research:

> Research is a high-hat word that scares a lot of people. It needn't. It's rather simple. Essentially research is nothing but a state of mind . . . a friendly, welcoming attitude toward change . . . going out to look for change instead of waiting for it to come.
>
> Research is an effort to do things better and not to be caught asleep at the switch. It is the problem-solving mind as contrasted with the let-well-enough-alone mind. It is the tomorrow mind instead of the yesterday mind. (Kettering, in Boyd 1961, 82)

If you have a problem-solving mind as a teacher, you are ready for research. If you welcome change and growth with your students, research can have a place in your professional life. The educational world is certainly in need of the tomorrow minds of teacher-researchers!

This is particularly true with the growing diversity in today's schools. At a recent education convention, noted educational activist Lisa Delpit was asked how it is possible to prepare teachers for the wide range of cultures, abilities, and talents that they will meet in any given classroom. She listed three key ingredients: The first is to be humble and recognize that you have much to learn from your students and their communities. Second, approach your teaching always with a sense of inquiry, framing questions about your students and their needs to guide your teaching. Finally, have a willingness to share your story. Other teachers need to know what you have learned and how you have gained your wisdom.

These three ingredients are the basis of teacher research. We approach our classrooms with humility and a sense of inquiry and wonder—and we make a commitment to add our wisdom to a knowledge base that educates others about the realities of teaching and learning. Teacher-researcher Tim Gillespie (2000) claims that our teaching narratives have become increasingly important:

> We need to tell our stories, because true classroom narratives offer an important alternative to other prevalent modes of discourse about school life. There are competing narratives out there about this profession of ours that are dangerous, and classroom stories resist and complicate them. (2)

Debates about the changing roles of teachers and the value of their research persist. The teacher-as-researcher movement is not without controversy. Those of us who believe in the power of teacher research have been constrained by conservative definitions of university researchers and federal policymakers. These debates are entirely predictable, if only because universities and public schools still have different beliefs when ascribing value to research, as Michael Patton (2002) notes:

> Debates about the meaningfulness, rigor, significance, and relevance of various approaches to research are the regular features of university life. On the whole, within universities and among scholars, the status hierarchy in science attributes the highest status to basic research . . . and virtually no status to formative and action research. The status hierarchy is reversed in real-world settings, where people with problems attribute the greatest significance to action and formative research that can help them solve their problems in a timely way. (223)

Teachers and many researchers who work in university settings will probably never fully agree on the value of different types of research. Ongoing debates about the value of teacher research remind us of an anecdote about Picasso:

> A story is told of a French railroad passenger who, upon learning that his neighbor on the next seat was Picasso, began to grouse and grumble about modern art, saying that it was not a faithful representation of reality. Picasso demanded to know what *was* a faithful representation of reality. The man produced a wallet-sized photo and said, "There! That's a real picture—that's what my wife really looks like." Picasso looked at it carefully from several angles, turning it up and down and sideways, and said, "She's awfully small. And flat." (Nachmanovitch 1990, 118)

Like Picasso, teacher-researchers are heading a revolution in modern art—the modern art of teaching. We are looking at research possibilities from new angles. We are redefining our roles, rejecting the small and flat impoverished models of research that attempt to "turn classroom inquiry into a pseudo-scientific horserace" (Atwell 1991).

We are also declaring the work of fellow teacher-researchers as invaluable, regardless of the value other researchers and policymakers may place on it.

Teacher-researcher Jane Doan writes about case studies, arguing passionately for trusting our values as teacher-researchers:

> The need to prove that case studies are valid in the scientific community stems from teachers' basic insecurities. We are forever trying to prove ourselves. Why can't we believe in ourselves enough to say that case studies are the way to do educational research? No explaining, no defending of ourselves, no worrying about accountability! Just, this is what we are doing. This is who we are.

This new stance is compatible not only with our vision of research but also with a vision of what teachers can be. This vision is not of passive teachers who perpetuate the system as it is, but of teachers who see how the system can be changed through their research.

"The growing awareness of the political 'stuff' that is inherent to teacher research is probably what stuck with me the most," reflects Gail Parson when she tells about her experience at a teacher-research institute. "I remember Mary Kay, sitting forward in her seat, jabbing at the air with one finger like she does, and saying with that enigmatic half-smile, 'It's a whole different thing to go to a school board or a curriculum committee and say, Based on my research. . . .' "

We think that once you embark on the challenge that is teacher research, you will be hooked. As Gail notes:

> Somebody had to stick her neck out and try it . . . and we did. It makes me appreciate what's happening now even more. The study I did . . . remains a huge pile of "stuff"—the compost for one rough article, and a source of more and more questions I have about how adolescents think and process information and make meaning for themselves. I showed the suitcase full of [copies of] journals, audiotapes, and field notes to a professor friend who said, "You did this as a working teacher??!!!" Damn straight, sez I. Want to meet a few of my *"working teacher"* friends? Wait till you see what they're up to!

We invite you to meet some of our working teacher friends and enter into the growing community of teachers who are testing the limits of educational research. Wait until you see what we're up to!

Research, like teaching, is a complicated and messy process. You cannot divide the process into neat linear steps, no matter how hard you try. We had some trouble constructing this text about the process of doing research, and it may help you to see some of the bones that are sticking out in this skeleton.

Books are linear, but the research process is _not_. As researchers, we do not necessarily start with a question and then move through data-collection procedures and designs to our findings and publication in a lockstep fashion. Nor do we wait to analyze data until all our data are collected; we are analyzing, writing, and reflecting right from the beginning. We urge you to use this book in the ways that will most benefit your own process. You may want to skip around; how you read this book should be based on where you are in your development as a teacher-researcher.

For example, if you have problems with writing, start with one of the last chapters, "Perishable Art: Writing Up Research." You will not be able to write down research notes or construct brief memos if you must first overcome an aversion to writing. In the same way, understanding data collection or research design will be difficult without a sense of the whole—how collection, analysis, and design can fit into your life as a classroom teacher.

We start with stories of beginning teacher-researchers and their struggles in "Try to Love the Questions Themselves: Finding and Framing a Research Question." This chapter takes you through the initial stages of deciding what to investigate in the classroom and how to frame the question so that information can be gathered effectively. Chapter 1 closes with some suggestions for getting started.

Chapter 2, "Form and Function: The Research Design," discusses the importance of designing the research to fit the area of investigation. You will read the stories of four teacher-researchers making decisions and solving problems as they refine their research designs.

In Chapter 3, "The Artist's Toolbox: Strategies for Data Collection," we detail the many ways to gather data in the midst of teaching. We share examples of the various ways that teachers log their data through field notes and teaching journals, as well as show strategies for collecting student samples, conducting interviews, and using the electronic media of videotaping and audiotaping to gather information.

Next, Chapter 4, "Pentimento: Strategies for Data Analysis," demystifies the process of making sense of that mountain of data. We present strategies for preparing data for analysis, narrowing the focus, isolating the important findings, and fleshing out the final categories.

In Chapter 5, "The Legacy of Distant Teachers: Creative Review of Literature," we discuss the implications of others' research on your findings. This chapter purposely follows data analysis, since a careful review of literature is most helpful _after_ categories are defined.

Chapter 6, "Perishable Art: Writing Up Research," takes you through the process of converting research into words for sharing with a wider audience. We suggest writing exercises and resources as well as a wide variety of outlets for published work. (These resources are extended in Appendix E.)

We discuss the importance of creating a teacher-research network and support group in the final chapter, "You Are Not Alone: Finding Support for Your Research." You will read tips from successful teacher-organizers for starting and maintaining these groups. We suggest strategies for writing proposals to fund research as well as smaller grants to fund classroom projects. Successful proposals and grants are included along with ideas for sources of funding.

There are several journals and websites that can aid teacher-researchers. We list these in Appendix E, "Resources for Publication."

We hope you enjoy the stories and research techniques of the teacher-researchers that follow as much as we enjoyed compiling them.

chapter one

Try to Love the Questions Themselves
Finding and Framing a Research Question

Always the more beautiful answer who asks the more beautiful question.
—*ee cummings*

The Dunne-Za, a branch of the Athabaskan tribe, say that a person who speaks from the authority of his or her own experience "little bit know something." Knowledge, the elders say, empowers a person to live in this world with intelligence and understanding (Ridington 1990). Dunne-Za men and women expect their children to gain power by observing the animals and natural forces around them through a series of quests called *vision quests*. Every person "knows something" from these experiences and from the stories that emerge from the quests.

The goals of teacher-researchers, like those of the Dunne-Za on vision quests, is to "little bit know something" about their students' abilities and learning strategies. New knowledge not only better enables teachers to understand students and their world but also empowers the learners themselves.

Teacher-researchers at all grade levels—from kindergarten to graduate level—are increasingly turning to qualitative or ethnographic research methods. Observational studies help the teacher understand the student's world from the *student's point of view* rather than from that of the teacher's own culture. Students are the informants in teacher research, helping us to learn both the recipes for behavior in their cultures and the learning strategies that they employ. And central to the role of informants is being an active collaborator in these research endeavors.

Teachers just beginning their own classroom research often feel overwhelmed; there is so much to study in their classrooms that they wonder how other teachers have known how to start. As Glenda Bissex writes, "A teacher-researcher may start out not with a hypothesis to test, but with a wondering to pursue" (1987, 3). All teachers have wonderings worth pursuing. Transforming wonderings into questions is the start of teacher research.

Finding the Question

Nothing shapes our research as much as the questions we ask. In the last few years, more teachers are investigating our own classrooms and with our own students, recognizing that finding and asking those questions are a natural—and vital—part of the way that we make sense of the teaching and learning in our classrooms.

In qualitative research, the questions come from real-world observations and dilemmas. Here are some examples of the wonderings that teacher-researchers we know are pursuing:

- How do my students' questions change after participating in science talks?
- How do students in my multiage classroom develop spelling strategies?
- What happens when my students attempt peer mentoring?
- What is the range of participation among the boys in my class during reading workshop?
- What happens when my students independently solve math problems?
- What happens when middle school students with autism are given the opportunity to socialize with one another two to three times a week in a socialization lab?
- How do students communicate their mathematical thinking during whole-group discussions?
- How does a writing workshop affect students' sense of social responsibility in a second language class?
- What procedures or activities promote or encourage students to revise their writing?
- What problems does a preservice teacher solve as she begins to teach without her mentor teacher?
- What happens when eighth graders choose their own reading material in a reading workshop situation?

- What language occurs in mathematics learning and what role does it play?
- How do children resolve problems on their own in their improvisational dramatic play?
- How do teachers of writing change their instruction after participating in a writing institute?
- How do students evaluate the reading and writing of peers?

The questions these teachers chose to pursue arose out of their classroom concerns; they were important questions for their teaching.

Kathleen Reilly (1995), a high school English teacher, recalls the moment she began to frame the question that led to her changes in practice:

> I think I know when it happened. . . . I was in conference with Matthew, and he said the usual, "I can't write for you; you're too serious." Right then, part of me imagined what it would be like if I were not the only one to read and think about his writing. Teacher-researchers pay attention to the "what-ifs" that occur, and I have learned to let myself push a simple question like this to the end of the thought: What if I were not the only one to read and think about Matthew's writing? I wanted his energies directed to growth, not to figuring me out. What if I could show Matthew that what I see in his writing is not restricted to just my view? What if other readers made comments? Where are the other readers who can help convince Matthew that his writer's voice is strong, but he may have relied too much on humor and not enough on substance? At seventeen, he was certain that the only way to success was to psyche out the teacher. I had a hunch student writing could change if I were not the only reader. (50)

Because of this hunch, Kathleen spent a year investigating what happened when the principal, peers, and parents of her students became collaborators in assessment. She describes the year that she was involved in this research as the best year she'd had in a long time "because I saw the way my students responded to the attention, support, and gentle prodding of other readers" (Reilly 1995, 51).

First-grade teacher Christina Randall also used her writing to focus on concerns about her interactions with students. But her observations led to much different questions:

> Going to lunch is one of the many hassles faced with youngsters in a portable classroom. We need at least fifteen minutes to wash hands, put on outer gear, and

clean our room. Usually we are keeping some other class waiting. Last week the procedure was much the same. On our way into the main building they spy it. The line stops. "What's that?" "Is that a starfish?" "What's that starfish doing on top of the clam?" "Lookit! I just saw that clam thing open its shell." Questions are being asked faster than can possibly be answered. We are all fascinated with the saltwater aquarium. I reluctantly pull myself back from the tank with a "Let's go, gang. We can come back later to look at the aquarium." The questions continued after lunch and throughout the rest of the day. Within days the aquarium begins to show up in writing.

In creating a language-rich environment for young children, I have capitalized on the interest in the saltwater aquarium. We wrote a group story, went to research materials, and returned to the main building with observation logs in hand. Teachable moment? As a teacher in search of stimulating topics, I could hardly pass it up.

Teachable moment. Developmentally appropriate practice. Workshop approach. Cooperative learning. Least-restrictive environment. Strategy instruction.

Buzzwords suggest that the transition be made from focusing on how the child succeeds with the curriculum to how the curriculum succeeds with the child.

But is success determined by the products of tests or the processes observed and documented? If the curriculum is rich and diverse in language-building activities, what about remedial services like speech and language therapy? Do children need to be pulled out for remedial services to work on specific skills?

Like Christina, many teachers have to do some wandering to get to their wonderings. Often questions for research start with a feeling of tension. Christina wants to look beyond faddish buzzwords and rapid implementation of new teaching methods to try to figure out what is really going on with language development in her students and what this means for the systems of intervention established in schools. Kathleen wants to understand how to help her students move beyond writing to please her. This involved working with others beyond the walls of her classroom and letting go of her control as her students' only audience.

It is not surprising that the root word of question is *quest*. Teacher-researchers embark on a new kind of vision quest as they look for research topics in their classrooms. They want questions to research that can lead to a new vision of themselves as teachers and of their students as learners. These questions often involve seeing students in new ways.

Jack Campbell, a teacher-researcher from Fairbanks, Alaska, realized he needed to take a closer look at his students and their culture if he wanted to help them become better writers.

> This past year, I've watched Native writers become confused because of the way their writing has been edited. When they receive feedback, either from their response groups . . . or from me, sometimes they lose confidence because they take the criticism "personal." When these criticisms occur in their experience-based writing . . . they seem to interpret their writing as being ineffective. When a novice writer offers an essay on his or her personal experiences, and these in turn are criticized, perhaps for legitimate technical reasons, their writing voices lose authority and direction. The critiques, without explanations, become forms of cultural tyrannies.

As Jack thought about changing his teaching to meet the needs of his students, he wanted to be able to document how these strategies affected his students. He crafted his teaching dilemma into the following question: *How can Alaskan Native writers establish a stronger writing voice?*

Elsa Bro found herself wondering about "how students choose protective spaces within the classroom." As an intern teacher with just one month in the classroom, she turned her musings into questions: "What happens when I ask these students to get into groups?" she wrote in her teaching journal. "What are the effects of doing seating assignments? How might 'changing places' literally and figuratively benefit them?"

Natalie Goldberg (1990) advises writers to be specific:

> Not car, but Cadillac. Not fruit, but apple. Not bird, but wren. Not a codependent, neurotic man, but Harry, who runs to open the refrigerator for his wife, thinking she wants an apple, when she is headed for the gas stove to light her cigarette. . . . Get below the label and be specific to the person. (3)

Goldberg stresses that the best way to create a vivid and true picture with words is through specific, tangible, concrete images. The same can be said of a good teacher-research question.

All these teachers started with specific instances of tension in their classrooms—a lack of trust in conferences, an inability to get students to line up, hurt feelings when suggestions were made. As these teacher-researchers thought about these tensions, they began to focus on larger issues of culture, learning, and school structure. The questions they asked were not aimed at quick-fix solutions to errors in classroom technique. Although asking these questions might help these teachers with their methods, the explorations have even greater implications. All involve understanding students and teaching in much deeper ways.

This attempt at new understanding often leads beyond the classroom door. Joan Merriam, a fourth-grade resource room teacher, was happy with the successes of her students; however, her case study of Charles started when she realized that everyone involved in Charles' schooling did not share her definition of success:

> On Parent Conference night, Charles' entire family arrived in my room at the appointed time. Charles chose some poetry books and took his younger sister to the couch and read to her while I talked with his parents.
>
> They had just come from a conference with Charles' classroom teacher, and concern was on their faces. Fourth grade is the first level in our school that assigns letter grades, so letters on the rank card were a new experience for them. Charles had received Cs in science, social studies, and spelling. Although his teacher had tried to assure them that C was average, they were not convinced. My glowing report of Charles' progress in reading and his grade of A did little to allay their fears. They were all too aware that *The Boxcar Children* in which Charles was reading so well was written at a third-grade reading level. While Charles' mom assured me that he was achieving success in my room, she was worried about what to her was a lack of success in the classroom. She asked me to predict when Charles would "catch up" to his peers and work at grade level. When he goes on to fifth grade, Charles will rotate among four teachers for classes. Both parents expressed concern that Charles might have difficulty "keeping up" with the rest of the class next year. While I did my best to reassure them that Charles was progressing, it was evident that they left the conference with some lingering doubts. That conference left me with some doubts as well. Charles' parents and I had been operating at different levels. I was excited at how far Charles had come, while they were very worried about how far he had to go. When writing Charles' progress report, I had only considered his success during the one hour a day he worked in my room. I needed to look beyond my room for ways to help him succeed in his classroom and at home.

As a result of that conference, Joan established two research questions worth exploring: *How could she help Charles attain a higher level of "success" in his other classroom? How could she better communicate with his parents about his progress?*

Joan was willing to look beyond the one hour Charles spent daily in her classroom to understand his needs. Jack's research question would take him into Native American culture so that he could better understand what criticism meant to his students. The answers to these teachers' research questions won't necessarily validate their teaching practices. More likely, these teachers will discover that they need to change how they work with students and how they view young learners.

Kathleen, Christina, Jack, and Joan are unthreatened by change. They all could have easily developed questions through their observations from a defensive stance, a determination to maintain the classroom status quo. Kathleen could have asked, *How can I make my students understand the importance of my conferences with them?* Christina could have asked, *How can I get students to spend more time on-task?* Instead, the research questions, if answered, will probably result in changes in the teachers—not merely in their methods, but in their teaching philosophies and attitudes toward students.

Framing the Question

"One purpose of qualitative methods is to discover important questions, processes, and relationships, not to test them" (Marshall and Rossman 1989, 43). To keep the research process open to continual discovery, the framing of research questions is critical.

The first consideration while framing questions is to make sure the question is open-ended enough to allow possibilities the researcher hasn't imagined to emerge. This rules out the kind of closed yes or no questions that are developed in experimental studies to test the differences between control and experimental groups.

Look again at some of the sample questions listed in the previous section, "Finding the Question." What do you notice about them? The patterns that you see in your colleagues' research questions can help you frame your own. You will notice that these questions are posed in a way that can be answered by descriptions and observations. The keywords are most often *how or what*, leaving the teacher-researcher open to describing the process and changes as they emerge. Framing the questions in this way helps make the research feasible for us as teachers in the midst of our teaching; we are not tied to a rigid procedure that may interfere with the flow of the classroom and with the changing needs of students.

When posing your research question for the first time, come back to what intrigues you in your classroom, what you wonder about. You might begin by thinking about a particular student who you are not quite sure how to help. What is working for her in the classroom and what is causing her problems? Perhaps poetry seems to be the one avenue that is meaningful to her. What is it about poetry that facilitates writing for her or other students? You might frame a question that allows you to follow and describe the writing behaviors of this student and others in the classroom in relation to the poetry that they read, write, and hear.

You might instead want to investigate classwide teaching dilemmas that have arisen, as Kathleen did in her question about expanding the audiences for her student writers or as Jack did in his question about ways to help his native Alaskan writers retain their voices in their writing. What are you puzzled by in your classroom? Are there *what-ifs* running through your mind begging to be explored? Teachers often need to rely on their intuitive hunches; trust these hunches to guide you in the genesis of your research question. Remember that research is a process "that religiously uses logical analysis as a critical tool in the *refinement* of ideas, but which often begins at a very different place, where imagery, metaphor, and analogy, 'intuitive hunches,' kinesthetic feeling states, and even dreams and dream-like states are prepotent" (Bargar and Duncan 1982, 3).

When you create your questions, build in enough time for observations to take shape and even for the nature of the questions to shift in focus. The questions we pursue evolve and become richer when we allow our ideas and observations to incubate. Harry Matrone reflects on his own research experiences and urges new researchers to give themselves the gift of time:

> As a result of my experience I'm wondering, shouldn't the first year of a teacher-researcher study be just doing observations—with the eye of the researcher—on things going on in one's classroom? Then, after making these observations, a teacher-researcher could identify an area to study during year two. I think my original question is being considered too soon. What I should really be looking at this year are the changes in topics that kids in my workshops experience over the course of a semester or two. Kids invest themselves in learning to the degree that their emotions allow them to. I realized a month or so into the school year

that I had put my eye on the cognitive sight before I had considered the emotional.

As far as discoveries related to my original question, while I may have set out in the beginning to check out the strategies kids develop when their instruction is less structured and directed, what I've really done is check out how well they can apply the procedures that I teach. The reality is that the choices my students have are much more limited than my original question implies. At this point, I'm less taken with the idea of trying to write on my original question than I am to write on some other area I've become more aware of. I feel good about the effort. I'm learning a great deal.

Teacher-researchers know that when it comes to research, the process needs to be as fulfilling as the final results. Finding and framing questions takes time and may involve lots of exploration through wonderings. But as Harry notes, much can be learned along the way. The benefits of teacher research *begin* with finding and enjoying the possibilities in your questions, not with analyzing research results. And the research cycle *continues* with new questions as well as possible answers.

Suggestions for Getting Started

1. Keep a teaching journal for at least one week, and preferably longer. Set aside some time at the start or end of the school day to write in this journal, reflecting on what you have noticed in the classroom. There is no specific format for this kind of writing; you may choose to keep a journal, a diary, or a record of observations. If keeping this kind of record is new to you, try timed practice writing for about ten minutes a day: Put your pen to paper and *keep your hand moving*, writing about the things that happened in your classroom. If you get stuck, write, "I remember in class today . . ." and just keep going. After several days of this kind of reflection, reread your journal entries and look for what surprises or intrigues you. See if there are some patterns in your concerns or delights that bear further inquiry.

2. Brainstorm a list of the things that you wonder about in your classroom. Write down at least ten things and don't censor your list. Make an appointment to get together with a teaching colleague to talk about your list. (We suggest meeting off school grounds—for lunch on a weekend or at your favorite café after school. Treat yourself to a comfortable and inviting environment in which to explore your research agenda!) As you sip some tea or share a meal, talk through your list. We find that just airing possibilities with a trusted colleague can help you focus on the area that really intrigues you.

3. Be specific in your concerns. Many teachers reject their first questions or needlessly broaden them. They don't always believe that their concerns are worthy of study. *What works well in writing workshops?* is a question we have been presented with more than once by teacher-researchers. This is a monumental question, too global for anyone to frame. But when we are presented with specific questions by teacher-researchers, such as *How are Julie's perceptions of her role in writing response groups changing over time?*, the question is often followed with, "But I know that's not important enough to study." For too long, educational research has tried to answer big questions with short-term, large-scale questions that ignore the complexity of teacher and student interactions. Your research will probably start from a different point—individual students and their needs in your classroom. The more specific you are, the easier it will be to develop research procedures.

4. Once you have narrowed your area, write down your question, *considering it a first draft*. Don't worry yet about how it is framed; just get it down on paper as a question. Write it as fully as you need to, as a whole paragraph if necessary. Give yourself permission to play with it, writing it in several different ways until you have all the information you want included in it. Now, read it again. Does it still intrigue you? Are you still itching to investigate this area? If the answer is no, look over your process and see where you lost your enthusiasm. Make sure you get that aspect back into your draft before you move on to the refining stage.

5. When you are ready to focus your question, look back over the sample questions in this chapter. Try beginning yours in the same way: "What is the role of . . . ?" "How do . . . ?" "What procedures . . . ?" "What happens when . . . ?" You may find that you need to make adjustments for your own particular question, but these stems are often a good first step.

6. Our final advice is the most important: Give yourself the time you need and the permission to modify your question as you continue your investigation. Carry poet Rainer Maria Rilke's advice with you as you begin your endeavor: "Be patient toward all that is unsolved in your heart and try to love the questions themselves" (1934, 14).

chapter two

Form and Function
The Research Design

The plan is the generator. Without a plan there can be neither grandeur of aim and expression, nor rhythm, nor mass, nor coherence. . . . A plan calls for the most active imagination. It calls for the most severe discipline also. The plan is what determines everything; it is the decisive moment.
—*Le Corbusier*

he Research Design presents the *how-to* of the study; it is the plan for engaging in systematic inquiry. Architectural design has much in common with research planning. As Le Corbusier (1946, 47) points out, a plan calls for both discipline and imagination simultaneously. A successful design must be flexible and creative, since the researcher continues to discover and refine further questions. Yet without a conscious effort to impose a meaningful order on your investigation, there is little possibility of answering the questions you have posed.

The architectural designs of Frank Lloyd Wright provide an excellent model for classroom research designs. Like Wright's designs, these research designs should be innovative rather than imitative and built around very special needs. Wright stressed the importance of designing a building for the site itself and for the needs of the clients. His most famous building, for example, is Fallingwater in Bear Run, Pennsylvania. This incredible structure is on a gigantic jagged rock in a ravine in the middle of a waterfall. The building is built around a huge natural boulder on which the client had spent many hours sunning himself. Wright built the whole structure around this core, using the boulder as the root of a fireplace and as the stable center of the cantilevered structures that support the building. Wright later said of the building: "That was a particular expression of a man's love for that particular site and the music of the waterfall" (Willard 1972, 107).

Wright looked for ways to solve the particular design problems at hand by focusing on both the context of the environment and the needs of the human beings involved. Teacher-researchers, too, build their designs around these two important needs. And they have a central *boulder* as Fallingwater does—the core theory around which research is planned.

As you plan how you will conduct your study, you are *designing* it. In this chapter, we will discuss the four basic problems you need to address in designing research, as well as special considerations for the demands of classroom research. These four basic problems are *finding a focus or question, determining what data are relevant, collecting data*, and *analyzing data*.

In the following pages, you will see how different teacher-researchers worked through these four basic concerns as they grappled with designing their studies. Sharon Early decided to look at one child in her research plan. Rather than focusing on an individual child, Scott Christian decided to consider the effects of response logs on his students' learning. Julie Ford decided to research the results of a school board decision to track her students by academic ability. Finally, Carolyn Bowden, a teacher returning to the class after several years in another profession, planned to look closely at the process of language acquisition of her second language learning (ESOL) students. We look at the four problems of research design through the prism of these teacher-researchers' planning. In addition, if you would like to see their entire plans, you can find them in Appendix A.

Finding the Research Question

You will be pleased to know that you have already tackled the first problem: *What is the question of the study?* This is clearly the most important starting point for the design. It often helps to write down, in draft form, the secondary questions that emerge from your primary question, as Sharon Early did. In August, Sharon planned research based on her wonderings about a particular student. "I know I will have a gifted child who is also autistic in my sixth-grade class next year," Sharon wrote. "I know that I will be doing a lot of reading and thinking about autistic children and about this student in particular in order to better understand him." In her design, she listed the following questions:

QUESTION: *How does a cooperative classroom influence an autistic/gifted child?*
- During focused small-group work, what are the social interaction patterns of this child? Of other students?
- How does this student's writing change?
- How do his attitudes toward school and his behavior at home change?
- How is my teaching style affected?

Sharon's focus has already narrowed through the framing of her initial question and the questions that surround it. Wright used a boulder for his stable center; *the importance of social interaction in learning* is the theoretical framework that is Sharon's boulder. She will focus on the learning of her autistic and gifted student through his interactions with others in the class as well as through changes in his attitude at home and at school. She will look at changes in his written work. Finally, Sharon will consider how this student's learning affects her own teaching and further interactions.

As you read the following examples of teachers setting down their questions, look for the theoretical bases that underlie their research as well as the follow-up questions that begin to frame their designs. It is critical that you know your own boulders—the core theories that define who you are as a teacher and inform your moment-to-moment decisions in the classroom. These theories will undergird any research questions in your design. Often these theories can be found by extending your central question with more specific questions.

Scott Christian found it helpful to begin his design by jotting down a series of questions:

QUESTIONS:
How do response logs reflect students' progress as readers and writers?
What conclusions can I draw from analyzing the progression of the responses over the school year?

These are the central questions that are the impetus of the study. However, I want to use the logs themselves to determine the specific question that I will look at for a given period of time. For instance, one of the following more specific questions may be selected during the year:
- How do students select books to read?

- How do they select topics for writing?
- What is the most difficult aspect of the writing process for the students?
- What patterns are developing in terms of the sophistication or risk-taking of the responses?
- What kinds of dialogue develop between the teachers and the students in the log and why?

Carolyn Bowden began by writing down her purpose and questions in this form:

Research Purpose

In 1968, each of my second-grade students spoke English as a first language—with the exception of Andrew, a native Navajo student. Andrew understood a great deal, but spoke only a few words of English—forced into silence in a strange world far removed from his home and extended family in Arizona.

As I return to a teaching career, my goal is to teach to the strengths and needs of each child in my classroom or group. As I observed and volunteered in classrooms during the past year, I realized I would need to begin to study Spanish and earn an ESOL (English for Speakers of Other Languages) Endorsement if I hoped to meet the needs of all students in today's multicultural classrooms. The experience of learning a second language has taught me much more about the process of language acquisition, speaking, reading, and writing, than any graduate course. I will never be truly bilingual, but I intend to continue studying Spanish. Linda Rief (1992) wrote, "Most importantly, I must model my own process as a learner"; thus my question:

Research Question: *How will a teacher modeling second language learning impact ESOL learners' English acquisition and literacy?*

Subquestions
- Will modeling serve as a bridge to learn more about ESOL students, their background, and their interests?
- Will English-speaking students develop an interest in learning Spanish language and culture?
- How will the classroom as a multicultural learning community be affected?
- How will the makeup of the peer study groups be affected? Will they be more diverse?
- How will my best efforts in language learning impact parent–teacher communication?

- Will modeling my process encourage "fearful" ESOL students to speak?

I have no doubt that these questions will produce new questions that may be more relevant and important to our teaching and learning classroom.

The tone of these designs is informal. The audience for your design is primarily you, but also other teacher-researchers with whom you work. Your design is a working plan for you, *not* a formal research proposal. (The main goal of research proposals is to convince others that you are capable of carrying out your research; for a discussion of research proposals, see Chapter 7.)

While listing possible surrounding questions works well for some researchers, others prefer to write more comprehensively about their questions and ideas. In Julie Ford's design, further queries are embedded in the narrative that follows her research question:

Research Question: *What impact does ability grouping have on academically low-level students and what is the extent of the impact?*

- In the grouping situations I have taught, students have made it a point to ask about the ability level of their placement. As a teacher, it has been far easier to tell a student placed in a higher group his or her level than it has been to tell a student placed in a lower group. I feel this was based on the student reaction I have encountered.
- I wonder about the differences I've noticed in students' reactions to the information they receive. How is a student's self-concept affected by ability grouping? Are peer relations impacted in any way?
- When I consider the teaching component of grouping, I recall faculty room chatter I've heard and the observations I've made. There have been teacher comments about the dropping of student expectations when the "lower-level" kids are taught. Those teaching the "higher levels," though, have instead talked about the exciting lessons occurring in their classrooms. Comments about student behavior also crop up in a discussion on grouping. Many of the teachers of these "lower-level" students appear to be less eager to instruct them than those who teach the average to high groups. I wonder how teacher attitudes impact student performance levels and how grouping impacts student behavior.

Each of the approaches used to define the research question in the design has unique elements reflecting both the learning and writing styles of the researchers and the particular questions they are pursuing.

Determining the Relevant Data

Listing the surrounding questions, as Sharon, Scott, and Carolyn did, or putting your further wonderings into narrative form, as Julie did, helps set the stage for the second problem to solve in your research design: *What data are relevant?*

To decide the range of relevant data, focus on the environment and the human beings involved. First, think of the settings. What are the *places* where you might collect data? What happens in these settings—what *events* occur? What *people* are involved? What *interactions?* What *physical evidence* (or artifacts)?

What data are relevant, for example, in answering Sharon Early's research question: **How does a cooperative classroom influence an autistic and gifted child?**

During focused small-group work, what are the social interaction patterns of this child? Of other students? The *relevant data* for looking at the child's interaction patterns in small-group work will include the conversations that occur during the group sessions. To see what patterns may evolve, Sharon will need data from several sessions.

How does this student's writing change? The data Sharon needs for looking at the changes in the student's writing will include *artifacts:* copies of his writing. The student's perceptions of his writing and changes in his process would also be relevant data.

How do his attitude toward school and his behavior at home change? To understand her student's behavior at home, Sharon will have to collect her data in the *home setting*. She will need to talk with and learn about his interactions with parents and siblings.

How is my teaching style affected? A *document* of Sharon's decision making and the reasons behind the ways she solves teaching dilemmas will be the most important data to look at to answer this question.

The amount of relevant data will depend on the scope of your study. Sharon is designing her case study to focus her investigation on a specific student's learning, while Julie Ford is investigating the effect of school policy on the school community. Julie's question—*What impact does ability grouping have on academically low-level students and what is the extent of the impact?*—will clearly need a great deal of varied data in order to assess the range of impact. Her narrative wonderings help point her to the places, interactions, and artifacts that are relevant to her question. The *places* she needs to collect data vary from classroom settings to the teachers' room. Varied classroom learning *events* will be important data. The *interactions* include student-to-student, teacher-to-student, and teacher-to-teacher. The *artifacts* might include examples of student work as well as records of behavior and attendance.

Use the lens of your beginning questions to help you look at the setting and people involved and to decide which data—from a world of possibilities—will be relevant. Keeping in mind what you want to study and why you need to study it will help you sort through all the relevant data to determine what you actually should collect. Miles and Huberman (1984) call this aspect of designing research "bounding the collection of data." They write:

> You begin by wanting to study all the facets of an important problem or a fascinating social phenomenon. . . . But it soon becomes clear that choices must be made. Unless you are willing to devote most of your professional life to a single study, you will have to settle for less. (36)

Your next step, then, is to make decisions about which data to collect, and how to analyze them.

Data Collection and Analysis

> And amid the immense number and variety of living forms, I noted that invariably the form expressed the function, as for instance, the oak tree expressed the function oak, the pine tree the function pine, and so on through the amazing series. And inquiring more deeply, I discovered that in truth, it was not simply a matter of the form expressing the functions but the vital idea was this: that the function *created* or organized its form. (Sullivan 1956, 114)

Frank Lloyd Wright built on Louis Sullivan's ideas, stressing that form and function should become *one*—"an organic whole designed to meet the basic human needs" (Willard 1972, 73). We think that this notion of design should be paramount in teacher-researchers' designs, especially as they consider strategies for data collection and analysis. How can data-collection and analysis procedures be as much a part as possible of the *organic whole* of the class? Just as Wright grappled with ways to fit his structures *into* and not *onto* the building sites, teachers who are conducting research in the midst of their teaching work to find ways to collect their data within the structure of their classroom schedule and activities.

In the next chapter, we will try to help you assemble a toolbox of data-collection techniques that might fit naturally into the structure of your teaching day. Chapter 4 shows how analysis can also be integrated into your teaching concerns. You will probably want to read through both of these chapters before attempting the final draft of your research design. However, we can begin by looking at ways that the teacher-researchers in this chapter created *organic* designs to meet the needs of the human beings within their classes as they made plans to collect and analyze their data. We want to give you a sense of the whole—entire designs of researchers—before you concentrate on the data-collection and analysis particulars of your research questions.

Sharon's question, you recall, focused on a single student for her case study of an autistic and gifted child. She plans to collect the following data:

Data Collection

- I will videotape this student during small-group work at the beginning, middle, and end of the school year.
- I'd like to have audiotapes of conferences with his mother and ideally, if she is willing, I'd like to have his mother journal about her son's behavior and how it reflects his attitude toward school. Perhaps the student himself will be able to journal and will be taped doing conferences.
- I will be journaling about my perceptions of this student and his social interactions, what I observe, what I learn.
- Copies of his writing will be collected during the school year.

Although Sharon's analysis plans are tentative, they provide her with a strategy and an organizational plan that will enable her to begin her analysis early. She appropriately calls this section of her plan Reflecting.

Reflecting

- I will analyze the type and frequency of interaction patterns as reflected on the videotape.
- I will review my journal entries at least biweekly, looking for and reflecting on patterns I find.
- I will compare the journal entries of his mother with my observations at school.

Rather than prepare a case study of an individual, Scott decides to study three of his language arts classes; he will investigate the value of response logs for his students. Under his Method section, he plans for both data collection and analysis.

Method

I teach three seventh-grade language arts classes. Each class will turn in their logs on a different day during the week. I will focus each evening on two or three logs from the class which strike me as particularly revealing or insightful. I will be keeping a log and will record excerpts from the logs, will reflect on them and generalize on the process and form until I see something specific to evaluate. I want to focus on one specific question each semester. In other words, the data will provide the question. As the year progressed last year, I found myself trying different techniques: dialogue entries with other students, modeling on the overhead, varying the time between when they were collected, altering my response, positive notes/calls, etc., to parents in order to alter the nature of response. I want to be more analytic in that process this year to determine what is happening, what I should do, and how effective my actions are in regard to the specific question. Once the specific question is determined (within the first two weeks of the quarter), I will also collect some very limited alternative data (e.g., brief questionnaires, comments from parents, comments from conferences and interviews, etc.). These will not be terribly involved but will mainly serve to support my conclusions as they develop.

As Carolyn designs ways to measure the effect of her own second language on the learning community, she benchmarks points in the year to collect data, including self-reflection, student surveys, and sociograms.

Data Collection

- I will keep a teacher journal of anecdotal notes and involve students as teacher-researchers.
- I will tape student writing table conversations every eight weeks.
- I will survey students in September and in May. Possible questions include:
  - Do you ask other people at your writing/reading table questions?
  - Who do you ask for help?
  - What have you learned from other students in the classroom?
  - Who have you learned from?
  - Have you helped Mrs. Bowden speak/read Spanish? If so, tell me about the time.
- Sociograms in the fall and spring.
- Videotape student groups at work on publishing projects.
- Work to develop a parent survey (but I need to research the questions, format, timing, translation, and cultural appropriateness, etc.).

Data Analysis
- I will review my teaching journal each week, noting significant learning events, social interactions.
- I will listen to the writing table discussion tape each quarter and note peer discussions in my teaching journal.
- I will review videotapes to see if other data patterns hold true here or offer different insights.
- I will analyze student surveys for trends/patterns.

These design plans meet Le Corbusier's criteria for good architectural design—they are imaginative and flexible. The teacher-researchers constructed designs that can be changed as the needs of the research change. Yet the designs are also disciplined, setting in motion the structure for beginning to collect the information to answer the research questions. Teacher-researchers understand that no amount of data or range of data-collection strategies will overcome those moments throughout the study when we sense we aren't collecting the right materials.

The best way to overcome those feelings is to make sure your design is individual—a good match to your work habits, the needs of your students, school constraints, and the unique aspects of your research question.

Julie's research design called for a range of data and for imaginative collection procedures. She made choices that both fit into her teaching schedule and would meet the stringent demands of her initial school board audience.

Data Collection

I intend to gather several pieces of data that will provide information on the social, emotional, and academic impacts of ability grouping. The methods for collecting this data are described below:

Surveys: Surveys will be given to students in both homogeneous and heterogeneous groups (as I teach both). Surveys will also be given to teachers who instruct students in these groupings. The surveys will be anonymous to provide an element of safety when responding. The surveys will provide me with information about the students' and teachers' feelings about both homogeneous and heterogeneous classroom situations.

Interviews: To get more in-depth responses, I will conduct audiotaped interviews of both students and teachers. Again, I will gather information from the students in the various grouping situations and their teachers. The interviews will provide emotional (self-concept), social (peer relations and views of others), and academic (students' and teachers' attitudes and viewpoints about academic abilities) information.

Sociograms: I will ask students of the varying grouping situations to list their individual choices for working partners and/or seating partners. I will ask students to first select choices within their classroom settings and then within the entire grade level. Information about peer relations will be the outcome of these sociograms.

Student work: I will look over the students' papers for a variety of reasons, including effort and quality.

Student records: I will look at attendance and behavior records of students from the different groupings.

Faculty room chatter: I will take notes on the informal chatter about the different groups that I hear in the faculty room. In a stressless situation (unlike an interview), teachers may be more free in expressing their feelings about grouping.

Data Analysis

The results of the *surveys and interviews* will be compiled and common responses will be looked for and listed.

For the *sociograms* I will record student choice results onto circular diagrams. Arrows will denote student selections so peer relations will be apparent. I will analyze the charts looking for specific choices between the differing groups. Do the students select in or out of their ability groups? Are there any trends?

As I look over the *student work*, I will record the patterns I find. I will look for different characteristics by group.

By ability group, I will list the findings from the *attendance and behavior records*. I will analyze the data I gather to see if similar information appears within each group. I will compare the results across groupings.

I will record the *faculty room chatter* in columns related to whether they are positive or negative comments. I will also make special notes of the academic expectations comments.

After gathering and analyzing these data, I will compile written pictures of the students in the various groupings. These written pictures will be compared so the impact of ability grouping on the "lower-level" students will be evident.

Even though you may not be familiar with the data-collection and data-analysis procedures of Julie and the other researchers at this point, what is important here is to consider how naturally Julie's question flows into data collection, analysis, and plans for presentation. Her central boulder is a clear purpose and theory of what needs to be studied. Once you have this central focus, it is much easier to bound your data-collection and analysis procedures.

Getting Support

Although getting support is not listed as a component of traditional research design, it is an essential one. Conducting classroom research—or any research—can be a lonely endeavor. You need someone with a listening ear who is sympathetic and attentive as you try out ideas and brainstorm solutions to problems. Your research compatriot needs to know the whole background of the research, beginning with the initial wonderings that frame the question. Because we have found such support essential in keeping our research going, we urge the teacher-researchers with whom we work to *write plans for support* into their research designs.

Scott Christian chose a colleague from his teacher-researcher support group as well as a wider audience of other teachers in his area who teach with a "workshop approach." He wrote this support plan into his design: "In terms of support, I will be meeting regularly with one of the members of my regional support group, as well as communicating with other workshop teachers. It is possible that the specific questions could arise from one of the researchers as well as from the logs."

Being a member of a teacher-researcher group is an extremely helpful way to be involved with other teachers and to get the kind of support you need (see Chapter 7). If you are not able to meet regularly with this kind of group, find a trusted colleague with whom to make specific plans to communicate regularly—preferably person to person. In conducting our first research studies together many years ago, the two of us met every Thursday for a working lunch. Each week we brought food, field notes, samples of student work, transcribed tapes, memos we had written, and often the problems we were trying to solve, as well as our questions about what the data might mean. These research chats often lasted all afternoon.

One of the most important benefits of these sessions is that they are a chance to engage in a kind of first-draft thinking. Talking through your ideas can help you formulate them more clearly. And meeting with a partner who knows your study almost as well as her own makes it easier to pick up where you left off, without having to explain all the particulars of your study. You can launch right into your dilemma or share the excitement of seeing your data begin to come together.

If face-to-face meetings aren't feasible, weekly telephone conferences, regularly planned letters, or the use of electronic media are other strategies. If your district is connected by a computer network, videoconferencing, or voicemail, you can use these to help build the support you need.

We suggest building your plans for support specifically into the time frame of your study, as many teachers do, by setting dates to meet with a support group or to share at monthly meetings with a school partner.

The time frames are necessarily tentative, of course. As you pursue your question and find that you need to adapt your design to follow up on an unexpected pattern, you would certainly need to make adjustments in the calendar you have set. While your schedule should be flexible, mapping out a time frame can be a useful strategy. Depending on the nature of your question, of course, time frames will vary greatly. Your calendar might be quite general or more structured, like Scott's (see Table 2–1).

THE ART OF CLASSROOM INQUIRY, REVISED EDITION

TABLE 2–1. *Scott's Calendar*

WEEKS 1–10	WEEKS 11–20	WEEKS 11–15	WEEKS 16–20
Get permissions. Formulate specific question #1. Keep teacher log, initial survey record.	Consider form and begin draft 1 of phase 1. By the end of the quarter have draft 1 complete. Discuss with other researcher.	Select question #2. Revise draft 1. Begin writing draft 1 of phase 2. Have phase 1 readable and understandable before the meeting.	Draw conclusions about process. Do final survey. Edit and revise both pieces. Final deadline for both pieces will be 7/1.

Getting Permissions

You will notice that Scott has built "getting permissions" into his design. He lists it as the first step in weeks 1 to 10. The key indicator for deciding whether you will need to get permission from your students and their parents for the data you will collect is *the intended audience for your data and your findings*. If you and other teachers in your school will be the sole audience, then you may not need to get permission for any of the data you will collect. (It is a good idea to check your particular district's policy, however, before assuming you have this freedom.) Research data include audiotapes, copies of the students' work, videotapes, and/or the observations in your teaching log or field notes. In this case, the data are essential *diagnostic* information about a particular student or your classroom community; the research is designed to give you information that will help you adapt your instruction to meet the needs of the students in your classroom, school, and community.

If, on the other hand, your research will have a wider audience than yourself and the other teachers in your school, you must get permission for copies of the students' work or for any slides, videotapes, or audiotapes that you plan to share as examples.

Remember, this includes *any audience beyond the teachers at your school*. If you conduct a presentation for teachers in your district, for parents and the community, for a college course requirement, or even for parent volunteers and aides at your school, you will need to have permission to share any of the classroom examples.

What does it mean to have permission? Essentially, it means that you are protecting the privacy of the students and families with whom you work. For example, you need to promise confidentiality in exchange for permission to

◆ Share a student's writing as part of an article you write.
◆ Show videotapes of response groups in action at a national or local conference.

Dear Parents,

This year, I will be looking carefully at the daily activities that make up the reading and writing curriculum in our classroom. I especially want to look at the thinking processes of children as they read and write. I'll be interviewing the children about their processes and about their reading and writing as part of my teaching as I always do. Occasionally this year, I'll also be audiotaping these interviews and conversations. When the whole class shares their reading and writing and discusses it, these conversations may also be recorded on occasion. The purpose of these recordings will be to give me a chance to examine the children's comments more closely and repeatedly in order to catch things I might miss if I only hear them once.

I'll also be making copies of some of the writing and drawings composed by the students, with their permission. I know the class will benefit from the better understanding we will have of the children's reading and writing processes.

In any reports using this research, a fictitious name will be used to protect your child's privacy. I would appreciate you signing the permission form below so that I may share the information I learn from your child with a wider audience.

Sincerely,

Classroom Teacher

_____   _____

Child's Name   Parent or Guardian

                                               _____

                                               Date

FIGURE 2–1. *Sample Permission Form*

◆ Share examples from transcripts you have taped, either in writing or by playing excerpts of the tapes themselves.

In many cases, because you will be planning to share with a wider audience—even if it is a local one—it is usually a good idea to send out permission forms

---

[Date]
To: [Child or parent's name and address]

I am preparing a book entitled [working title of book, and editor's name if you are not main author], to be published by [Heinemann] in or around [month and year].

We would appreciate your permission to include the following material by [child's name] in this and future editions of this work:

[Provide description of child's drawing or writing. It helps to include a copy of the material for which permission is being sought.]

The child's real name will not appear in the finished book. [If you plan to use a pseudonym instead of the child's real name, you may want to state what it is here.]

Two copies of this request are enclosed. Please sign both copies and return one to me, keeping the other for your files.

Thank you for granting permission for the above-named material.

[Your signature]

[Your name and address, typewritten or printed]

I (we) grant permission for the use of the material as described above.

_____   _____

Date   Signature, name, and address of person granting
                      permission
                      (parent or guardian, if author is a minor)

FIGURE 2–2. *Standard Student Permission Form*

early on in your research. The simple form in Figure 2–1, used by a teacher we know, can be adapted to your needs.

We believe that the students themselves should also be asked about making copies of their work. We have found that they are usually delighted and sometimes want you to copy *all* of their work!

If, however, you need to request permission from a parent *after* you have written up the research and are about to share it or publish it, you might use a publisher's form like the one shown in Figure 2–2.

Choosing fictional names for students in your research is the customary procedure. Whether you fictionalize the setting itself depends on your research question. Since Julie will be presenting her research before the school board, she will not change her town's name, but she will change the names of all the teachers and students involved in her study. On the other hand, if she decides that her research has larger implications and plans to share it with a national audience, she may need to expand her use of pseudonyms to the town, school, and perhaps herself as well. (In most cases, teachers *do* list their school and the town in which they work, changing only the names of their students.)

Final Thoughts

Setting down a design for your study reminds any teacher-researcher of how many questions we have about teaching, of how our profession is always in movement, and of why we are always tentative about what we know. According to Rubin and Rubin (1995):

> The qualitative researcher has to have a high tolerance for uncertainty, especially at the beginning of the project, because the design will continue to change. . . . At no point in the research can the [researcher] say, okay, from here on out, I can operate by rote and know in advance each step of the way. You always have to be prepared for multiple possibilities. Perhaps more important, the researcher has to be confident enough and curious enough to welcome challenges to his or her preconceptions. You can't do this kind of research well if you are afraid of making a mistake or finding out that you were wrong about something. (41)

The design is a way of formalizing your intention to dig deeper into one question or one piece of your curiosity about teaching and your students. And like every aspect of the research project, the design will continue to evolve in large and small ways once you begin to collect and analyze data.

Research Permissions and Confidentiality

Permissions and Confidentiality

Issues of when to get permission to do research and what must remain confidential vex researchers. The situation only becomes more complicated for teacher-researchers. Here are some tips for thinking through permissions and confidentiality for classroom-based research projects:

◆ Get permissions from parents for students to participate in any research project you might publish someday, or present in a public setting. It always helps for parents to know that your classroom is inquiry-based, so the form also becomes an informational tool.

◆ Use a permissions form that grants rights for multiple published uses, in worldwide settings. If you are unsure where to begin with a permissions form, contact any publisher whose work you enjoy and they will send you a standard form that can be mimicked. Many publishers also provide these forms on their webpages under "Author Guidelines."

◆ Always err on the side of caution in disguising student names. Students will sometimes want to have their real names used. You need to think through who might be hurt, however unintentionally, if you do use real names. A good compromise is to have students pick their own pseudonyms for the project. Kids often have favorite names at any age they would prefer to their own.

◆ Share some of your dataset with parents when they come in for conferences or to chat informally about their child's work. Bring some of your data to meetings with other teachers and administrators. The more they see this is a natural part of your teaching life, the more comfortable they will be with permissions forms that come home.

Extensions

1. Look again at the research designs of Sharon, Scott, Julie, and Carolyn. As you reread these teacher-researchers' questions, brainstorm answers to the following design queries for each example, just as we did for Sharon's question in this chapter:

   ◆ In what *places* might data be collected?
   ◆ In these settings, what *events* take place?

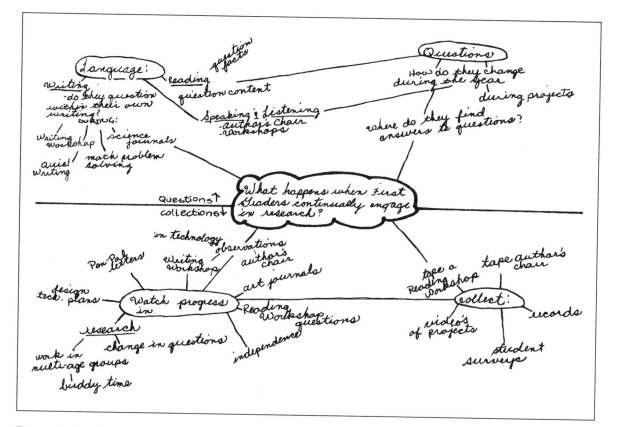

FIGURE 2–3A. *Ostrow's Brainstorming*

How do inquiries change during the following activities:

>Writing Workshop
>Reading Workshop
>Author's Chair
>Quiet Writing
>Problem Solving
>Journals
>Research

Where do my students go to find answers to questions?
In what situations do my students seek answers to inquiries?
What effect does multiage groupings have on their ability to question and
find answers to questions?

I will watch progress in the following areas:

>Writing Workshop
>Reading Workshop
>Author's Chair
>Use of Technology Journals
>Design Technical Plan
>Pen-Pal Letters
>Projects

I will observe the changes in questions and inquiries of my students
throughout the year.
I will observe my students in their multiage groups and with their buddies.

I will collect the following data throughout the year:

>Periodic tapes of Reading Workshops and Author's Chair
>Videotapes of projects
>Individual records

>I will give student surveys about progress in research.

FIGURE 2–3B. *Ostrow's Design Planning*

- What *people* are involved?
- What *interactions*?
- What *artifacts*?

2. Now return to your original research question. List possible surrounding questions, or try a timed narrative free-write to explore other aspects of your question that you wonder about. If your process is more visual, try a webbing exercise such as Jill Ostrow's (see Figures 2–3 a and b). After you have your questions down on paper, brainstorm answers to the queries in extension 1.

3. Swap your research questions with a colleague or two and use the "Research Brief Response" guidesheet (see Figure 2–4) to begin to frame questions for each other. Once again, we encourage you to make time outside of school in a comfortable atmosphere to really talk through these questions. Include some time to discuss the theoretical framework—your *boulder*.

Research Brief Response

I am responding to the brief of _____

A connection I make between your brief and my own is . . .

What I find most interesting about this design is . . .

Something I wonder about is . . .

After reading your brief, one change I might make to my research brief is . . .

FIGURE 2–4. *Research Brief Response*

THE ART OF CLASSROOM INQUIRY, REVISED EDITION

4. Brainstorm to come up with several individuals who could serve as your support system. Is there someone in your school or in the building where you work with whom you feel comfortable enough to share work in progress—someone who will suspend judgment? It may seem an odd requirement, but try to choose someone who shares a similar sense of humor. This can make all the difference in a successful long-term collaboration. If there is no one at your school, think of colleagues you know from classes you have taken or from within a support group.

   After you have chosen one or more compatible colleagues, make some specific plans to meet on a regular basis. Be sure to keep it "do-able"—will one phone call a week and one Saturday morning a month work for both of you? What about one planning or lunch period at school per week? You can either meet face to face or draft a letter during this time. You might not need to meet that often if you have a strong support group that meets monthly or bimonthly; however, it will still be helpful to have a colleague "on call" to discuss research issues as they arise. After you have made some tentative plans, *write them down* as part of your design.

5. To gather the information necessary to answer your question, how much time do you think you will need? Try to be as realistic as possible in your assessment of your time needs, taking into account both the nature of your question and the other demands on your time—both professional and personal. You need to be flexible about the time frame you set on your timeline, but it helps to set deadlines that are realistic enough for you to take them seriously. Once again, it helps to commit these plans to paper.

6. Who will be your audience for the answers to your question? If you will need permission to share any of your data or findings, write out a form as part of your design. The sample forms included in this chapter can be adapted to meet the needs of your research question.

7. Try the "Questioning Your Research Plans" activity in Figure 2–5 (see pages 34–35) to consider alternative points of view as you complete your design.

Questioning Your Research Plans

Imagine you have just spent half an hour explaining your research project to your mother or father (pick a parent who isn't an educator). What questions might she or he ask you about your project?

How would you respond to these questions?

Imagine explaining your project to a colleague who has a very different philosophy of teaching and learning (think of a real person you know). What questions might she or he ask you about your project?

How would you respond?

FIGURE 2–5. *Questioning Your Research Plans*

Imagine explaining your project to one of your students. What questions might she or he ask?

How would you respond?

Imagine explaining your project to a school board member. What questions might she or he ask?

How would you respond?

FIGURE 2–5, continued. *Questioning Your Research Plans*

chapter 3

The Artist's Toolbox
Strategies for Data Collection

When the only tool you own is a hammer, every problem begins to resemble a nail.
—Abraham Maslow

Research is both art and craft. Artists have vision and faith in that creative vision. At the same time, they also have many tools to help them make that vision come to life. They are adept at manipulating the tools of their craft, and through practice, they develop a keen sense of how different tools can inform and complement their vision.

As you read this chapter, envision yourself as a carpenter with an empty toolbox or as an artist with a bare studio. What we are attempting to do is fill your toolbox and scatter palettes, brushes, and cloths throughout your studio. Carpenters and artists do not use all of their tools at the same time. They develop favorite hammers or brushes that get used daily. But even though they may use few of the many tools available, they do know what is available—the different implements that will help them explore their crafts fully.

In the same way, the more data-collection tools you have, the better equipped you are to answer any question. Some of the tools are tried and true, essential to a researcher. Few teachers can undertake a research project without some sort of note taking—it would be comparable to a carpenter trying to build a house without a hammer. Other data-collection tools that will be presented, such as sociograms and various surveys, are much more specialized. You may never need them to answer the questions you develop, or they may be just the tools you need to refine your question and better understand the workings of your students.

Collecting data can be exhilarating and discouraging at the same time. We experience the same feelings that Corrine Glesne (1999) writes about when we collect data, no matter how many times we have been through the process:

> During data collection, expect to feel—at the same time or in close sequence—that you are not learning enough, that you are learning more than you can ever deal with, that you are not learning the right stuff, and that you are learning great stuff but do not know where it will lead or how it will all fit together. (41)

This chapter is about particulars—the tools you can use to collect data. As you read about these tools, we challenge you to think about the important whole—how research strategies can fit into your classroom routines. Before presenting the many tools that teacher-researchers can use, we want to show you how tools inform the work of one artist, Rachael Wentworth.

Rachael is a young painter who works in Portland, Maine. She wrote to us about how she uses tools to support her work. In her analysis, she gives us a sense of how the tools fit into the whole of her artistic process:

> As a painter, it's important for me to explore my subject visually before picking up a tool to make marks. The first tool I implement is my eye. I stand in total silence surveying my set-up, searching for that very moment that excites me the most. That point usually evolves into what the painting is about. Once I have that spark of excitement—tempered by a quick realization of what is occurring in the scene as a whole, I begin to make a preliminary drawing.
>
> I like to use lightweight, soft vine-charcoal on paper to map out my compositional ideas. I start with a quick five-minute gesture drawing, letting the charcoal disintegrate as it touches the page. If I want a big area of dark value, I use my hands and fingers to mush the charcoal into the surface. I am going for what's essential here—I edit nothing; I just enjoy what initially happens without manipulating or judging it.
>
> Once I'm loosened up, I go on to lengthier drawings. I use rigid compressed charcoal, and at first, I use it on its wide side to initiate big bold areas and provide myself with structure. With each added mark, my eyes are constantly readjusting to what the work now needs (an eraser for a mismeasurement, a cloth to smudge a large area so that it unites with the rest of the piece, my palms to rub

the charcoal in) . . . here I am the manipulator. I challenge nearly every first guess until my drawing feels whole.

I do several drawings—exploring my subject from every angle before committing to the one view that feels most exciting to me.

Now I'm ready to paint! My glass palette is huge and provides me with plenty of smooth surface to mix my oils. I use a big, flat palette knife and mix big, satisfying piles of paint for at least an hour before I put anything on the canvas. I mix and mix and mix! I watch the colors evolve, and I constantly compare them with the color I observe in my still life. I try to make the colors true to my vision.

I apply the paint first with a wide brush mixed with turps to wash the canvas with large, generalized areas of color. I later get more specific with smaller brushes and palette knives. I alternate tools to get the varying effects that I search for. Sometimes I paint for hours and end up scraping it all off with a razor blade only to repaint over it with a second guess. Often I must take out the one thing that I love the most in order to make the painting work as a whole. Painting is exasperating and exhilarating; it calls for me to be both subjective and objective. I always take the time to step back and watch what's evolving. There's no room for impatience. I must always surrender my ego in order to give into what the painting is asking for. I take out more than I leave in, and I depend on faith in my vision to carry me through to the work's fruition.

There are many connections between Rachael's process as a painter and the work of teacher-researchers. The most important tool you have as a researcher is your eye and your view of classroom life. You need to look hard and deep at yourself and students at work. Many of the data-collection techniques that follow help researchers get different views of classroom life. For example, if you are having trouble making sense of a scene through the notes you take, you may want to do some interviews or tape transcription to help you refocus. If your interviews narrow your view of classroom encounters too much, you may want to return to the *broad strokes* of rapid note taking.

Rachael also emphasizes the importance of taking time to let the *true vision* emerge. There are few shortcuts in becoming comfortable with different data-collection techniques. Rachael may work for hours or weeks on a painting only to end up discarding it. She accepts this, in part, because she enjoys the process of her work. There is a sense of fun in her mixing of paints and playing with bold charcoal strokes. The process of data collection should be fun. We find that we learn so much day to day as we collect and analyze data that the final results of our research become less critical. As Don Murray (1990) writes, the joy should be in the doing—not the done. We find that teacher-researchers enjoy testing out a variety of data-collection techniques, if only because the techniques keep the process fresh and fun.

Don't be overwhelmed with the data-collection possibilities presented in this chapter. If you are new to teacher research, you may have trouble imagining how you will have the time or the energy to collect so much data in so many different ways. Realize now that you don't have to use all the techniques here. Some of the most insightful and elegant analyses of classroom life by teacher-researchers were completed using only one or two data-collection techniques. You may read through these possibilities and want to use many of them. But as you look back at your question and begin to design a research study, it is probable that only two or three data-collection methods will be necessary.

This is as it should be. There is a danger in too much data collection. Educational ethnographer Harry Wolcott (1992) says it succinctly: "The answers to my best questions do not lie solely in the accumulation of data." (72)

Rachael uses a few specific tools most often and in specialized ways. Her work is dependent on those charcoal strokes. In the same way, you may also begin to use one or two techniques presented here in specialized and specific ways over time. That is part of the excitement of teacher research. Most teacher-researchers develop their own specialized techniques of interviewing or note taking.

On the other hand, if you are a veteran teacher-researcher, you may find new possibilities for collecting data in this chapter. It is easy to fall back on one or two familiar collection methods, never realizing that there are other ways of framing and collecting information in your classroom. The information here may add a few tools to your research repertoire.

The broad categories we present are teaching journals and note taking, student work, classroom artifacts, interviews, and audiotape and videotape transcription. Within each of these categories there is a range of data-collection tools to consider when designing your project.

At the end of this chapter, we include exercises to use before beginning research, to help you understand how each data-collection tool might be used in your design. We give rough estimates of how long it takes to complete a set of field notes or a tape transcription, but only you can determine your pace—it may be faster or slower than ours.

Most important, remember to make this handbook work for you. Do not feel that you have to read the chapters in order. (If a linear reading of these chapters isn't helpful, circle around what comes next.) If you get bogged down and/or confused by the different data-collection techniques, you may want to move back to the chapter on finding a question to reconsider how collecting data can inform your initial wonderings. Or, you may want to move forward and look at more of the whole—how data collection fits into a research design and analysis—before you consider the particulars of how to use data-collection tools.

Rachael's final advice to herself is the best advice for teacher-researchers. Be patient, and trust that the research process will eventually make sense to you.

Note Taking

The most common method used for data collection is note taking. Unfortunately, the model for note takir.g presented in qualitative research is usually that of the full-time ethnographer. Ethnographers have different goals or purposes for their work than many teacher-researchers.

An ethnographer will visit a research site, whether it is a classroom, a local bar, or a hut in the African bush, and attempt to understand the culture before her. This understanding comes through observation, listening, and copious note taking. Each day hours are spent writing down what is seen and then extending and expanding these observations.

There are obvious problems in using the note-taking methods of full-time ethnographers as a model for teacher research. The research you do should never be at the expense of your teaching; it should inform and enhance your performance as a teacher. Giving over hours, or even one hour, of your day to note taking can detract from your performance as a teacher. But if note taking is integrated naturally into your classroom routines, it can inform both your teaching and your research.

There is a good alternative to the ethnographic model of note taking. Teacher-researchers we've worked with often have note taking processes closer to those of writers. A notebook is an essential tool for many writers; in these notebooks, they jot down a phrase, a quick sketch of a scene, a wonderful quote from another writer. The notes are incomplete by design, meant to serve as a jog to the memory or a catalyst for more focused writing later.

Busy teachers, in a similar vein, will write down just a phrase or two to remind them of a critical incident. Vygotsky (1962) noted that there is a "world in a word." By capturing the essence of an event through a word or two on a sticky note, teacher-researchers can save key data points to amplify later when they have more time to write. Ralph Fletcher explains the value of a writer's notebook as a "safe place" to risk any kind of new thinking:

> Your writer's notebook gives you a safe place to ask: *What really matters? What haunts me? What in my life, in this world, do I never want to forget?* Your notebook is an open invitation to care again about the world, and to bring those concerns into the full light of consciousness. (1996, 13)

The principles that teacher-researchers need to follow in note taking are the same ones you use in working with students. Start with what you have, with what you know about what works with note taking and build on that. There are three note-taking strategies that teacher-researchers find most helpful in their work. These include using anecdotal records as part of the database, taking notes or keeping a journal while working with students, and setting aside a time when students are not present to record classroom events.

Anecdotal Records

Many of the records you keep as part of "kidwatching" evaluative strategies may be useful without any revision. Detailed notes from small-group math investigations, science talks, or whole-class writing discussions may be ripe for analysis already. You may not need to revise these records. At the same time, just knowing your research question will probably cause you to consider that concern more as you take notes.

Some common anecdotal records include daily notes about conferences, "status-of-the-class" sheets (Atwell 1991), weekly lists of students who have read to the whole class, or small-group logs of current events discussions.

Tailoring your anecdotal records to meet your research needs may not involve much revision of your recordkeeping. For example, Chris Randall already kept status-of-the-class lists during her writing workshop. Her research question was *How does work in integrated units affect the genres and topics chosen in writing workshop?* Chris decided to revise her status-of-the-class form to include two new columns. She added a small space to take notes on the genre or topic if there seemed to be any connection between the writing and the work from a unit. She also added a column to note whether she would need a photocopy of the work for her research.

With the new form, it was easy for Chris to scan the genre column quickly each week and month and note rough percentages of fiction and nonfiction genres for each child. At the end of the project, Chris added up the numbers for the class and quantified the uses of different genres for each child and for the class as a whole.

This new form complemented anecdotal records Chris already used to note events during writing conferences. These records were also useful in her research (see Figure 3–1). Like Chris, you will quickly develop your own shorthand in your notes, connecting them to your specific research topic.

Fifth-grade teacher Barbara Owens also adapted the ways she was taking notes to match her teaching style. She began keeping anecdotal records on her students in a separate book. When problems with this format arose, she made the necessary accommodations. She writes:

> It was soon apparent that the journal was never at hand when I wanted to write so I switched to "quick writes" on my lesson plans. I have always done lesson plans on computer and keep current lessons in a binder on my front work table. Included is a space with blank lines to record absences, behavior concerns, etc. It was convenient and easy to use that space as well as the back of the page to do a quick write. These were then used to complete weekly reflective pieces. The space for writing at the end of the lesson plans has been expanded to accommodate quick writes. It's easy to sit and complete even a few minutes of writing since they are available with my lessons as I reflect and revise.

Note-Taking Methods and Skills

The teacher-researcher has some of the same constraints as the professional ethnographer or writer in taking notes. Sometimes it is hard to take notes intensively and still maintain a role as teacher in the class. For this reason, many teacher-researchers rely on brief, intense periods of note taking during their teaching day. You may decide to take notes during silent writing periods in writing workshop. Even though this note-taking period is short, a remarkable amount of information can be gathered over the course of a year in these ten-minute chunks.

Debbie Miller (2002) labels a small notebook for each child in her first-grade class with the child's name. She keeps these notebooks in alphabetical order in a basket, pulling the five in the front of the basket each day. Debbie makes sure she jots some notes on each of the five children in their individual notebooks during reading and writing workshop that day. At the end of the day, these notebooks go to the back of the basket. This ensures that Debbie takes specific notes

Writing Status 9/4 - 9/17

Date	Student	Topic	F	WF	Draft	References Used	Notes	Copy
9/4	~~~	absent ~~~	~	~	~	~~~~~~~	———	
9/5		Dinosaurs		✓	D1 ✓	Dinosaur books from class library		✓
9/6		Ponies	✓		D1 ✓			✓
9/9		Dinosaurs		✓	D1 ↙	Dinosaur books from class library		✓
9/10		Dinosaur Story		✓	D2 ↙	Dinosaur books from class library		
9/11		Little Girl	✓		D1 ✓			
9/12		Curious George	✓		D1 ✓	Curious George books from class library		
9/13		Clifford	✓		D1 ✓	Clifford books from class library		
9/16		Clifford	✓		D1 ↙	"		
9/17		?					Searched for topic	

(Reading)/Writing Conference

Name Jane   Date March 9

(Book)/Piece Bored-Nothing to Do! by Peter Spier

Lesson: Jane read once to class helper. She read easily. She remembered to read slower. We talked prior to reading about pausing at punctuation (,.?!) She did well remembering to pause as well. Read more sentence to sentence rather than word to word.

Questions: Were illustrations more important to Jane in this book? How much attention does she pay to illustration.

Notes: Read book to first graders

FIGURE 3–1. *Randall's Conference Record Forms*

on every child each week. If a child is absent, she flips the notebook upside down in the basket so that she is certain to take more extensive notes on that child the following week.

Some teachers choose onsite, or in-class, note-taking times based on moments when they want the attention to be turned away from the teacher. For example, multiage teacher Jill Ostrow kept detailed notes of whole-class calendar math sessions. Research shows that students focus their attention on the teacher during whole-class discussions regardless of who is talking or leading the discussion. Most teachers would prefer to have attention focused on the students who are sharing their work or solving a problem. Jill sat at the back of the group, quick to comment on work or to step in and discipline the group if necessary. But much of her time was spent with head down, noting the contributors and the range of topics discussed during this time. Children could not gauge her reaction easily, and they soon learned to attend to the child who was leading the group at the calendar rather than to Jill.

The note taking during this time served two purposes. Jill compiled a detailed record of math concept development by analyzing these daily discussions. At the same time, she taught students implicitly that the person sharing at the moment should be the focus of attention.

Determining when notes can be taken during class is the easy part of a difficult task. What to write is truly challenging. Many teachers think of note taking as *scripting*. In this definition of note taking, only what is seen is written down, often as quickly as possible. The teacher is trying to be objective—not adding any kind of reflection or interpretation to the events. When we work with teacher-researchers and have them take notes for ten minutes in their classrooms, we frequently read notes like Joan Merriam's (see Figure 3–2).

Trying to interpret what these notes mean becomes an enormous task for a teacher-researcher. When we were learning how to do research, becoming skilled as a note taker seemed an almost mystical undertaking. Anthropologists we worked with shared many war stories from their time in the *field*, but little of their growth process in developing note-taking skills. We were told we would learn by doing when it came to note taking, but we often felt lost in that *doing* phase. There were thousands of incidents and details that could be recorded in the field. We often had no idea if we were recording the right details in the right way.

We have since learned a few strategies that have helped us hone our skills as note takers. Joan's "scriptlike" notes are what is known as *raw* data. A big part of the analysis chapter will deal with how to bring raw notes to a cooked state

FIGURE 3–2. *Merriam's Class Notes*

(see Chapter 4). *Cooking notes* is the process of reflecting on what you are seeing shortly after you first write your notes.

It may be helpful to present just a few examples of ongoing cooking that can occur with notes even during the earliest data-collection phases. If you learn to cook your notes a bit as you collect them, you will see your note-taking skills develop rapidly. Learning to take notes is the process of training your eye to look for incidents that delight, jar, confound, or confuse you during the day. You must learn to gauge your reactions and then quickly determine possible sources of those reactions.

One way to begin the cooking process is to leave a wide margin on the paper, as Joan did in the following example (see Figure 3–3). After you write your initial raw notes, take some time to reflect on what you are seeing and make notes on the right side of the page. When Joan reflected on her observations, she found herself focusing on the changes in Brandy as she developed as a poet.

Another cooking method that can be used as soon as you begin to collect data is William Corsaro's field-note coding system, which is based on the work of Claude Lévi-Strauss (1968). This scheme enables teachers to explore a range of functions for notes as they record class interactions. The teacher-researchers we work with find this scheme enormously helpful in moving from scripting to thoughtful analysis.

Corsaro (1981) identified four categories for his notes from the field—*field notes, methodological notes, theoretical notes,* and *personal notes.* These four categories can help you find new directions for your work as you *cook* your notes.

Field notes (FN) are direct observations of what you are seeing in your classroom or at a research site. Much of what shows up in Joan's raw notes would be considered field notes. FNs include who is being observed and the context of the observation.

Methodological notes (MN) are observations involving the research methods you are using. You may note that you are having trouble writing down conversations as children work in small groups and decide that you need to place a tape recorder at a workstation. You may not understand the interactions between two children and decide that you need to interview one of the children later. Any notes that involve changing your research method should be labeled *MN.* These notes may include changes in where or how you are taking notes, the technology you are using in your research, or how you work with co-researchers (colleagues, students, or classroom aides).

Theoretical notes (TN) are notations involving theories about what is happening in the field. These theories can be personal hunches about what is happening, or they can include references from research literature that support what you are seeing.

Personal notes (PN) are references involving events in your life or in the lives of your students that may affect what you are seeing. It is helpful to note if you

Cooked Notes

Observer: Joan Merriam

Site: 5th Grade Classroom

Thursday, March 28

This class has been writing poetry. Their
teacher, Gwen Smith and I have been trying
some of the ideas presented in Georgia
Heard's book, For The Good of the Earth
and Sun. Right from the start, we told the
kids they were "guinea pigs" and that we
would be learning along with them. They
seem to like that idea. At the close of
class on Wednesday a few students felt their
poems were finished. Others needed some
time to complete their poems. We decided
to set aside the first 15 minutes of class
on Thursday for completion of poems
in progress.

Poetry in Progress — If I write up some of this, here's a possible title.

I sit down near Lucinda who is working to
"shape" her poem. Brandy has completed her
poem and offers to help.

Brandy: I can help you Lucinda. Remember
that stuff about white space ?

Lucinda: Well, sorta.

Brandy: Um, it works. I tried writing
my poem different ways to see what looked
best. I'll show you. Whad'ya write ?

Lucinda: It's "My Sister, the Pain"

Lucinda (con't) Just ideas about how she's
in trouble a lot. "My sister - always in

*I'm pleased that Brandy offered to help Lucinda. Sometimes Lucinda is a loner.
The mini-lessons we have been doing each day are having an effect. Brandy is willing to shape her work in different ways to see what "looks like a poem" to her.*

FIGURE 3–3. *Merriam's "Cooked Notes"*   *(Continues)*

trouble. First its the babysitter. She
cries when my mother leaves like a fussy
baby. She always gets what she wants.
She blames it on me when she gets in trouble
and it makes me mad." I guess I like
the ideas but it isn't a poem yet.

Brandy: Yeah, my sister is a pain , too.
I hate when I have to babysit her. Um,
let's see, Mrs. Smith said look for
extra words you don't need. What else ?
Oh, yeah, she said keep the good descriptions.
How 'bout we underline the good stuff ?

Lucinda: OK, let's see (underlining and
calling out at the same time) "My sister
the pain - - fussy baby—— cries a lot
gets what she wants - - - " How's
some of that ?

Brandy: OK Keep those words and let's cross
out some of the other words and read it again.

Lucinda: "My sister the pain". Oh, I think
I'll try "my sister" on one line and "the pain
on the next. (begins to furiously write)
"always a brat". No, I won't use that part.
She is a brat but it doesn't sound good.

Brandy: Now we have what is looking like
a poem. Try "fussy baby" on one line and
"cries a lot" on the next. Are you
sure this isn't my sister you're writing
about ?

Lucinda often choose to read about sibling rivalry. This poem may be an outlet for some of her feelings.

I'm pleased to see that Lucinda recognizes her ideas are good, but they need shape in order to become a poem.

Great! Now Lucinda realizes she is not alone.

Students are utilizing some ideas from mini-lessons. Brandy doesn't always appear attentive, but she remembers the information.

In the beginning Brandy couldn't see the value of re-reading her poem. Now she's advising others to re-read! Completing one poem has increased her confidence.

Now Brandy is the authority! I like the way the girls are working to shape the poem while also commiserating about the trials of dealing with

FIGURE 3–3, continued. *Merriam's "Cooked Notes"*

Lucinda: (Writing and talking at the same time)
Well, we wouldn't be any better off if we
traded sisters, would we ? (giggling)
Oh, yeah, she's short, so I tease her about
that. Lets' see, "The shortest of the family"
Now listen while I read it so far.

> My sister
>
> The pain
>
> Fussy Baby
>
> Cries a lot.
>
> Gets what
>
> She wants.
>
> The shortest of the family.

Well, it doesn't really end, does it ?
Brandy: Well, you need to sort of finish it.
Mrs. Merriam told us to try to include feelings.
How do you feel about her ?
Lucinda: She's a brat, but we decided we
wouldn't write that. She makes me so mad.
OK, that's it. I'll write that.
"She makes me mad."
Brandy: That sounds like the end, hey, we
did it !

When I talk with
Lucinda about her
piece I will ask
her to go back
to her first poem,
which she discarded
unfinished. In it
she was forcing a
rhyme which didn't
work "sister, mister
etc. It will be
interesting to see
which feels more
like a poem to
her now and
why.

FIGURE 3–3, continued. *Merriam's "Cooked Notes"*

are suffering from a raging headache or from your latest argument with your teenage daughter the night before you started these field notes. If something happened at your school or in the life of a student that may alter what you are seeing, it should be noted. You may not look at this particular set of field notes for days, weeks, or months. When a set of notes doesn't make sense or the mood seems off, there are often personal reasons for the discrepancies or problems. A brief personal note can help you remember those influences well after the events. The following chart gives you a sense of the kinds of questions to ask yourself as you try to cook your raw notes using Corsaro's scheme.

Methodological Notes (MN)

Are there places in my notes that call for changes in the way I am doing research?
1. Where I am taking notes?
2. How I am taking notes (shorthand, jargon, setup of page)?
3. The technology I am using (tape recorder, videocamera).
4. How I am working with co-researchers (colleagues, classroom aides, students)?

Field Notes (FN)

Am I describing the field fully?
1. Who is being observed?
2. The context of the observation:
   a. What is being done (curricular or social)?
   b. Why is it being done (curricular or social)?

Theoretical Notes (TN)

What theories am I developing or supporting through what I am seeing?
1. Personal theories (hunches about why students are engaged in specific acts)
2. Theories in research literature (citations I make of other researchers' work or sources that can be linked to mine)

Personal Notes (PN)

What in my life, or the lives of the students, is affecting what I am seeing?
1. My moods, events in and out of the classroom, my mental and physical health
2. The moods, health, and personal events in the lives of colleagues or students in the field

One point needs to be made about personal notes: These notes must *never* appear in the permanent records of students. It is all right to generalize or speculate as part of your research base. But administrators are leery, with good legal reason, of hunches about connections between school performance and home lives appearing in permanent files.

Here is an example of how one set of field notes was cooked using Corsaro's codes:

FN: *I sit down next to Kelly, who is busy writing and drawing.*

RUTH: Can you read this to me?

KELLY: *You* read it. (The words are: "MORE ERCH KMAK")

RUTH: I can read "more." Is that "er"?

KELLY: (*smiles*) You guess the clues.

PN: *I felt frustrated. I wasn't sure what she had written, and I couldn't guess the clues. She just kept smiling! So I tried to read, "Kmmak"?*

FN: *Kelly finally gave in and told me it said, "More earthquakes."*

KELLY: I saw it on TV. You're supposed to sit in doorways when there's an earthquake, then it won't hurt you. This was on a new TV show. You had trouble, but Mom and Dad will guess very quickly 'cause they saw the show with me. It's an episode.

TN: *Kelly understands that knowing the context is an important part of decoding a text. Interesting the way she wants to turn the tables on me and have me "guess the clues."*

FN: *I go over to Paul and try to ask him about his writing, but he tells me, "It's a secret." Susan is still writing about her brother. At 9:10, she loudly announces, "Better stop writing, the big hand's on the two."*

TN: *Susan seems to be the class organizer—self-proclaimed. She takes on the role of making sure that everything runs according to schedule.*

FN: *After recess, Linda shared reading with the whole class, which is on tape, as is the whole-class writing share.*

MN: *As recess closed, I was finishing up some copies on the copier, and the children were intrigued: too intrigued. I think it delayed whole-group reading share, and I need to remember not to do copying while class is in session.*

Teacher-researchers, in addition to leaving wide margins, also double-space their notes. This is important even with handwritten notes. You will need that space for later analysis.

As you take notes, don't forget visual aids. Depending on your research question, it may be important to note the location of individuals at specific times. Use of physical space can tell a great deal about social relationships. It may be helpful to draw a diagram of your room and make multiple copies, as in the example in Figure 3–4.

If you keep the room diagram handy, you can note where students work and with whom they work on a daily basis. Important patterns showing the use of space and social interactions may emerge over time.

A second note-taking strategy that is helpful for many teacher-researchers is to take notes *after* observing students. *Mental notes* and *jotted notes* can be extremely helpful. When you are talking with a student or observing a classroom event, you are not always in a position to write; however, you can still direct your mind to remember certain aspects. By making mental notes, you will be able to put down on paper later what you are seeing now. You can also preserve some of your mental notes, using jotted notes—the little phrases, quotes, and keywords that you put down during the observation at inconspicuous mo-

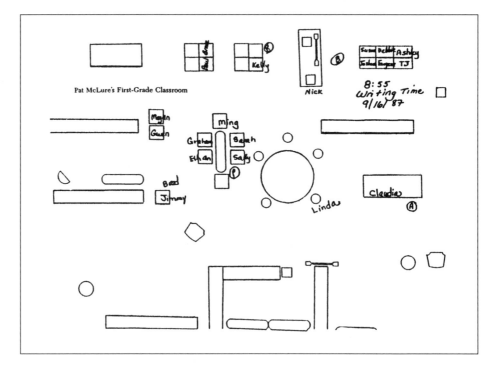

FIGURE 3–4. *Classroom Diagram*

THE ART OF CLASSROOM INQUIRY, REVISED EDITION

ments. These jottings give you something physical to refer to when you sit down to record your field notes.

You may find it even more helpful to set aside ten minutes immediately after students leave the room to write down what you have seen. You may choose a time when students are with specialists, at recess, or on their way home. Write down everything you can remember from the time you've just spent with students, calling up your mental notes and referring to any you've jotted. If you get stuck, write "I remember" or "I saw" or "I was surprised at" to get yourself started again.

Many teachers are surprised at how much more relaxed and reflective they are when they write their notes at a quiet time. But there is a danger in this note-taking strategy. If you decide to take notes after students leave, you must keep this time sacred. Too frequently, the best intentions are lost when colleagues come in to chat or when an activity must be prepared before students return. You must choose both a realistic time for doing this kind of note taking and a location where you will not be interrupted or distracted as you write.

We have found that teachers are most successful in developing consistent note-taking routines when they are working with another researcher. Many teacher-researchers exchange a teaching journal with a colleague daily or weekly. When a peer is expecting to see some notes from you, you may be more consistent in your note taking.

Don't be afraid to look for co-researchers outside the classroom as well. For their study of the literate behaviors of Deborah's third-grade students, Deborah Dunham and Carolee Gates enlisted parents to log students' home literacy. Eleven parents volunteered to keep these logs.

"We asked the parents to record briefly any reading or writing they saw their children doing at home," Deborah explained.

> We emphasized briefness, asking for only a phrase telling us what the children were doing, where they were doing it, and how long the activity lasted. I think we were successful because we provided parents with the logs and a manageable task. Many people aren't that comfortable as writers, and we didn't force them to try to write detailed observations.

The parent logs were a critical component of this research project. Carolee found that the parents were surprised at what they saw: "Many parents said they hadn't realized how much reading and writing their children do every day until they started looking closely at them. We were surprised at the variety of tasks, too."

Before you begin collecting data through note taking, talk about your project with colleagues, parents, and students. All the teachers we have worked with have found that other teachers and parents are interested in their research when they hear about it. Someone in your community will want to get involved. Having an extra pair of eyes to help cook your notes and a partner with whom to exchange a log will make note taking a more pleasant task.

It takes time to improve note-taking skills. If you are a novice note taker, think about how you tackle other new programs in your classroom when you plan how you will develop your skills. Few teachers can radically reform every aspect of classroom life annually. Most fine teachers we know choose one or two curricular components to improve at a time. For example, you may be working hard at fostering more collaboration in your classroom or at developing hands-on strategies in your math program.

In the same way, you can develop your note-taking skills by focusing on one or two aspects at a time. Here are some skill areas to consider. If you tackle them one at a time, focusing on seeing improvement over weeks or months, you will be surprised at your improvement.

Focus on particulars E. B. White's advice, "Don't write about Man, write about a man," holds here. Try to include the details that will spark your memory later in remembering whole swatches of events and dialogue. It is difficult at first to know which details are going to be the telling details—the ones that are critical in your findings.

It may be helpful to think about only one particular at a time as you work on this aspect of note taking. For example, you may concentrate on spatial relationships one day, focus on gestures and nonverbal communication another day, and add diagrams and sketches to your words the next day.

Write fast Don't edit or revise when you first take notes. As you begin to cook your notes, you will know how you need to refocus or redirect your note-taking energies. Too many teachers do not allow themselves to be ungrammatical, sloppy, disjointed, obtuse, and rambling in their notes. If parts of your notes *don't* ramble off into nowhere, you are probably censoring yourself too much. If you are writing notes after the fact, a word processor is invaluable. Sitting at the word processor in your classroom also gives colleagues a sense that you are doing something important and this curtails interruptions.

Write down actual quotes in the students' dialect Work hard at trying to include the actual words of students—their diction and syntax. Too many quotes from children in classroom research have a homogenized, middle-class, flat newscaster cadence to them. They don't quite ring true. Try to get the words in dialect from your students down on the page. Tape recordings and transcriptions can help in this area, but you may not always have a tape recorder (or the time later to transcribe the actual quotes). Get in the habit of listening carefully for the exact words of students.

Don't censure what you write with your teacher's eyes You may not want to record some of what you see in your classroom if you think it reflects negatively on your teaching. But remember, what frustrates a teacher often fascinates a researcher. If you want to get a new sense of your classroom, you must write down the good and the not so good.

Incorporate your own literacy into your note-taking strategies When you work to make meaning of what you see, what do you rely on? Teachers whose literacy is very visual often find drawing to be a useful note-taking tool. Karen Ernst uses drawing as a way of *seeing* in her classroom research:

> On the first day as a new researcher, I was awkward and self-conscious, and unconsciously reached for my familiar way of interpreting—drawing—as a way to begin my observation. Drawing helped me look at the classroom, helped me concentrate, focus on the details, and gave me a record of what I had noticed. . . .
>
> I imagined that my pen was touching the child or object instead of the paper. Through drawing, I could feel the energy of two girls mirroring each other's actions (see Figure 3–5).
>
> My main method of collecting data was through recorded observations in my spiral "Sketch Journal" in which I used drawings and writing working together. . . . As I drew Brooke, robed in her green-striped smock, working at her table on her painting, I focused on her painting, and that focus led me to interview her, her words filling the spaces around the drawing. Together, the words and drawing captured the moment and Brooke's process of making meaning.

Researchers we work with find that their notes are usually the most important data source. Suzanne Pelletier considers her teaching notes to be the key ingredient in her findings:

> [The journal I keep includes] what I call prewonderings. What might be a straight observation may surface again in another form, which may cause you to become

FIGURE 3–5. *Ernst's Drawing from Classroom Research*

aware that there may be some kind of a pattern. From those patterns come the wonderings, which in turn may lead to hypotheses, rather like the spring rains, which form puddles, and streamlets, and rivers. Journals allow us to trace those rivers up- and downstream. We discover things about ourselves as we journey. Do we portage when we come to rapids along the river, do we take risks and attempt to ride them out, or do we give up?

Learning to take notes well never ends. At times, the process can be frustrating. But ultimately, no other data source is more important for tracing how you come to see your classroom and research question in new ways.

Note-Taking Supplies

When we read accounts of classroom research, and talk to fellow teacher-researchers, the one tool that is cited again and again as the most important is the teaching journal. But each teacher who relies on one has told us that there isn't one right way to keep one—and stresses that you have to find a way to use it that meets your needs: the paper might be lined or unlined, the notebook large or small.

In her book *A Trail Through the Leaves*, Hannah Hinchman (1997) writes about the gift her journal, over the years, has become for her in understanding her environment:

> Before I closed the covers on Volume One, I had discovered that the journal was my most powerful ally in crafting the kind of life I wanted. I was building a scaffolding of choices and attitudes, forging affinities, discovering what colors, places, times of the day I could truly call mine. The journal, with its patient rumination, has acted as the great bringer of order, again and again. . . . [T]he mere act of writing has allowed me to step outside the bleakness, in the act of capturing it. It has been the field of resolution and the renewal of vows. (14)

Teacher-researchers love to prowl through office supply warehouses to see what is new in the recordkeeping game. We are always looking for the perfect notebook or paper pad to support our work and manage the unmanageable. Supplies are important; you can waste precious hours sorting through notes that are not organized to meet your research and teaching needs.

In terms of physical tools for note taking, we recommend a few that are helpful. The first may be the most ubiquitous—sticky notes. How did we function without them? When taking notes in the midst of students, you may find the little note pads to be less intrusive than a bulky notebook or clipboard. Using sticky notes also allows you to determine later the best place to put them.

Loose-leaf notebooks also solve some of the "where and how do these notes fit in" problems. You can't always be sure that space allotted for different

Starting—and Sustaining—Teaching Journals

Make the Journal Your Own

Choose a journal that feels like a good fit for you. There is a range of sizes and kinds of binding available, pages that are lined or unlined, and notebooks with both lines and blank spaces or pages to accommodate a mixture of drawing and writing.

Set the tone for your journal by creating a personalized first page, with a quote, poem, drawing, notecard, or example of student work to greet you when you open the pages.

Keep the journal in a handy place, whether it's a pocket, backpack, or desk drawer, ready for the moments when you have a chance to write in it.

Paste in notes from students, sticky notes, invitations, postcards, poems.

Make goals you can accomplish for writing in your journal. (A minimum might be a goal to write in your journal at least twice a week for at least five minutes each time.)

You'll probably find that you're able to write at various times during your teaching day: while students are doing writing, during planning times, or even during one lunch period per week.

It's also useful to write early in the morning or at the end of the school day, or even after supper, as a time to reflect on what happened in your classroom—and what you make of it. Set aside a brief time that works for you, and stick to it.

If writing on a computer is the best way for you to get your thoughts out, print out what you've written and tape it into your journal so that you'll be able to reread it in an easily accessible place.

Use your journal during odd moments to compile lists, make plans, record events, ramble, draw.

Lower your standards and give yourself permission to write, as Natalie Goldberg suggests, "the worst junk in the world."

Experiment!

Try out advice from other writers on ways to keep your notebook, strategies for writing, and even potential writing assignments to give yourself. The following books are wonderful resources to start with:

Fletcher, R. 1996. *Breathing In, Breathing Out*. Portsmouth, NH: Heinemann.

Goldberg, N. 1990. *Wild Mind: Living the Writer's Life*. New York: Bantam Books.

Heard, G. 1995. *Writing Toward Home: Tales and Lessons to Find Your Way*. Portsmouth, NH: Heinemann.

Hinchman, H. 1997. *A Trail Through the Leaves: The Journal as a Path to Place*. New York: W. W. Norton.

Lamott, A. 1994. *Bird by Bird: Some Instructions on Writing and Life*. New York: Doubleday.

kinds of observations in spiral-bound notebooks will be adequate as your research progresses. Teacher-researchers also find some of the newer index-card notebooks to be useful because the cards can be sorted and tabulated in a variety of ways.

Some teacher-researchers have rediscovered carbon paper as an important data-collection tool. Carbon paper is inexpensive, and the newer papers are less smeary than previous versions. Carbon paper can be easily inserted underneath notes being written to parents or students if a supply is kept within reach. This is an easy and inexpensive alternative to photocopies, especially since teacher-researchers often need only one copy for data collection. Carbon paper is great in a pinch when you want a second set of notes and know before you start writing that a copying machine is not easily accessible.

The issue of photocopies is an important one for many of us; schools sometimes hawkishly guard the use of them. At the same time, we can understand the reluctance of some administrators to allow unlimited use of the machines. We have seen even the most expensive ones run into the ground at educational institutions. It seems to be an axiom that no matter how sturdy the machine, a collective of educators will find ways to overwhelm it. Few teacher-researchers can depend on a photocopier being available and in good working order when they need it. You need to have some alternative plans when it comes to making copies; for example, you may want to request funds for an inexpensive photocopier through a local grant competition. Small sturdy copiers are available for under $500 now. For more information about getting funding for your work, see Chapter 7.

Saving Student Work and Classroom Artifacts

An important data source for any teacher-researcher is student work. Good teachers develop incredible memories. Just the sight of a reading log or student draft of writing can often jog your memory, recreating the experience of how it was created within the classroom context.

A recordkeeping practice that is good for any teacher, but essential for the researcher, is to *save everything*. Do not allow student work to go home unless you are assured of having it returned to you. Most researchers we know allow only limited samples of work to go home. If you want to chart student progress and change, follow students' daily work.

There are ways to share work with parents and still ensure that you keep it for your own recordkeeping and research. First-grade teacher Pat McLure had students pick out a favorite piece of work from the previous week each Monday. These pieces went home in bright and sturdy envelopes, which were to be returned on Tuesday. Parents and students quickly learned that Monday was the day when the envelopes would be opened, shared, and celebrated and then returned on Tuesday.

Date stamping of work also becomes critical in research. It is not enough to save student work—you need to know when it was produced. If you work with young students who have trouble remembering to date their work, you might want to assign date stamping as a regular class chore. One student can be responsible each day to go around with a mechanized date stamper, marking each student's work in a place on the paper you designate.

Student work isn't the only data source within the classroom. Artifacts include anything within the classroom or school that might be useful to your study. You may choose to make copies of the curriculum guide, save notes from the principal or colleagues, or photograph bulletin boards before materials are removed from them. Teachers should also consider what leaves their room and is lost forever; for example, notes sent home to parents may prove to be an important source of data for many studies. You may want to make copies of these before they are given to students.

The following are some classroom materials that may be worth saving for your research:

◆ Student reading (in all subject areas): journals, book lists, projects, responses to peers
◆ Student writing (in all subject areas): journals, drafts, published pieces
◆ Student projects and displays
◆ Schoolwide correspondence from principal
◆ Correspondence from central office
◆ Notes from colleagues, parents, and/or specialists
◆ Flyers for schoolwide events
◆ Newspaper accounts that reference the school or district during data-collection period

As you sort through classroom artifacts, remember the teacher-researcher's creed: *When in doubt, save it.* You can always have a file or box marked "miscellaneous" for these materials. You might also create files, using the headings just listed, to help you access the data later. Over time, the size of your classroom artifact collection may become enormous!

Interviews

"The job of the interviewer," according to teacher Ken Macrorie (1987, 50), "is to launch the speaker and then sit back and wait for surprises." Many teachers are already master interviewers. If you use workshop formats in your classroom, you spend large chunks of your day questioning and listening to students. You can build on these skills in collecting interview data.

Being intentional about listening closely in interviews can be intense work. Language researcher Sandra Koyritzin (1999) compares the magic of interviewing to the unique qualities of two French horns playing together:

> When two French horns are perfectly in tune, and when they play two notes of a chord, you can hear a third horn sounding triumphantly between them. And, between each horn and imaginary horn is the echo of yet another horn, resonating and ethereal. To hear these horns is awe-inspiring. . . . As I see it, an interview is like working toward, and then magically hearing the third horn. In fact, the very word *interview* implies that it is created between two, a negotiated glimpse of the beyond that comes when two people are able, for a moment, to hold themselves in perfect tune. . . . But you cannot effortlessly hear the third horn; you have to listen carefully, adjust your breathing, strive to be one with the other horn player, taste her spit. You have to try to let go of your ego, to give up your own pace, and dwell within the performance of others. (27)

There are two types of interviews to consider as part of a research design—formal and informal. *Informal* interviews occur throughout the data-collection process. They are often spontaneous, born of daily interactions in your classroom. You are probably already adept at probing students during workshops to understand their learning processes. The informal interview is an extension or adaptation of conference routines (see "Interviewing Children" practical tip on page 63). Conference questions and student answers become an important part of your data-collection routine.

Many of the common questions asked during workshops are research-oriented. Asking students why and how they do work, and getting them to analyze those processes themselves, helps you enlist students as co-researchers. The focus in this section will not be on informal interviews, since most teacher-researchers are able to weave information from these interactions naturally into their anecdotal records and field notes.

Process interview questions can be traced to the Atkinson, New Hampshire, research project completed by Donald Graves, Lucy Calkins, and Susan Sowers in 1980–1981. The researchers repeatedly asked individual students questions, such as *Where did you get the idea for this piece?* or *What are you going to write next?*, in order to understand students' writing processes. Within a few weeks, they found that the *students* were asking each other these questions regularly! Because the questions evolved from a research project, they can help teacher-researchers ferret out some of the thinking undergirding the work of their students.

Carla Bragan wanted to look at the influence of home on her first-grade students' literacy. During conferences in writing workshop, she would ask children standard questions about where their ideas came from and what they planned to do next. But to understand home–school literacy links, Carla decided she needed to get information from parents too.

She devised a series of interview questions for parents and children and compared the responses (see Figures 3–6 and 3–7). These interviews allowed Carla to hypothesize about the classroom behavior of students, and she included these hypotheses in her notes (see Figure 3–8).

Carla also chose to chart some of the responses of parents (see Figure 3–9). By visually representing the information, she came to some important realizations. One was the discrepancy between male and female role models for reading in the home.

You may also want to do some more formal whole-class or small-group interviews at various stages in your research. These can be done orally with students or parents, or in written form. Two of the most common formal interviews are *surveys* and *sociograms*.

Surveys

Before you begin your research, try to determine which formal interviews you will use. *Baseline data*, or information you collect at the beginning of the project to determine the "starting point" of understanding, can play a critical role in your findings later on.

Interviewing Children

One important tool for the teacher-researcher is interviewing—asking questions to bring out the information we couldn't learn without getting inside our students' minds. Through conferencing, many teachers find themselves interviewing daily, and this is a skill that can be honed. One of the key skills for interviewers is to be able to ask questions through a casual, conversational approach. In this way, interviewing has an improvisational tone that allows the interviewer to come to an interview with an idea of what to ask, but ready to adjust the sequence of questions or build on a person's answers. For example, ninth-grade teacher Virginia Shorey reports that she often begins her interviews with comments or questions such as, "What you were telling me the other day was really interesting" or "I didn't have a chance to ask you about this before, but can you tell me a little more about. . . ." Then she continues to ask open-ended questions that follow up on her students' responses.

Here are some interviewing tips that will help you help you learn from your students:

✦ Listen actively. Pay attention to what the child says, but also how she says it—the word choice, syntax, and context of her comments. Show you're listening through your body language such as nods, smiles, or looks of surprise.

✦ Be flexible in your questioning. If the child looks puzzled by your question, rephrase it or ask another. Don't be restricted by questions you may have planned to ask.

✦ Allow the interview to continue long enough so that important points are able to surface. This may not occur until you have talked with a child long enough to get him involved and interested in the conversation.

✦ Write down key information. You'll be able to jog your memory later if you note descriptive words for the voice, actions, and expressions of the child you are interviewing. This will be helpful even if you are using a tape recorder.

Good interviews often begin with a kind of skeletal framework and adjustments emerge as the conversations take shape. The key ingredients are listening, respect, and asking genuine questions.

Literacy Survey for the Parents of the First-Grade Children

1. Have you ever told your child a story? Ex. A story about when you were a child?
2. How often do you read to your child? What determines whether or there will be a story?
3. What is the setting of this story time? Is it always the same?
4. Do you read factual or fictional stories to your child? Give two examples of each.
5. Does your child ask to be read to?
6. Has your child heard any other adult read? If so who?
7. Does your child track (follow along with his or her eyes or finger) when you are reading?
8. Does your child fill in the missing word if you stop reading?
9. Does your child have any books that he or she can call his or her own? Where are they kept?
10. Are there books, newspapers, and magazines within your child's view? List two of each available.
11. Are there paper and pencils available to your child in your home? If so, where are they kept?
12. Does your child like to make letters and numbers when you are writing (model after you)?
13. Do you allow your child to write at this time?
14. Does your child see you reading? If so, what?
15. Does your child see you writing? Ex. Grocery list, invitations, letters, stories, poems, or in a journal?

FIGURE 3–6. *Bragan's Interview Questions for Parents*

Recently, surveys have been used more and more in all realms of education research. It's important to realize that surveys are a helpful, but truly limited, tool in getting a full sense of any environment or culture. As Patton (2002) notes:

A questionnaire is like a photograph. A qualitative study is like a documentary film. Both offer images. One, however—the photograph—captures and freezes a moment in time, like recording a respondent's answer to a survey question at a moment in time. The other—the film—offers a fluid sense of development, movement, and change. (54)

Literacy Survey for First-Grade Children
 1. Has Mom or Dad ever told you a story?
 2. How often does Mom or Dad read to you?
 3. When is story time at your house?
 4. Do you see Mom and Dad reading?
 5. Do your parents read stories to you that are true or make-believe?
 6. Do you read along with Mom or Dad?
 7. When they pause, do you fill in the missing words?
 8. Do you have any books that are yours?
 9. At home, do you see books and newspapers and magazines?
10. Can you get paper and pencils and crayons when you want to write?
11. When Mom and Dad are writing, do you like to make numbers and letters too?
12. Do Mom and Dad let you write when they are writing?
13. Do you see Mom and Dad writing?
14. Do you go to the library?

FIGURE 3–7. *Bragan's Interview Questions for First Graders*

Our advice with surveys, as well as interviews, is to view them like the photographs Patton describes—useful snapshots of a moment in time that must be pieced together with other data to get a true picture of what is happening in your classroom.

A number of survey questions, which teacher-researchers find helpful, have already been developed by educators. Many teachers use the Burke Reading and Writing Inventories (Weaver 1988) (see Figure 3–10 on page 68) to gather baseline information about their students.

The following interview of a student by Georgianna Ellis (GE) demonstrates the use of the Burke questions. By seeing how one student responds to the survey questions, you should be able to gain a sense of the multiple ways the responses can be used. There are many possibilities for using this information with case studies or for charting out whole-class responses to the Burke Inventory, as Carla did with her interviews of parents.

Student Interview
GE: When you are reading and you come to something you don't know, what do you do?

	Stephen
	↕
Child Questionnaire #6	Do you have any books that you call your own?
Parent Questionnaire #6	Does your child have any books that he/she can call his/her own?

Stephen	Mom & Dad
↕	↕
Yeah, I have hundreds . . . My brother's only got five cause he doesn't like books.	Yes

Mrs. Bragan
↕
For Stephen the printed word has been a challenge but the signs are all there . . . he wants to read.

	Stephen
	↕
Child Questionnaire #11	Do you see Mom & Dad reading?
Parent Questionnaire #11	Does your child see you reading?

Stephen	Mom & Dad
↕	↕
Afternoons, Saturday mornings, lovebooks, fishing books, Atlas— to see where to go fishing	Yes

Mrs. Bragan
↕
I found it curious that Stephen recognized the Atlas as a book with information that would show his Dad where to go. I do notice Stephen at the globe oftentimes just twirling and pointing to places he recognizes. I wonder if that interest comes from seeing the Atlas at home.

FIGURE 3–8. *Bragan's Hypotheses from Interviews*

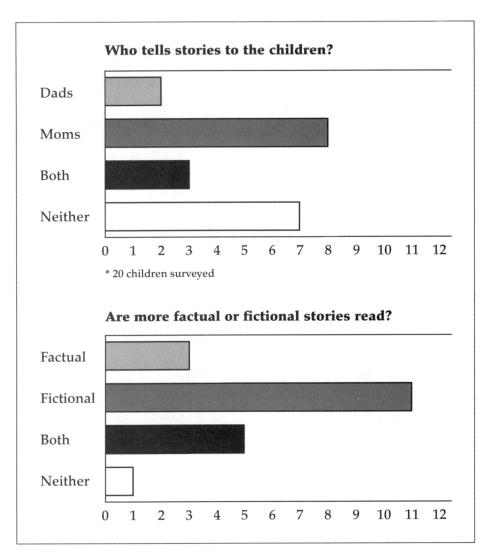

Who tells stories to the children?

Dads

Moms

Both

Neither

0 1 2 3 4 5 6 7 8 9 10 11 12

* 20 children surveyed

Are more factual or fictional stories read?

Factual

Fictional

Both

Neither

0 1 2 3 4 5 6 7 8 9 10 11 12

FIGURE 3–9. *Bragan's Charts from Interviews*

RA: Um, I try to sound it out and if I can't, I come and ask the teacher.

GE: Who is a good reader you know?

RA: My mother. She's a very fast reader.

GE: What makes her a good reader?

RA: She's a really fast reader. She reads all sorts of newspapers and stuff to us and she really reads fast and she doesn't mess up a word.

Burke Interview Questions

Name _____ Age _____ Date _____

Occupation _____ Education Level _____

1. When you are reading and you come to something you do not know, what do you do? Do you ever do something else?
2. Who is a good reader that you know?
3. What makes him or her a good reader?
4. Do you think that she or he ever comes to something she or he does not know when she or he reads?
5. Yes—When she or he does come to something she or he does not know, what do you think she or he does about it?
   No—Suppose that she or he does come to something that she or he does not know. Pretend what you think she or he does about it.
6. If you knew that someone was having difficulty reading, how would you help that person?
7. What would a teacher do to help that person?
8. How did you learn to read? What did you or someone else do to help you learn?
9. What would you like to do better as a reader?
10. Do you think you are a good reader? Yes   No

FIGURE 3–10. *Burke Interview Questions*

GE: Really? That's good. Do you think she ever comes to a word she doesn't know when she reads?

RA: Yeah, big long words. She can spell superfrazalistiexpedaiosios (?) in [no] more than five seconds.

GE: When she does come to something she doesn't know, what do you think she does about it?

RA: Probably looks it up in a dictionary.

GE: If you knew that someone was having difficulty reading, how would you help them?

RA: Well, I'd probably go out and buy some memory-help tapes or read books or stuff to help them.

GE: What would a teacher do to help that person?

RA: Probably give them some extra work, help, or ask them if they want to stay after a couple of days and [get] help.

GE: How did you learn to read?

RA: How did I learn to read?

GE: Do you remember? How you learned to read in kindergarten? Did you learn to read in first grade?

RA: First grade.

GE: OK.

RA: The teacher was kind of hard, but no matter what . . . how many I got wrong she just slapped down a dictionary in front of me and said, "Well, the first letter is D, right," and she punched a cassette dictionary—it's like a computer dictionary—and she reads it out to me and you have to say it.

Other research designs require formulation of new survey questions. Cyndy Fish, a resource room teacher, and first-grade teacher Lynne Young decided to do a collective study of parent and student understandings of mathematics. The teachers were in the midst of changing their math program and they wanted to determine whether their changing concepts of math curricula mirrored student and parent understandings. They developed surveys for students and parents in order to get a sense of initial understandings and personal histories with math. The following is an example of a home survey they developed for parents.

Fish/Young Math Surveys for Parents

We are conducting a brief survey to find out what experiences people have had with math during their schooling.

There are certainly no right or wrong answers to this survey. Please answer as honestly and thoroughly as you can. We hope to use this information to help your child's experiences with math be even more meaningful than ours were.

If you should need more space, feel free to use another piece of paper or the back of this sheet.

1. What is math?
2. Do you like math? Why or why not?
3. What experiences did you have in math during your school years?
4. How is math important in our lives?
5. Is math important in your occupation? Why or why not?

6. How do you use math on a daily basis?

7. What is your favorite part of math? Why?

8. What is your least favorite part of math? Why?

9. What do you, or did you, find to be the easiest part of math?

10. What do you, or did you, find to be the most difficult part of math?

11. If you were having a problem in school with math, what would you have done?

12. When you got out of school, did you still see math as being important in your life?

13. Do you feel that math education is the same today as it was when we were in school? Why or why not?

14. What changes, if any, would you like to see in math education today?

15. What words or pictures come to your mind when you think of math?

After having teachers try out any new research technique, we ask them to reflect on what they would change if they were to use the technique again. Reflecting on their survey with parents and children, Cyndy and Lynne took stock of what went well and what they might change.

"Our response rate to the parent survey wasn't as high as we would have liked," Lynne explained after compiling responses. "We asked too many questions." They used the same questions in slightly different form when they surveyed the children. Cyndy noted that some of the survey questions for the children were confusing to them: "A few children said that math is 'when you eat food in school.' We hadn't realized how many math activities in kindergarten and first grade involve cooking and eating. One child even said, 'You know you're finished with math when you're full!'" The survey did give Cyndy and Lynne a sense of the children's histories as learners.

Cyndy and Lynne realize that as their research takes shape, some of the survey questions and responses will prove to be unimportant. One thing researchers often discover is that they do not have a sense of what they should have collected at the start of the project until they are well into their research. This is the great dilemma in qualitative research. You usually do not know what you are looking for until you find it. Then, you need to be able to chart the route to that unexpected destination through the data you have collected and describe it clearly.

Surveys can also give you a sense of where to begin in your research. Gail Covello wanted to research the many roles that teachers take on in their professional lives. She didn't know where to begin to explore this topic. She decided to survey teachers in and out of her school to get a sense of the possibilities for her research.

Gail Covello's Survey of Teacher Roles

1. What types of teacher "roles" enhance children's exploration?
2. What types of teacher "roles" allow for individuality in the classroom?
3. What types of attitudes encourage or promote open communication and sharing of children's inner feelings?
4. Under what type of care do children feel safest (stricter than home, matching teacher to parent, authoritative, nurturing)?
5. How is it that at times one feels matching child to teacher will bring out the full potential and a blossoming of the child?
6. When teachers identify themselves on a continuum, describing teacher role and philosophical positions, is it advantageous to encourage, nudge, confront, question?
7. Do teachers need time to visit each other's classrooms and expand their repertoire of roles by getting a wider vision of how another teacher operates in his or her classroom?
8. Can I ask children to describe the role of a teacher?
9. Can I ask parents to describe the role of a teacher?
10. Is it true that how teachers perceive themselves rubs off on the children (positively or negatively)?
11. Does how a teacher perceives herself or himself manifest itself in the way she or he responds to children?
12. How do we encourage "reflective" thinking and practice within our schools?
13. Can a school's philosophy help identify and strengthen an individual teacher's roles in the classroom?
14. What kind of teacher do children like to have?
15. What characteristics make for "my favorite teacher" (books: *Best Teacher in the World*, *Miss Nelson Is Missing*)?
16. Who was your favorite teacher (or teachers) when you were in school? What qualities made up your favorite teacher?
17. Did your teachers influence you to become a teacher?

From this survey, Gail discovered more than seventy roles that teachers perceive they take on during the school day (see Table 3–1). "This survey helped me see what I needed to observe and ask in my research," Gail said. "I could then understand what other data-collection strategies might help me."

TABLE 3–1.

MULTIPLE ROLES OF A TEACHER

Friend	Ego booster	Confidant	Role model
Motivator	Co-learner	Father/Mother	Wonderer
Interpreter	Teacher	Writer	Reader
Counselor	Explorer	Questioner	Housekeeper
Suggester	Food dispenser	Cook	Hugger
Ego builder	Musician	Exclaimer	Clothing checker
Doctor	Learner	Listener	Nurse
Praiser	Aide	Secretary	Thinker
Modifier	Mailperson	Change agent	Health monitor
Aerobics teacher	Picker-upper	Skills builder	Problem solver
Supporter	Dispenser of knowledge	Mediator	Talker
Shuttle bus	Clown	Educator	Surrogate mother/father
Facilitator	Caregiver	Guidance counselor	Janitor
Dentist	Nurturer	Guide	Disciplinarian
Instuctor	Initiator	Psychologist	Observer
Actress	Nutritionist		

Resource person (for many needs)	Liaison between home and school community
Atmosphere director (temperature, behavior, room)	Pseudo-family member/part of the team
Support person and educator to parents	Facilitator of services needed
Cross-curriculum educator	Caretaker (of kids in many ways)

If you do plan to survey parents, other teachers, or the general public, you may decide to take a tip from professional survey researchers. People are becoming more and more inundated with junk mail, newsletters, and school missives in their daily lives. Response rates to surveys are often poor simply because it is easy for these papers to be lost in the shuffle. One way to get people to notice a survey is to provide a reward or incentive. Many mass-market surveys include some sort of token or contest entry form to encourage you to reply—for example, a completed survey being entered in a raffle, a small gift that is attached to the form or forwarded on receipt of the survey, or even the enclosure of a dollar bill.

We doubt that many teacher-researchers can afford to enclose dollar bills or raffle tickets for cars in their surveys. However, we have seen dramatic increases in response rates when teachers attach a few stickers to the form, with a note that the small gift is thanks in advance for filling out the survey. This is a good use for those stickers that book clubs continually forward to teachers. Teacher-researchers we have worked with have seen a jump in response from a rate of 25 percent to 75 percent participation when they use this technique. You may also choose to have parents fill out the surveys at an open house or parent-appreciation night because you can collect them onsite.

Sociograms

Another type of formal interview useful for baseline information is the *sociogram*. This chart of class relationships is derived from interviews with each member of the class. Developed by Jacob Moreno (1953) as a way to understand peer networks and relationships, a sociogram can be useful when your research involves determining who has power in your classroom. Sociograms are also helpful with case studies since they enable the researcher to perceive the case study child within the social context of the class. We have simplified Moreno's techniques for teacher-researchers, so here is how the sociogram works.

You develop questions to ask each member of the class; the child is to respond with the name or names of classmates. You meet with each child and say, "I want you to give me first, second, and third choices in response to this question." Then you give the sociogram question. You might ask, "If you could work with anyone in the class, whom would you work with?"; or "If you could play with anyone in the class, whom would you play with?"; or "Who is good at spelling in this class?"

You need to interview young children individually at a table or desk some distance from the others in the class. If you are working with students who are nine or older, you may instead choose to have them fill out brief response sheets at their desks.

You should complete your interviews in as little time as possible. The less time students have to discuss the questions, the better. As you ask the questions, you need to make sure you record (1) the name of the child you are interviewing, and (2) the numbered responses for each question.

For example, your tally sheet might look something like Georgianna Ellis'. She asked her students: "Whom would you choose to work with on a social studies project?" On Georgianna's chart (see Figure 3–11), she plotted the children's choices.

Unlike informal or conference interviews, your purpose in preparing a sociogram is not to get at the root issue or process of students. It is important that you do not veer away from the sociogram question to pursue an interesting or confusing response. For example, if a child cites a student with whom she just

	Jordon	Polly	Joseph	Susan	Edith	Eric	Ashley	Patrick	Linda	Hannah	Adam	Bridget	Clay	Nathan	Lori	Alice	Todd	Sherri	Dan	Kim
Jordon														1			2		3	
Polly			1				2											3		
Joseph						3					1		2							
Susan							2					1			3					
Edith							1		3			2								
Eric											3		2	1						
Ashley									1	3		2								
Patrick			1				2						3							
Linda										2			3		1					
Hannah									1				3		2					
Adam							3							2	1					
Bridget							3		2	1										
Clay			1				3					2								
Nathan	2						1					3								
Lori							1		2									3		
Alice							2			3					1					
Todd	2												1						3	
Sherri							1						2		3					
Dan	1													2				3		
Kim									3			1			2					

First choice = 3 pts.   Second choice = 2 pts.   Third choice = 1 pt.

STARS	MID-RANGE	LOW-RANGE	ISOLATES
Ashley (12, 7)	Clay (10, 5)	Dan (6, 2)	Edith
Bridget (12, 7)	Eric (9, 4)	Sherri (6, 2)	Kim
Linda (12, 6)	Adam (9, 4)	Todd (5, 2)	Alice
Lori (12, 6)	Hannah (9, 4)	Patrick (3, 1)	Polly
	Nathan (5, 4)	Joseph (2, 2)	
	Jordan (5, 3)	Susan (1, 1)	

First number in parentheses denotes point total for first, second, and third selections. Second number in parentheses denotes the number of classmates who chose this individual.

FIGURE 3–11. *Ellis' Sociogram Tally Sheet*

had a fight as someone she would like to work with, you may want to ask her later in the day why she made that choice. But in a sociogram interview, you want to move briskly, noting only the names of the children in the response.

After completing the tally sheet, you must assign a point value to each response. *A first choice gets 3 points, a second choice gets 2 points, and a third choice gets 1 point.* For example, in response to Georgianna's question, Polly chose Sherri first, Ashley second, and Susan third. Joseph chose Patrick first, Clay second, and Adam third. Let's look at Georgianna's tally sheet again. On the right, she outlines the Stars and so forth. The first number in parentheses after each name is the point total for each child (first choice = 3 points, second = 2 points, third = 1 point). The second number in parentheses is the number of children who chose the student.

After you know the point values for each student, you can then chart the relationships in the class. For Georgianna's final sociogram, see Figure 3–12.

Notice that Georgianna gives brief directions for reading the sociogram at the bottom of the page. With any chart or graph, you should be sure to provide directions or an example of how you interpreted the data. In reading the sociogram, arrows point toward the child chosen; for example, find Kim on the sociogram. Kim chose Linda first, Lori second, and Bridget third.

When you have gathered your information, chart it out on the page and begin to interpret what you see. Here are some of the terms used in analyzing sociograms (Sax 1989):

◆ A *cleavage* is formed when two or more segments of the class fail to nominate each other. Many teacher-researchers find cleavage between girls and boys in their classes (i.e., girls tend to pick girls; boys tend to pick boys). A distinct cleavage between boys and girls occurs in Georgianna's sociogram.
◆ *Cliques* consist of individuals who select each other and tend to avoid other members of the group. Nathan, Eric, and Adam are an example of a clique in Georgianna's sociogram.
◆ *Stars* are the members of the class who are selected most often. Ashley is a star in Georgianna's sociogram.
◆ A *mutual choice* is two individuals who select each other. Lori and Sherri are mutual choices in Georgianna's sociogram.
◆ An *isolate* is a person not selected by any other member of the group. Alice and Kim are examples of isolates in Georgianna's sociogram.

An isolate may not necessarily be someone who is disliked or undesirable. For example, Anne Crane was doing a case study of a girl named Linda,

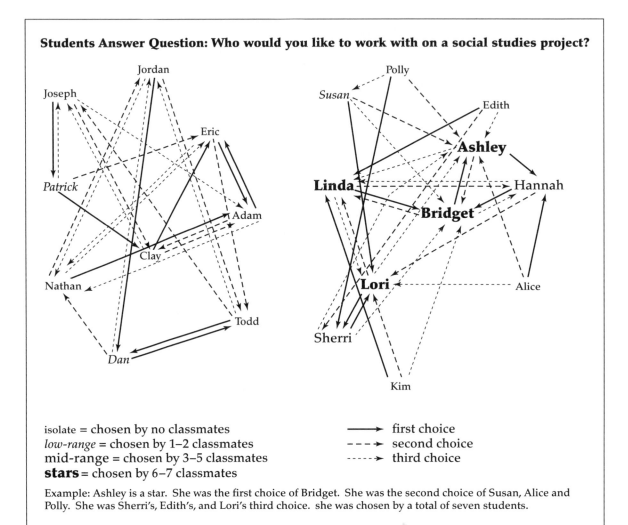

Students Answer Question: Who would you like to work with on a social studies project?

isolate = chosen by no classmates
low-range = chosen by 1–2 classmates
mid-range = chosen by 3–5 classmates
stars = chosen by 6–7 classmates

→ first choice
- - → second choice
----→ third choice

Example: Ashley is a star. She was the first choice of Bridget. She was the second choice of Susan, Alice and Polly. She was Sherri's, Edith's, and Lori's third choice. she was chosen by a total of seven students.

FIGURE 3–12. *Ellis' Sociogram*

identified as an isolate on a sociogram with the question, "Whom do you like to work with?" Before inferring that students disliked Linda, Anne decided to ask students another question, "Whom would you not want to work with?" Since Linda was also an isolate on this sociogram, Anne could see that Linda was not disliked; she just was not noticed by many class members.

You must use some caution in doing sociograms for a class. This is one data source that should not be open to students. *You also need to disguise the names of students in all of your sociogram figures and charts*. In addition, use positive sociogram questions as much as possible. Students should not spend class time identifying classmates they reject unless this information is critical for your research. In Anne's case, it was very helpful for her to ask students to identify classmates with whom they did not want to work. In realizing that Linda was not noticed by her classmates, Anne was able to develop strategies to help Linda become part of the mainstream in the class.

There are also some limits in using sociograms. The following are the key limitations (Sax 1989):

1. The reasons for selections or rejections cannot be known from the sociometric choices but have to be obtained from other sources, such as interviews with students.
2. The interpretations of sociometric choice patterns must be based on other kinds of information about group members.
3. The isolate is not necessarily a withdrawn and unhappy child, although that is a possibility. Similarly, the star may not always be well adjusted and happy.
4. The isolates and stars in one group may not be rated as low or high in another. The nature of the group is an important determinant of sociometric choice.
5. The nature of the questions asked of students is another determinant of choice. (175)

Every sociogram is unique. Responses will vary according to the social make-up of your class and the questions you choose to ask. You may have some groups with many children at the extremes of being stars or isolates. You may have other groups of students in which social relationships are fairly equal.

One of the most important purposes of the sociogram tool is to identify the extremes in the social network—the isolates and the stars. Knowing the limits can help shape your data collection and save you time. As researcher Berg (1989) writes, "A star may hold the key to deeper penetration into the lives and perceptions of inhabitants of that setting. Sometimes a single gesture or word from a star will open more doors than weeks and weeks of attempts to gain access to these portals" (71).

There is no question that completing a sociogram is time-consuming and not suited to all designs. At the same time, a physical representation of social relationships in the classroom is an invaluable tool for many teachers in understanding the underground workings of their classroom—the social networks that play such an important role in children's learning.

Possible Sociogram Questions

Research Question	Sociogram Question
What benefits do students derive from peer conferences?	What classmate is most helpful to you during peer conferences?
How do whole-class share sessions influence the writing of students?	What classmates do you like to have read their writing to the class?
How do pull-out programs influence students' attitudes about the abilities of their classmates?	Who is a good writer in our class?
How do social relationships outside of class influence student choices in class?	Whom do you like to play with on the playground?

Audiotape and Videotape Transcriptions

Audiotapes and videotapes are wonderful resources for teacher-researchers. But there is a danger in collecting too much of this information. Even with a transcribing machine, audiotape transcription is painstaking work. You must plan to spend one hour of transcription time for every seven minutes of tape you collect. Plus, the time you need for tape transcription multiplies if you do not have a transcribing machine.

As with all data sources, you will probably end up collecting more information than you need. As you collect, be sure to analyze and sort as well. Label the tapes carefully and then transcribe the bits and pieces that are necessary for your research.

Think carefully about whether you need audiotapes and/or videotapes. We have seen researchers leave tape recorders running at all times in different parts of the room (see "Using Tape Recorders for Gathering Data" practical tip on the next page). Sometimes a video camera is left running in one corner of the room. This practice would be analogous to writing raw field notes without attempting any analysis or *cooking* during data collection. Raw tapes, with no thought to the purpose or function of the data, can result in too much data and too little focus by the end of the study.

Using Tape Recorders for Gathering Data

Tape recorders can be a tremendously helpful tool in collecting data: They record the sound and speech exactly and give you, as the teacher-researcher, a chance to hear everything multiple times, recognizing patterns that you might miss if you only heard them once. Also, if you are relying solely on your notes, you can't record everything and are likely to inadvertently change words or phrases or miss a telling detail. Like any technology, though, tape recorders work best if you are both knowledgeable about your equipment, and well prepared for the situation in which you will rely on it. Here are some tips to help you gather the data you need with confidence.

Know Your Equipment

◆ If you own your own tape recorder, refamiliarize yourself with its use and have your manual handy. Don't assume it's "plug and play."

◆ Find out what the power source is: batteries, electricity, or both. Are the batteries rechargeable? The batteries themselves will probably tell you how long you can plan to record on one set. If you are relying on batteries alone, be sure to bring enough for your whole taping session.

◆ Microphones:
  – Built-in: Most likely, your recorder will have a built-in microphone. It is best to position the microphone as close as possible to your informant. It also helps to place the recorder on a piece of foam rubber if you find you're picking up a lot of surface noise from the table.
  – External: Even with a good built-in microphone, you will not be able to position the recorder to clearly pick up all of the conversation. We recommend purchasing an additional external microphone to help you out of these dilemmas. Especially in the case of small groups or class discussions, it is helpful to use a omnidirectional microphone—one that will pick up sound from all directions. An added benefit is that the recorder can be placed on a different table, out of the students' sight. Check with your local vendors to find the external microphone that works best for your needs.

◆ Tape stock: Use name brand, high-quality tapes. We have found that generic brands will not withstand the rigors of many fast forward/rewind functions. Also, avoid using anything longer than a C90 cassette (45 minutes per side).

◆ Go to the area where you will be making the recording. Set the recorder up and conduct a test recording. Talk into the recorder in a normal tone of voice, rewind, and play it back to make sure the sound is clearly audible. If possible, conduct a short test to make sure the microphone will pick up all the participants' voices.

We suggest that you make the tape recorder a familiar part of your classroom. The more used to the equipment your students are, the more comfortable they will be with it and the more natural your recordings will be. If you are recording one-on-one with students, it's helpful to talk conversationally with them first, allowing them to hear their own recorded voice and satisfying their curiosity before your data collection begins.

To determine how audio- and videotapes can inform your research, start with your question. For example, Grace Hoffman did a case study of a student who seemed to have trouble being accepted by peers. By taperecording his interactions in small groups, she was able to note specific behaviors and incidents that alienated him from peers.

Audiotape transcription can be frustrating at first. You cannot be sure of the quality of the tape you will receive, and the unexpected is the norm with audiorecordings. This proved to be true for teacher-researcher Lynne Young when she first tested out taping techniques:

> I placed [audio]tape recorders in our teachers' lounge [with teacher permission] in two different locations, and all we got was static and conversations that I could not decode. Then I decided to tape two groups of children in my classroom at opposite ends of the room. Parts of the two conversations overlapped each other, and on one of them we got lots of coughing from one of the girls who had a bad cough. Not much else could be heard. . . . I finally decided I was taking this too darn seriously.

Over time, Lynne adjusted the placement of the tape recorder. She narrowed the focus of the study and the number of audiotapes collected as her data collection continued. Many researchers also find it necessary to purchase a new tape recorder to get adequate audio quality.

In presenting excerpts of transcripts from your research, you may want to use some simple transcription markers. Table 3–2 presents some standard marks used by linguists.

Most teacher-researchers we have worked with prefer to use these marks sparingly. The goal in adding transcription marks to your texts should be to enhance understanding of the language used. Since most readers of teacher research are not professional linguists, using all of the marks can hinder a reader's sense of language in the classroom; however some prove to be helpful in presenting tape transcription.

An example of how Susan Gaudet used transcription markers selectively in her work is shown in Figure 3–13. If you do use markers, always begin your text by defining these markers, as Susan does.

Three markers are used most often by teachers. The use of ellipsis dots to denote pauses in speech helps readers gain a sense of the rhythm and pace of conversation. Teachers are often curious about wait time and pace of instruction, and ellipsis dots convey a sense of time and pace.

TABLE 3–2. *Key to Transcription Conventions*

.. noticeable pause or break in rhythm (less than 0.5 second)

... half-second pause, as measured by stop watch

an extra dot is added for each half-second of pause, hence,

.... full second pause

..... second-and-a-half pause, and so on

<u>underline</u> marks emphatic stress

CAPS mark very emphatic stress

musical notation is used for amplitude and appears under the line:

p piano (spoken softly)	*ff* fortissimo (spoken very loudly)
pp pianissimo (spoken very softly)	*acc* spoken quickly
f forte (spoken loudly)	*dec* spoken slowly

The above notations continue until punctuation, unless otherwise noted

/?/ indicates transcription impossible

/words/ within slashes indicate uncertain transcription

[brackets] are used for comments on quality of speech and context

⌈Brackets between lines indicate overlapping speech
⌊Two people talking at the same time

Brackets on two lines⌉
　　　　　　　⌊indicate second utterance latched onto first, without perceptible pause

---

Another transcription marker used frequently is brackets placed between lines to indicate overlapping speech. This marker shows when a child is interrupted, often leading to a change in topic. Finally, the # or /?/ mark denotes words that are mumbled or misunderstood. This marker helps readers know when speakers ramble or mumble while speaking. It alerts readers that something important may be missing.

One of the purposes of the transcription markers is to give a sense of nonverbal communication in the classroom. The more you can give a sense of the context surrounding conversations in your classroom, the more powerfully the classroom's atmosphere will be conveyed to readers.

Key to Transcription Symbols

. . . half-second pause

an extra dot is added for each half-second of pause, hence,

. . . . one second pause

. . . . . one-and-one-half second pause, etc.

/?/ transcription impossible (each question mark indicates an unintelligible word)

[Brackets] used for comments on context

[Brackets between lines with text underlined indicates that the underlined texts were overlapping; that is, the speakers said the underlined text at the same time.

Numbers refer to number of utterances by parents

Q signifies a question was asked by one of Cameron's parents either seeking information, checking for understanding, or probing for instructional purposes

Ⓠ indicates the question is in statement form with rising intonation (ellipses were not included here if the question form could be inferred)

Analysis of Parent/Child Talk

The following discourse took place while Cameron and his parents were eating dinner. Much of the dinner discussion focuses on a friend who has lost his job and the upcoming funeral for Cameron's great uncle. At the beginning of this transcript, Cameron has expressed his concern to his mother about something on his plate. The opening statement is Mom's response to Cameron's concern.

MOM: That's O.K.[1] It's just the peeling.[2]
CAMERON: Huh?
MOM: It's just the peeling.[3] That's all right.[4]
DAD: David's pretty much given up on 'em.[5]
Ⓠ Q MOM: He has?[6] What's he going to do?[7]
Ⓠ DAD: Try to find another job.[8]
Ⓠ MOM: Up here?[9] . . . There are other companies that do whatever they do?[10]
DAD: / ? /.[11]

FIGURE 3–13. *Gaudet's Transcription* *(Continues)*

MOM: Doesn't Aerofusion do it for all the ·
DAD: Yea.[12]

Q   MOM: airplanes?[13]
DAD: /?/[14]
CAMERON: What is this?

Q   MOM: They call it what?[15]
DAD: Aeroconfusion.[16]

Q   MOM: Oh, really?[17] [Chuckling]
CAMERON: What is this? . . . What is this? . What is this? . . . . What
             is this? . . . . What's this Daddy? What's this?
DAD: . . . . little seeds.[18]

⌈ CAMERON: Little seeds.
Q   ⊢ MOM: If they do it for all airplanes, then how[19]
⌊ CAMERON: Look, Mommy, little seeds.

Ⓠ   MOM: Oh, little seeds?[20]
⌈ CAMERON: Umm.
⌊ DAD: They don't do it for all of them[21]. . . . They just do certain types
          of things.[22]

MOM: Does Eastern have their own air .
⌈ DAD: Yes.[23]
Q   ⊨ MOM: plane mechanics and stuff?[24]
⌊ DAD: Yes.[25]

ⓆQ   MOM: Oh, they do?[26] . . At the airport?[27]
DAD: Mm-hmm.[28]

Q   MOM: Well, what does Aerofusion do?[29]
⌈ DAD: Specialty stuff.[30] Aerofusion is mostly[31]
Ⓠ   ⌊ MOM: Like routine maintenance,[32] or like that?[33] If there's a
Ⓠ   problem they send it to them?[34]

DAD: Right.[35] [Cameron begins pounding on something.]

Q   MOM: Oh, really?[36]
DAD: Specialty is heavy welding.[37]
⌈ MOM: So actually he's in a better job.[35] He's in a higher /?/ class.[39]
⌊ CAMERON: [Talking to self] Here. Thank you. Thank you very. You
          like cream.

Q   ⌈ DAD: / ? / there?[40]
⌊ MOM: For pay.[41]

⌈ CAMERON: You like cream.
Q   ⌊ DAD: He's just a regular flight mechanic.[42] You know?[43] Yea, he's in a
          position where he could get a job supposedly if there's openings.[44]
⌊ CAMERON: [Babbling] Have a ice cream. You eat it. / ? ? ? ? /

FIGURE 3–13, continued. *Gaudet's Transcription*

Collecting data through videotapes presents some unique opportunities beyond audiotapes. By recording the actions as well as the sounds of classroom life, you will have a record of nonverbal interactions, which adds an often-neglected element to your data. Judy Fueyo's study of the nonverbal aspects of literacy in a first-grade classroom was aided immensely by her videotaped segments recorded at the block area, for example. Also, the videotapes of Pat McLure's writing conferences with individual students helped her develop principles for conducting successful writing conferences that included the kinds of questions asked as well as other aspects, such as maintaining eye contact and mirroring a student's reactions. These findings resulted from using video as a data-gathering tool.

On the other hand, the transcription involved in video analysis is time-consuming and many layered. We urge researchers to think carefully about their reasons for including the use of video for this very reason. If you do decide you need to videotape, it is often best to begin transcribing the tapes *after* you have begun to form categories so that you can deal selectively with the wealth of data in transcription. We will return to issues of transcribing video- and audiotapes as part of the data-analysis procedures described in Chapter 4.

Photography as a Tool for Research

More and more teachers are turning to photographic documentation as a data-collection tool to help them understand their classrooms. Cameras are portable and fairly unobtrusive and can capture moments in a classroom that might go unremembered. One way teachers can begin to collect data using photographs is as a complement to written observations because they can jog your memory of incidents in the classroom. Like other data-gathering tools, pictures can help you notice what is going on with fresh eyes and help you focus. Depending on your research, you might document: Who sits where during different times of the day? How do they use their bodies? Whom do they work with?

JoBeth Allen and Linda Labbo (2001) show another powerful use of cameras in teacher research: enabling students to participate in the process of data collection and analysis by using themselves and their photographs as objects of inquiry. As their students select pictures representing their lives and draft narratives for their pictures, the world beyond the school becomes part of the classroom community—and text. This can deepen the class's knowledge and inform your inquiry. To create a class definition of literacy, for example, one teacher gave her students a digital camera, with each student having the camera for one week. The assignment was to "take pictures that represent your understanding of literacy." After each student had downloaded her pictures onto the computer, the class created a webpage with a rich mosaic of pictures from their lives, which in turn informed the teacher about her students' growing understanding of the complexities of literacy. Assignments like this invite students into inquiry, and they help us all see research questions through a new lens.

You can't really understand the tools of data collection until you test them out. As you test them out, you will also experience a continual sense that you are not gathering enough, that you are just scratching at the surface of what your students know, or that you might not know enough about your classroom. Writer Annie Proulx (2001) describes this sense in her own research for novels:

> The digging is never done because the shovel scrapes at life itself. It is not possible to get it all, or even very much of it, but I gather what I can of the rough, tumbling crowd, the lone walkers and the voluble talkers, the high lonesome singers, the messages people write and leave for me to read. (190)

If you are planning to attempt some teacher research, the following extensions will help you learn which tools are best suited to your questions. We urge you to work with a colleague or small group in testing out these data-collection techniques.

Extensions

Some of the following exercises work best if they are completed with a colleague or colleagues. For more information on forming a support group of teacher-researchers or applying for grants to buy specialized equipment, you may want to skip ahead to Chapter 7.

Note Taking

1. Look at the classroom records you keep now. Are there any simple revisions that could be made to extend your daily records as a data source?
   a. Adding a column to *cook* what you see later in the day?
   b. Adding a column to note what needs to be copied or collected?
2. Try out each of the note-taking strategies
   a. onsite
   b. after the fact

   What difference do you see in how you collect information? Are you more or less reflective? What do you tend to concentrate on in your notes?
3. Try Karen Ernst's Sketch Journal as a way to take notes. Without looking at your paper, do a line drawing of a student in your class. If this is uncomfortable for you, with a partner, brainstorm strategies you use to approach other tasks. For example, are you a mapmaker or list writer? Find ways to include these strategies in your note taking.
4. Add a wide margin and make a pact with a peer to *cook* each other's notes for a week using Corsaro's *FN, MN, TN, PN*. What is the difference in your cooking? What does it say about the differences between your perspective on the classroom and that of your colleague?
5. Videotape two short segments (5–10 minutes) of classroom interaction. Working with a group of peers, show one of the segments and take notes as quickly as possible as the segment rolls, leaving a wide margin. After the segment is completed, exchange notes with a colleague and add Corsaro's *FN, MN, TN,* and *FN* markers to your colleague's notes in the blank margin.

   After completing this exercise, roll the second segment, not allowing any notes to be taken during the viewing. After the segment ends, write down what you have seen for ten minutes, writing as quickly as possible and leaving a wide margin. Exchange with a colleague and go through Corsaro's coding process again.

   Talk about the patterns you see in the ways you take notes and the implications these have for note taking as a strategy in your research.

   (Note: This exercise can be done with any videotape segment. Sometimes it is interesting to use segments from outside of education—for example, brief excerpts from a wildlife program.)
6. Do the same videotape exercise, but this time add diagrams or visual aids to support your words. Compare your choice of visual aids with what a colleague adds to her notes.

Student Work

1. Take a look at the way you organize student work. Is there a better way to arrange work folders to assist in your work? Discuss this issue with your students—they may have helpful ideas.
2. Take a look at your recordkeeping system. Is there a way to add a column to a standard recordkeeping sheet to support your data collection? You might add space for brief notes, or a checkpoint for work that needs to be photocopied or a student who needs to be interviewed.

Interviews

1. Try the Burke Inventory with two students and then do a ten-minute free-write analyzing what went well and what confused you. What student answers were alike? What student answers were different? What are the possibilities for research? Try revising the inventory to explore other aspects of student literacy, such as scientific literacy.
2. Devise a four-question survey for your students and then chart out one of the answers. Compare your chart with that of a fellow teacher-researcher. How did each of you present the information?
3. Think about how your students respond to you as you ask open-ended questions. Do their responses change over time? How? Why? Do a ten-minute free-write after student interviews to explore this issue and then exchange with a colleague for discussion.

Tape Transcription

Transcribe a five-minute segment of talk without any markers. After printing the transcription, try to use some of the transcription markers from the chart in Figure 3–13. Have another teacher-researcher try the same exercise with another unmarked transcription draft. Which markers did he choose? Why?

Sociograms

Try to think of a time in your classroom day when it might be possible for you to complete brief sociogram interviews. Complete the interviews. We find that it is best to do the tally sheets and graphs in a support group the first time. You can answer each other's questions as you make sense of the data. Bring large chart paper and lots of erasers—you will need them!

4

Pentimento
Strategies for Data Analysis

Old paint on canvas, as it ages, sometimes becomes transparent. When this happens, it is possible, in some pictures, to see the original lines: a tree will show through a woman's dress, a child makes way for a dog, a large boat is no longer on an open sea. That is called pentimento. . . . Perhaps it would be as true to say that the old conception, replaced by a later choice, is a way of seeing and then seeing again.
—Lillian Hellman (1973)

Data analysis is a way of "seeing and then seeing again." It is the process of bringing order, structure, and meaning to the data, to discover what is underneath the surface of the classroom. In seeking to explain the material you are collecting, you enter into a dialogue with it, questioning it further, finding newer meanings and different rhythms. There are layers on layers of portraits in your classroom; some of the rich complexity can be brought into focus when you see underlying designs that help explain these pictures of learning in a deeper way.

The good news about data analysis is that it is fascinating work. Biologist Gary Lynch describes data analysis as one of his greatest joys:

If I have any strengths as a scientist, one of them is this: I love to pore over the data. . . . I just sit there and analyze it this way and that. Graph it this way, graph it that way. I can sit with data for hours, just as happy as can be. That's the secret of doing science. You can't imagine how profoundly important it is to sit and go through that material, and go through it so you can really understand . . . to gain it at an intuitive level. (in Johnson 1991, 28)

How can we—like Gary Lynch—make friends with the messy, time-consuming, and ambiguous task of analyzing data? It is a good starting point to get our fears and concerns out into the open—to ponder what it is about data analysis that stops some researchers cold. Teacher-researcher Suzanne Pelletier found it helpful to write about her concerns:

Sometimes I worry that I will become so self-absorbed in looking, collecting, and questioning that it will interfere and I will become so self-conscious that I will look at everything too closely. It was reassuring to read that other teacher-researchers go through the same thoughts. I love the comment that one T/R said, "My categories seem to mean maybe something." I identified with the teachers who were "confused, unsure, overwhelmed, discouraged" when they began the process of attempting to analyze their data. Active learning is messy; understanding this can help us to identify with our students who are going through this process too.

Suzanne works through some of her worries by writing about them. She finds solace in knowing that she is not alone in her struggles, and she recognizes that active learning is inevitably messy.

Some Northwest Native American tribes "speak bitterness" about negative past experiences and present concerns in order to get them out in the open. Giving voice to the bitterness helps individuals to name nebulous worries more specifically and to realize that their concerns are often shared by others in the community; it also helps bring some solutions and understanding. Talking and writing through experiences and fears about analyzing data can be a very useful strategy for teacher-researchers.

Like Suzanne, Cyndy Fish used her teaching journal to express negative feelings:

Janet Emig [composition researcher] writes that "making a paradigm shift requires not only a cognitive change but the courage to make the change." Being a perfectionist, this statement holds a lot of truth for me. I have the cognitive awareness, but because I have to do everything perfectly the first time, I tend not to have the courage to make the changes. I have started more projects over or even changed what I intended to do because I couldn't get it to look or be what I thought was perfect. I tend not to try new things unless I know I can be an expert or be perfect at it the first time. This sets me up for either not trying new things or not meeting my high expectations, no matter how unrealistic they are. I am getting better, but I still have a way to go.

Cyndy recognizes that the task of analyzing her data will require her—and other teachers like her, who are confident, perhaps even perfectionists at their craft—to delve into something that is messy, awkward, and unknown.

Gary Lynch, Suzanne Pelletier, and Cyndy Fish all hint at three important concepts that, though seldom discussed, can make all the difference in successful and creative data analysis. *Patience*, a willingness to make *mistakes*, and *playfulness* can lead us to a deep *seeing* of the underlying patterns beneath surface appearances. As we share more specific strategies and exercises for analyzing data, we will come back to the importance of giving yourself permission to take the time you need, to risk making mistakes and thus learn from them, and to play with your data.

As you are analyzing your data, essentially you are *theorizing* about what you have observed and collected. The Greek root of the word *theory* means "to contemplate" or "to see." Constructing theories is the art of contemplating what you see.

As we have stressed throughout this book, the entire process of research is recursive. Data analysis does not begin after collection has been completed; rather, it is a part of your research from the very first day. For beginning researchers, it is important to keep this in mind because there is a tendency to keep different aspects of the research process separate, focusing on one completely and then moving on to the next.

It is critical for you to weave data collection and analysis together throughout your study. In his book, *Case Study Research*, Robert Yin (1989) tells the unfortunate story of a colleague who continued to accumulate masses of data month after month, not knowing what to do with the mountain of evidence he had collected. In the end, it remained simply that—an untidy mountain of data, with no meaning to anyone, the researcher included.

What often seems intuitive in research findings really can be traced back to themes and patterns that emerge as one collects the data. That's the most challenging job for a teacher-researcher—to figure out what codes to use in looking at data, and then to determine if the codes point to a pattern or theme.

Richard Boyatzis compares this process to the work of the !Kung hunter in the Kalahari. He notes that these hunters are able to grasp the travel patterns and the condition of the animal and its feeding habits by carefully analyzing tracks, noting everything from the depth of the print to its thickness. As Boyatzis (1998) notes:

> To the uninitiated, the tracking skill of the !Kung seems magical. A thoughtful observer might use words like "natural" or "intuitive" to describe the capacity of the hunter. To those of us who do not spend hours studying animals in the bush, it appears to be an effortless process and the exercise of a capability with unconscious ease. It does not seem to be the deliberate exercise of a skill or a process of analysis. (8)

In the same way, teacher-researchers are often building on years of *tracking* student responses and behaviors, depending on their previous experience of understanding and analyzing even subtle nuances of change in individual kids. It can seem like a step backward to have to find ways to code what we've come to understand and assimilate quickly and nearly unconsciously. We doubt !Kung warriors will ever start leaving sticky notes in pawprints with scrawled annotations to attest to a finding. Better analyses of the tracking process aren't essential for final success, which is measured in fresh meat for the tribe.

But teacher-researchers do have to be a little more deliberate in how they come to specific findings, if only to avoid becoming what Shirley Brice Heath (1998) describes as "delusionally anecdotal." Heath notes that her own work is rich in story, but she was always certain there were many other related stories—experiences that could have been counted, weighed against each other, and verified in her notes before she presented a finding through an anecdote. There is a danger in presenting a compelling story or experience that backs up what we want to find in our research—even if that finding isn't supported by other data.

In this chapter, we show ways to prepare data for analysis first and then explain several analysis strategies. It is difficult to write about the mental processes—the intuitive leaps and the "aha" moments—that allow us to see our data coming together in new patterns. Few people write about their research findings as they unfold, and it is hard to reach back into our minds to recover the stages of discovery as they occurred. Because we know our own processes best, we will include several examples from our research here. We invite you to compare your processes with ours as you look closely at your data—seeing it, then seeing it again.

Preparing Your Data for Analysis

The process of preparing your data for analysis is important on many levels. You will quickly accumulate large masses of information. You need to organize this mountain in a way that helps you access relevant data readily. In addition, the process of organizing the data has other benefits. The physical act of spreading everything you have collected across the living-room floor or dining-room table gives you the lay of the land. Handling materials again always helps make unexpected connections. Doing the mundane groundwork of organizing the data helps free your mind for those "aha" creative leaps. The following sections discuss some ways to begin organizing different kinds of data.

Field Notes and Teaching Journals

We suggest starting with your field notes or teaching journal. The way that you set up your format for field notes has "made room" for your beginning analysis. Your *raw* notes—the ones gathered firsthand, such as jotted notes, observation notes, drawings, or tapes—are first converted into *cooked* notes. Your teaching journal may be an example of cooked notes if it includes your reflections as well as the observation notes themselves. Your journal might also look more like a writer's notebook, with brief phrases or descriptions of scenes and events in your classroom.

Audiotapes and Videotapes

Your cooked data might also include transcripts of the tapes you have recorded and intend to analyze. Although many researchers hire someone to transcribe tapes, we strongly urge teachers to transcribe their own tapes. We find that playing back hard-to-understand sections and actually hearing the words again in a setting where they may be played and replayed allows a kind of reflection that is extremely valuable. Many teacher-researchers listen to research tapes while commuting to and from school or doing other activities, or use a portable tape player to listen initially when time allows.

We have already discussed some of the transcription marks that help you as you physically transcribe the tape (see Chapter 3). Another transcription technique that is less time-consuming is topic analysis. Some research questions do not require that every word of a conversation be analyzed. They may require only a presentation of the person who controls the topic or an analysis of when a case study or case studies are involved in conversations.

Karen Achorn found it most helpful to note who controlled topic change in her transcription. Ronnie is clearly in control of introducing topics that relate to discussions of his goals, as the transcript shows (see Table 4–1).

There is an added challenge in preparing transcripts of videotapes. So much is going on that it is necessary to replay the video several times in order to transcribe the action as well as the words. Depending on your reasons for using video as part of your database, you might begin by making a running transcript of the audio portion first, as you would for an audiotape. One fairly easy way is to transcribe the audio in one column, leaving a wide second column so that on second viewing, you can record the general action. For example, in the video transcription in Figure 4–1 (see page 96), the audio portion was transcribed on the left and the handwritten notes on the right were written in after a second viewing.

This transcription was important in showing Pat the ways in which she interacted with children during writing conferences. She began to notice patterns in her responses (i.e., repeating back comments that Nathan said and maintaining eye contact) that worked to encourage Nathan to tell more. Looking at the

TABLE 4–1. *Achorn's Topic Analysis*

Flow of Topics in Discussion of Ronnie's Goals

DIGITAL COUNTER	TOPIC	PARTICIPANTS	HOW IT CAME UP
001	Goals	All	R: I want to be a toxicologist.
020	Decision to become a toxicologist	All	R: mentions Tim Landry and "Auntie's" influence
040	Dinosaurs	All	R: Most third graders "don't know it yet"
060	How to prepare to reach goal in Gr. 3	All	R: "teach others"
080	Experiments	All	R: talks of mixes
100	Rotten wood experiment	All	R: "magnifying, chlorophyll"
120	Other goals	All	R: interested in writing, would write all the bad things about Mike O
140	Brother	All	R: hits, kicks "really not a good kid," must be something about being seven
160	Self-esteem	All	R: dissected then ate a sunfish to improve himself
180	Taking Chances	All	R: risk is good, "I'm a lucky guy!"
200	Most Exciting Event in Life	All	R: I climbed Mt. Katahdin

nonverbal as well as the spoken events was necessary in order to prepare Pat's videotapes for analysis. For more information on the use of video in teacher research projects, see the practical tip on page 96.

Student Samples

In most cases, the only preparation that you make of a student sample is to get a clear photocopy of it. If you have access to a good scanner, you can also scan

---

Pat: Don't you remember which fish you were writing about?

Nathan: Um. . .oh! *(reads)* "My swordtail jumped out of my fish tank last week."

Pat: Ohhhhh.

Nathan *(reading):* "My Dad saved it."

Pat: He was able to save it? Get it back in?

Nathan: Yeah, he dunked. . .right. . .

Pat: Dunked it right back in? How are you going to keep it from doing that again?

Nathan: We got a cover.

Pat: Oh. . .*(pause)* So he can't jump out again?

Nathan: No.

Pat: No.

Nathn: My Siamese fighting fish--he can't see the cover--he tried to go up. . .

Pat: Does he?

Nathan: Last night he bumped his nose.

Pat *(laughs):* He bumped his nose on the cover?

P. points to fish on page, smiles and watches page as N. reads.
Kim approaches and stands next to desk,
N. looks up at P.
P. meets his eye, then looks at page

N. looks up at P. after reading. "it."

P. & N.: eye contact
Kim waits
N. uses hand motions.

P. & N. maintain eye contact. P. leans forward on arm.
N. continues to gesture.

Kim stands next to desk, holding book.

P. & N.: eye contact.

P. & N. laugh

FIGURE 4–1. *Video Transcription*

THE ART OF CLASSROOM INQUIRY, REVISED EDITION

Nathan: Right.

Pat: Oh, it looks nice, Kimberly. Mmm. It is nice, isn't it? Yeah.

Kimberly: I want to read it to Kristin.

Pat: OK, that's a good idea. *(To Nathan)* So, what else do you have about your aquarium? That's interesting. I like that.

Nathan: That's where I tried to spell aquarium, but I got kind of mixed up,

Pat: Oh, . . .All right. Mmm-hmm.

Nathan (reads): "I got. . .here, I have an aquarium. It has lots of fish.

P, turns to K, smiles, touches book.

P: Eye contact with Kim, then k8 N.

P: Eye contact w/ N, points to book.

N. pauses, looks at book, looks up to look at P, but she is looking at page. N. re-turns to page to read.

FIGURE 4–1, continued. *Video Transcription*

the images into your computer. For some of these samples, however, it might be important to have the copy in the colors in which the student created it. For young children's work especially, it is often helpful to *trace* the student work onto an overhead using permanent markers. We have found numerous benefits in using this practice.

First, just as in transcribing your own tapes, paying careful attention to a student's work by tracing each of her marks on the page helps you to notice things you might otherwise miss and to ask important follow-up questions of the author. Second, in any future sharing of this artifact, you have a clear, projectable copy for the small audience of your teacher-researcher support group or for a larger audience of parents at your school or participants at a local or national conference. It is also important to date each sample and number it chronologically. You can also make color photocopies, but we usually use this technology sparingly, as the cost can add up quickly.

As you prepare your data, you begin to analyze as well. We suggest that you read through your written data each week and begin to note categories in the wide margins you have left. It may be helpful to have another teacher who is familiar with your work do this too. Figure 4–2 shows a sample page of field notes

The Use of Video in Teacher Research Projects

In the last few years, the use of videotaping as part of teacher research data collection has increased dramatically with the advent of smaller and cheaper digital videorecorders. Videotaping has the potential to give teachers insights into untapped aspects of their classrooms. Kindergarten teacher Andie Cunningham's research focuses on her students' work during their "movement workshop" time; video is a natural choice for her data collection. If you need to look at the role of body language, or facial expressions, or want to take a closer look at several things that are happening all at once that might go unnoticed in a busy classroom, then collecting and analyzing videotapes will be an essential tool to add to your research toolbox.

A note of caution: There is a temptation to set up a video-camera in a corner and simply record everything. The stacks of tapes pile up quickly, and it can take hours or days to review and make sense of the data. We hope the following suggestions will help you use videotapes in your research to good advantage.

1. *Decide specific uses for the video you are planning to record.* Ask yourself the question, "What information will video give me that other forms of data collection won't?" For example, if your research question is about children's understandings and behavior during daily Author's Chair sharing times, video will provide you with the words and actions of both the author and her audience. Audiotaping in this case would only provide half the data you need. On the other hand, for data from a typical writing interview or conference with a student, an audiotape would provide the information that you need and could be transcribed more efficiently.

2. *Catalogue your data in preparation for analysis.* Initial cataloguing is vital for videotapes, and much quicker and more useful than transcribing the whole audiotrack of each tape. You can make a running guide as detailed or as sparse as you need. When we catalogue videotapes, we go through them quickly the first time, mostly writing down phrases to serve as a memory jog. We use a simple cataloguing sheet with two columns for the time and a description of what is happening on the tape so that we can find our way back to it. To use a simple cataloguing sheet like this, first rewind your tape and set the time counter at zero. (The typical time counters record minutes and seconds and are automatically set at zero at the end of rewinding.) The two columns might look like this:

Time	Description
5:05	Conference with Marissa
10:29	Morgan, Tessia, and Carly, writing

We also find it useful to put a star next to segments we want to review more closely later.

3. *Choose a key episode to code and analyze closely.* After you have reviewed your starred items, or found an episode that is representative, transcribe the audiotrack first. It can save time to make an audiotape of the sound portion of your videotape so that you can use a transcribing machine to create a transcript of the verbal part. After you have a column for the verbal, you can watch the videotape and fill in the nonverbal elements that are occurring. For example, in the research question that focused on Author's Chair, you might have four columns:

Author		Audience	
Verbal	Nonverbal	Verbal	Nonverbal

After analyzing your representative example fully, it isn't necessary to do this with all your videotapes. Instead, you can view them again in terms of what you learned from your close analysis of one event.

Jeff and Alex are back at Jeff's desk looking at something else.	
Jacob has picked up another book and is reading it now to Keith.	**Bonding**
I walk over to Ashley's desk. She is writing a book called *The Mystery of the Dog on Valentine's Day*. She says the title of the story used to be *Valentine's Day*, but it needed a better title.	**Genre?**
Tiffany, sitting across from Ashley, says to me, "Give me some ideas for my first page." She's writing a story about a new baby. I ask her why she decided to write a story about a new baby, and she says she wishes her mother would have another one. I ask her what she thinks she could write about a new baby. She says she knows everything to write except for the first page. (Boy, I can sure relate!) I tell her that when I have that problem I write everything but the first page and then I come back to it. She starts writing on the second page.	**Topic** **Process**
Barrett comes up to me and says he wants to share his muscleman story with me. (He has read it to me before—but now he has changed some ideas in the story.)	**Teacher–Child Bonding versus Child–Child Bonding? Sub-Categories**

FIGURE 4–2. *Power's Field Notes with Hubbard's Tentative Categories*

from one of Brenda's early studies, with Ruth's tentative comments/categories in the right column.

Notice the notations of words such as bonding, genre, and topic. These and some phrases represent a first-cut through the field notes and are a way of beginning to organize them. One category that emerges on these pages is *bonding*. Initial categories may or may not become important categories for later analysis, but they give the researcher an idea of what is in the notes.

The example below from Ruth's research is part of a transcript of an audio-taped conversation, combined with two examples of student work referred to in the tape transcript (see Figure 4–3).

Excerpt from Field Notes, October 9

RUTH: Ms. Winterborne showed me your journal, and I'm interested in what you're writing. Can you read this to me? (*see sample 1*)

Figure 4–3. *Chuck's Drawing*

CHUCK: (*reads*) "Watch out!"

RUTH: Can you tell me about what's going on?

CHUCK: He's . . . um . . . this is his little brother.. He's going "Help," but say-ing "Watch out!" And his mother and father clear back there (*he gestures to a space off the page*) might hear him.

RUTH: So, his mother and father are off the page? This looks like an alligator or a crocodile?

CHUCK: Crocodile.

RUTH: Gosh! I like the way you wrote the words coming right out of his mouth. What's that mark for? (*points to exclamation mark*)

CHUCK: Um—for him, he's telling him. Telling him to watch out.

RUTH: Uh huh. And so what does that mark do?

CHUCK: It shows that he's telling.

RUTH: Do you know what it's called?

CHUCK: Called an explanation mark?

RUTH: Hey, that's great! You do know a name for it! I was also interested in this page. Can you read it to me? (*see sample 2*)

CHUCK: (*reads*) "I'm waiting."

RUTH: That looks like a telephone.

CHUCK: I'm back there. The arrow's pointing down at me.

RUTH: This is you . . . and where are you?

CHUCK: Right there.

RUTH: I mean, are you in the house?
CHUCK: Yuh.

There are several ways to organize samples to go with the field notes. One way is to combine them, numbering them together as shown in Figure 4–3. Another way is to have one folder or binder for the samples and another for the notes, but with each numbered consecutively so that you can find your way back to them—for example, FN (field notes) 1–125; S (samples) 1–50. As you read Ruth's field notes, for you can turn to the binder of samples and easily refer to Chuck's drawings.

Indexing

You've collected several sets of field notes or written observations regularly in your teaching journal. You've transcribed tapes, and you've reread your notes regularly, jotting notes in the margins. Before you're too far along in this endeavor, it is important to begin to *narrow your focus*. We have found *indexing* your observations early on to be an important first step. When you index your field notes and observations, you create a table of contents of sorts that lists the many categories you noted as well as the pages in your field notes where they occur. Listing these on one page helps clarify what you have already begun to observe, pointing to themes and categories that call for further notes, observations, and samples.

The first step is to go back through your notes to date, reading them and making notes in the margins—perhaps adding new notations to earlier notes that have been sparked by later observations. Then, on a separate piece of paper, list the categories and themes you have noted and each page on which these categories appear. After completing this index, jot down a few paragraphs about what you have noticed from these categories. What categories intrigue you? What have you learned from this exercise? Where do you need to focus your energies for further data collection?

This process can be very simple or quite complex, depending on your data sources, level of research experience, and personal quirks. We'll give you a few different examples next to show a range of possibilities for starting the indexing process.

Debbie Glazier, a reading specialist in Bangor, Maine, decided to do a case study of Andy, a student who she and the regular classroom teacher were struggling to teach. She kept a teaching journal of observations about Andy in class and during one-on-one sessions. Debbie decided after a few weeks to begin to index her notes:

> One day, in the middle of October, I was rereading my notes from the previous few weeks. I had set up my journal to write on only the left side of the page; the right side is for comments. I picked up my pen and started making plus (+) signs next to all the times Andy was "with" us: reading a book, writing in his response journal, listening to a read-aloud, or speaking in an appropriate classroom situation (asking or responding to questions, etc.). I put a minus (–) sign next to all the times he did not appear to be "tuned-in."
>
> Reading through these new additions to my journal, I began to add words and phrases, noticing if Andy was focusing his attention on another student, an object on his desk. Next to the pluses, I noted what specifically drew Andy in to an activity: a tape recorder, a student reading her story in the Author's Chair, a picture book read-aloud with plenty of humor.
>
> It was a turning point in my classroom-based research. I wrote in my journal on September 6, "It's going to be important for us to get Andy to read and write for longer periods of time." This was the initial period when I was recording how many seconds or minutes he actually stayed with an activity. That particular day, he stayed less than two minutes with a book he had chosen to read.
>
> I'm still using clock time to emphasize the length of time he is able to sustain an activity, but my emphasis now is on the positive happenings in Andy's responses. Because of the daily journal entries with the quick pluses and minuses right next to the descriptions of activities, I feel we have a "fast and easy" way of retrieving the day's high points. What enables Andy to be successful today drives tomorrow's decision making for teaching. (Glazier 1996, 114)

Debbie indexes her notes using only two codes—the plus and minus signs, but the indexing leads to connections across the data. In addition, it is enough of an organization scheme to allow Debbie and the classroom teacher to find immediate uses for the data in shifting instruction to meet Andy's needs.

Indexes are commonly used to discover which themes are emerging as most prevalent in a study. After several weeks of taking field notes for a case study of a student struggling in a middle school English class, Bonnie Wood indexed her notes and saw the following categories emerging:

Category	Pages
Teacher directives	2,3,4,5,8,10,14,15,17,18,38,39,42,43,44,45
Teacher's use of whiteboard and overhead	1,17,19,21,22,40,42,44
Classwork	1,2,39,42,43,44
Homework	18,28,35
Teacher movement	1,3,18,41,43,45
Disabilities	1,12,45
Restlessness	2,4,8,9,11,12,14,15,18,20,21,39,40,41,43,44
Yawns	1,2,3,40
Boredom	1,2,4,5,21,22,23,40,41,44
Abrupt exits	14,16,19
Students writing in class	19,22,26,42,43
Mechanics of writing	25,28,29,30,31,32,33,34,37
Writing is fun	26,27,28,30,36
Writing is hard	28,31
Learning to write	26,34,35
Fiction	27,29,33
Nonfiction	28
Student–student socializing	1,8,9,10,12,15,25,39
Student–student interaction: schoolwork	2,24,29,32,34,41,43,44,45
Teacher–student interaction	2,3,4,5,10,18,20,21,22,23,38,40,41,42
Students sit quietly	8,13
Students' concern about grades, performance	11,18,19

Category	Pages
Other people seeing writing	29,32,33
Setting	1,17, 38,39
Conversations outside class	7,11,24

After indexing her notes, Bonnie did some free-writing and drawing (see Figure 4–4), thinking about what these categories might mean:

During my interview with my case study student, Ashleigh, we talked about writing. She said many interesting things, especially about the conflict between writing for fun and writing when it's hard, when you have to worry about mechanics. At this stage, I was sure that the way to help Ashleigh was directly about writing and confidence in writing.

Incorporating my other field notes, however, I see that the primary pattern or conflict is deeper than writing. It is about control, really, even power. Who has the dominant role in the classroom?

While observing in the classroom, I was very aware of student interest. When did their eyes light up? When did their expressions change or go slack? What was happening (or not happening) in the class when their movements were lethargic?

Lack of motivation often gets blamed for student disinterest. Motivation is just one of the blurry variables that animates a student. I saw these tensions in my notes too:
- Physical movement versus lack of movement
- Rules and mandatory work versus socialization, fantasy
- Student native abilities and disposition versus expectations imposed on students
- Teacher control and choice versus student control and choice

The last points to the issue of control again. (I picture people's spheres of control like the fluid force fields in *Star Trek: The Next Generation*. They bend and change and flow, constantly balancing the movement within them and the outside world's movement.) I sense that if the students felt truly in control of their own immediate destinies in the classroom, motivation would be a moot point. This theme comes out strongly in Ashleigh's thoughts on writing and in students' physical and cognitive reactions to classes, classwork, and interactions with teachers and each other.

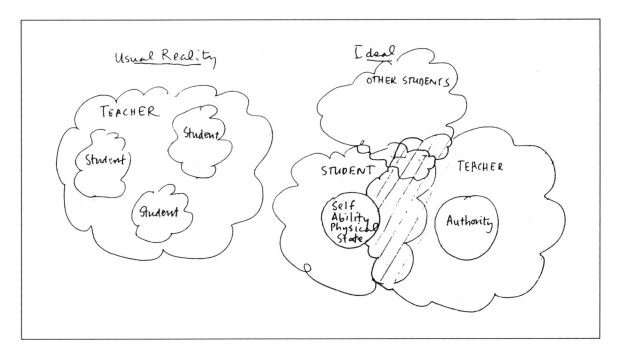

FIGURE 4–4. *Wood's Usual and Ideal Reality Drawing*

Initial indexing is somewhat akin to cleaning out the attic. A lot of stuff needs to go into some kind of bin or box. Some of what you find turns out to be unimportant. As a researcher, you never discard, but you can mentally set some of the information aside.

You are also organizing the information in a way that makes sense. In the attic, you might start with random piles, separating clothes from garden tools and old photo albums. Eventually, you might organize clothes further—into boxes labeled with each family member's name or according to size.

Bonnie makes a first pass through her data, like that first pass through the attic. But as she sees and sees again, she realizes there is a specific area that may be emerging as a category. Power or control among teachers and students is something she will pay more careful attention to in the data that she continues to collect. If she had not taken the time to analyze some data in the midst of her study, she might now have trouble making sense of all she collected.

Susan Hay didn't want to make the mistake of becoming too specific early in her categorizations of field notes collected for a case study. She soon found herself focusing on the importance of meaningful tasks for her students. Susan's pass through the data also caused her to analyze which data-collection strategies were most appropriate. She realized that interviews were the most effective collection tool for this particular case study.

Categories and Themes in Field Notes

Category	Pages
Background Information (BI)	1,2,11,14,18
Classroom Environment (CE)	1,11
Characterization (CH)	1,6,14,15,18
Class Routines (CR)	2,6,11
Individual Student Behavior (ISB)	2,3,6–10,12,13,19
Teacher Directives (TD)	2,3,7,11,12,19,20
Teaching Strategies (TS)	2–4, 8,9,12,13,16,17,19–21
Learning Styles (LS)	16,17
My Interactions with Students (MIS)	3–5, 11,12,14–17,19–21
Student Questions/Responses (SQ/R)	2,3–5,7,9,12,14–17,19–21
Procedures/Tasks (P/T)	2–5,8–10,11,13,19–21
Student Social Interactions (SSI)	7–10,11,19,21
High School Culture (HSC)	16

It was difficult to categorize my field notes. I did not want to draw premature inferences. For instance, Individual Student Behavior was originally in two separate categories: Student Engagement and Student Disengagement. But as I went over my notes, I realized it is not right to judge whether or not students are engaged based on their apparent behavior. Just because a student is fidgeting or staring at the floor doesn't necessarily mean she is not paying attention. I had also separated Student Social Interactions into the two categories of Off-Task Student Interactions and Student Social Interactions. How can I distinguish between the two? *Off-task* has a negative connotation. By my categories, I was implying that some forms of socializing were good and others bad, a judgment I wish to stay away from. I believe it is natural for adolescents to desire social interaction, and teaching strategies should tap into this desire rather than suppress it. The social interactions I observed occurred when the task was obviously not engaging the students. . . . Whose fault is that? The student's or the teacher's?

How can teachers provide meaningful tasks for students? How can teachers keep students engaged, and is this even possible all the time?

I learned the most from my interview with my case study, Kim. The main issue seems to be matching teaching strategies with student learning styles. My field notes point to this. . . . When the students are expected to sit still and listen for a long period of time, their behavior indicates restlessness, distraction, boredom. Kim stressed how important it is for teachers to vary their teaching strategies, because "most teachers . . . just lecture and have you read the book." From talking with Kim, I also got the feeling that she believes most teachers are out of touch with the needs and interests of students; she revealed a critical lack of dialogue, resulting in mutual estrangement. As a teacher, I hope to be able to establish a dialogue. I want to get constructive feedback from my students so that I can better meet their needs and interests.

Suzanne Pelletier did case studies of two students in her reading resource room. The first-grade teacher, who was the regular teacher for these students, exchanged a research log with her. When Suzanne went through her log early in the study to find information about the two case studies, she was surprised to realize that one child was barely noted in the log. "I talked about this child every day with that teacher, but I guess it wasn't natural for me to write about him in the log," she said. "I found I had to do extra interviews with other adults who worked with him, as well as additional observations, to gain the data I needed for the case study."

If you focus more closely on one or more case study students within your research project, as Bonnie, Susan, Debbie, and Suzanne did, you may find it helpful to create an additional notebook or folder for each case study. To look at the emerging categories in relation to her five case studies, Ruth created a notebook with a section marked for each child. Every week she reread her field notes then highlighted each child's words in his or her designated color (i.e., Kelly—orange, Paul—green, Ming—pink, Graham—blue, and Claudia—yellow). This way, she could very easily find references to these children when needed. For example, in reviewing the way the children responded to others in the whole-class share sessions, she could quickly find the comments they had made in response to others, as well as the stories they had shared about themselves.

At the end of each week, Ruth turned to the highlighted sections and recorded the categories with the corresponding field-note page numbers on index cards for each child. For example, in Kelly's section, she recorded the page numbers (FN 8, 9, 10) and the categories (writing concept/context; writing history; home/school). (See Figure 4–5.) These acted as a modified table of contents for the data on each child. Other information in this case study notebook included self-portraits, samples from reading folders, excerpts from special projects, as well as any memos written about these children.

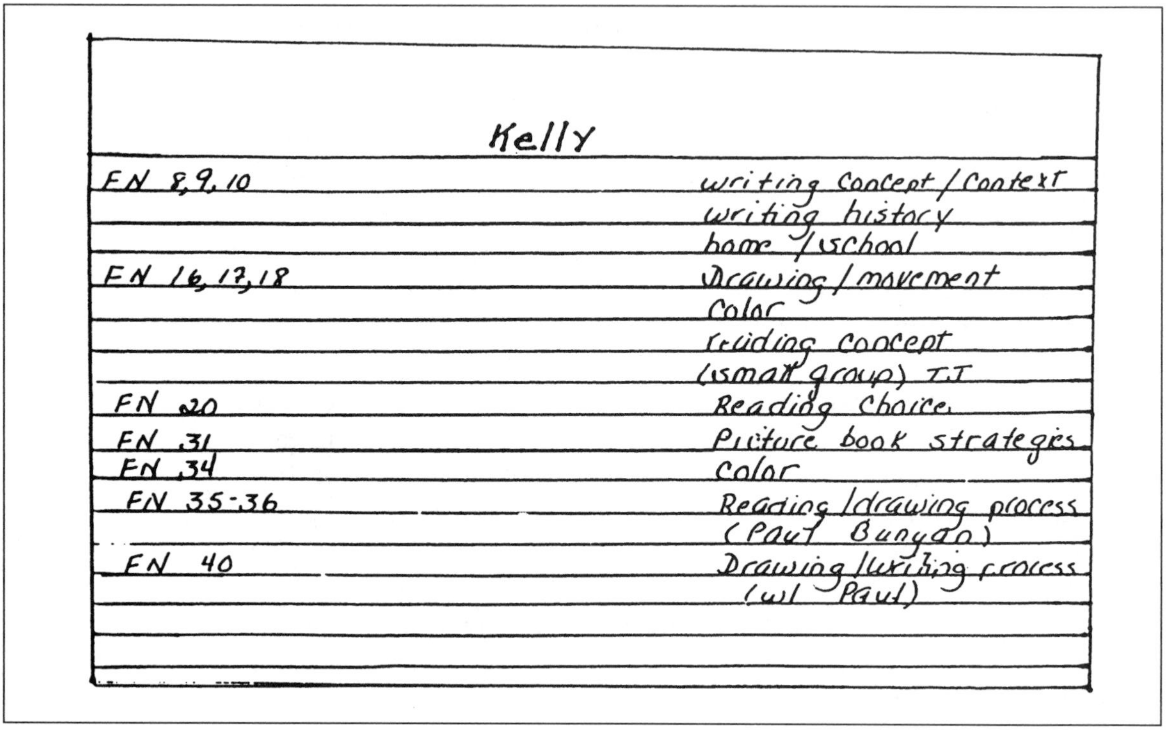

Kelly

FN 8, 9, 10	writing concept / context
	writing history
	home / school
FN 16, 17, 18	Drawing / movement
	Color
	reading concept
	(small group) T.T
FN 20	Reading Choice
FN 31	Picture book strategies
FN 34	Color
FN 35-36	Reading / drawing process
	(Paul Bunyan)
FN 40	Drawing / writing process
	(w/ Paul)

FIGURE 4–5. *Case Study Categories on Index Card*

If you use a computer for your notes, you can also easily access information about each case study child by using the Search or Find utilities that are a part of many word processing programs. For example, if you are doing a case study of Brian, you simply do a search for each reference to "Brian." You can then analyze and code all specific references to him within your computer file or start a separate file with categories or codes related to Brian's actions. Many of the more sophisticated word processing programs, including Microsoft Word, have tools for highlighting sections of text in different colors, as well as making sticky note comments in the margins; these functions are often right on the main toolbar. Tools like these are useful for trying out potential codes or themes on soft copies of notes in the computer before printing out hard copies for your files.

Narrowing the focus of your study can also *change* your methods of tape transcription. After she had begun her analysis of student responses in literature discussion groups, Shirley Kaltenbach decided to code the students' utterances according to cognitive levels of thought. Rather than creating her own categories in this case, she decided to use Bloom's taxonomy because it is one with which other teachers would be familiar and has been used often to look at texts' cognitive levels of comprehension. In this case, Shirley transcribed her tapes in a format that allowed for the analysis she was preparing to do (Kaltenbach 1991). (See Table 4–2.)

To assist in your work, you may choose to collect your data on worksheets with categories already delineated. For example, in Julia Crowl's study of home literacy, she asked parents to fill out a simple worksheet after each of her visits (see Figure 4–6). Julia also filled out the sheet. This enabled Julia to start with a database of dialogue, events, and actions.

This approach is akin to beginning your attic cleaning with labeled boxes or bins. By beginning with these categories, Julia could then determine dialogue, events, and actions that were common or critical during her home literacy visits. Eventually, new categories within each category emerged.

TABLE 4–2. *Kaltenbach's Coding of Student Utterances*

STUDENT	UTTERANCE	CLASSIFICATION
1	What does moon, ug, poet mean?	Knowledge
5	A poet is a person who writes poems. Do you do I wonders in class?	
1	Ya.	
3	I've got a wonder. If he's the moon, I don't know why someone would give him a nightgown, because it doesn't have arms.	Analysis
2	It would just fall off.	Analysis
1	It wouldn't fit him.	Analysis
2	It's not a him, it's a her.	Comprehension
1	Oh, it wouldn't fit her, because I think the moon is bigger than the earth.	Analysis
2	The moon is not bigger than the world. It's much smaller, believe me.	Evaluation

NAME: _____	DATE: _____
EVEN START APPOINTMENT	
I SAW:	
I HEARD:	
I SAID:	
I DID:	

FIGURE 4–6. *Crowl's Worksheet*

Analyzing Student Work

When looking at student samples, it is usually impossible to quickly jot categories you notice on the samples themselves. In this case, many researchers choose to use separate pieces of paper that can be attached, such as large, lined sticky notes. You might group the samples according to the categories that have emerged from your other sources of data, then store copies of these samples in folders marked by category.

Ruth's study of the underground literacy in a sixth-grade classroom depended heavily on student samples. The messages the students wrote comprised an important component of their daily lives. The written notes fell into three main categories: social, informational, and "silly"—as Kelly, the sixth-grade informant who assisted Ruth in the sorting, called them. The notes from the different categories were sorted and stored in separate envelopes labeled with the

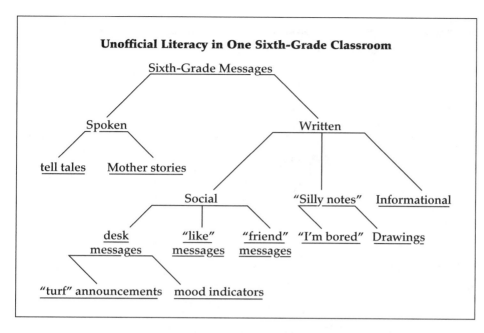

FIGURE 4–7. *Hubbard's Category Chart*

three main categories. Later, the largest category—social written notes—was further subdivided (see Figure 4–7).

Jeff Wilhelm (1996) also enlisted his middle school students to assist in the analysis of student work. This task, however, was a bit more daunting than categorizing writing samples because the study involved student reading. Jeff found it useful to view videotapes with students to gain their insights:

> I often videotaped students creating or presenting [story representations], visual protocols, story dramas, on occasion dance, and quite often an array of visual artwork that they used during and after their reading to help them create and represent the meanings they were making with text. Often, I would view the videotapes with students and have them explain what it was they were thinking, feeling and deciding as they were creating their responses. (57)

Ultimately, Jeff and his students were able to come up with ten different dimensions of responses to reading, which then served as a tool for indexing and analyzing subsequent data. This process of viewing and categorizing responses proved to be transforming not just for Jeff, but for his students too:

> As we co-researched our reading together, we were phenomenologists monitor-
> ing our own experience of reading. We were ethnographers observing and study-
> ing the culture of engaged reading. And finally, we were action researchers,
> continually asking "What-if?" and testing new ways of researching and respond-
> ing. We were continually experimenting as we tried new strategies, moves, and
> stances as we sought more powerful and fulfilling ways of being together with
> texts. My classroom, filled with researchers, became a giant project of possibility.
> (60)

Memos

Writing can be an important tool to begin to think things through and to share these ideas with a colleague. A *research memo* can be a writing tool for the re-searcher. Glaser (1978) defines a memo as "the theorizing write-up about codes and their relationships as they strike the analyst while coding. . . . It can be a sentence, a paragraph, or a few pages" (43).

But where to begin in writing to make meaning, when there is so much data, and so much of it might seem random or unfocused? Deborah Meier (1995) writes about "intellectual habits of mind" that she developed with colleagues when she worked as a principal in New York City. These habits of mind are also useful frames for starting the data-analysis process through writing about spe-cific data:

> It was all very well to refer to "habits of mind," but the phrase seemed too abstract.
> We didn't want an endless laundry list either, so we wrote down five. . . . They are:
> the question of evidence, or "How do we know what we know?"; the question of
> viewpoint in all its multiplicity, or "Who's speaking?"; the search for connections
> and patterns, or "What causes what?"; supposition, or "How might things have
> been different?"; and finally, why any of this matters, or "Who cares?" (49)

Take one of Meier's questions, and then apply it to one bit of intriguing data. Why should anyone care that third period had such odd behavior during your Civil War role-plays? Who did most of the speaking during a whole-class discussion? How do you know that Justine's critique of your new reading group format was really valuable? You'll find that sometimes linking one of Meier's questions to a datapoint leads to a deadend, but more often than not, you will make new connections or find yourself traveling down new roads in your analysis.

We suggest writing memos early in your study. It helps you begin to work with the data and to put what you are learning into a form accessible to you and to others. Memos are a way of capturing your thought processes as you collect data and of beginning to think about how you will present your findings to others. They are also a way to begin to play with the data and to have some fun with it.

In George Johnson's (1991) fascinating chronicle of the processes of three researchers studying the workings of the mind, *In the Places of Memory*, he notes that the essence of theory building is to be able to "connect the bits and pieces of seemingly unrelated data into a story" (46). Beginning to weave research incidents and insights into a tale through memos—musing on what story the data might tell—is important for classroom researchers as well.

Librarian Marcia Taft was investigating the choices children make in their library books. She recorded observations and conversations in her teaching journal and then wrote a memo to share with her teacher-researcher colleagues:

> Kim watched as Stephanie signed out her book and asked, somewhat condescendingly, "Are you going to read that again?"
>
> "Sure, I like it. I like her books. Besides, I read it the first time because I saw your name on the card. You've read it three times," Steph answered defensively.
>
> Since these are two avid fifth-grade readers, I wondered about this book, expecting to see the latest Anastasia, or, knowing these girls, perhaps one of our new fantasies. It wasn't a medal winner, or even Judy Blume's biography, but an amusing adventure mystery by a clever writer, Marjorie Sharmat—not a new book.
>
> Because the girls, usually comfortable classmates, were glaring at one another, I intervened. "Hey, there's nothing wrong about reading a book over again, especially if you don't have to."
>
> "Right. I have books I read over and over again."
>
> "So do I, even mysteries, even when I know how they'll end."
>
> Saying that I felt the same way, I tried to find out why.
>
> "Because they make you feel good," said Stephanie.
>
> "Because I don't have to worry that I'll be bored," added Kim.
>
> BOR-ING is one of her favorite words right now.

"Tell me some titles," I prodded, regretting the librarian tone.

"Oh, *A Summer to Die* and any Anastasia," Steph began.

Kim added, "*Peppermint Pig, Bridge,* and of course *Charlotte's Web,* but I hated *Trumpet of the Swan.* I never finished it."

"I only got to the third chapter for a long time. I finally finished it for the Book Club," added Amy.

Here was a new tack. Remembering how I disliked *Trumpet,* I poked some more.

"It was dull, nothing ever happened."

"I wasn't interested in the boy, or the swan. I just didn't care what happened to them." Not exactly literary criticism, but strong reasons, it seemed.

I started to suggest that the books we reread are books which touch our own lives or experience, but they were excitedly telling me about a book they had both read, reread, and read again since last spring, *Owlstone Crown,* by X. J. Kennedy.

"Why, was it because you met the author?"

"Well, I do like to remember the way his voice sounded when he read his poetry," mused Kim.

"And," Steph went on, "I like opening my book and seeing how he autographed it. I feel it's really mine, almost for me. And the story is creepy, and funny, and sad. Sometimes at night before I go to bed, I have a lot of books from school and the library around my room, but I don't feel like any of them. I read my *Owlstone* book again. But you know, Mrs. Taft, what you said about liking, because the same has happened to you? Well, I've never known any stone owls."

Later: Some points stood out as I was writing and rereading this last journal entry:

1. Often kids read a book because their friend recommends it, or the friend's name is on the card, presumably looking on that friend as a reliable critic. (Not quite the same as the current "hot" book; the "in" best-seller of adult cocktail conversation has its counterpart in school libraries.)
2. A book doesn't have to be funny or an easy read to be a favorite. This should be obvious, but I do get tired of being asked for a funny, short book.
3. When does a book become personalized, "mine"—one I return to again and again? This seems important to think more about.

Phyllis [another teacher in the school] suggested that the Kennedy book became a favorite because of all the excitement surrounding the Kennedy visit and the way several teachers used it in the classroom, rather than because of any intrinsic magic in the book.

Pam [yet another teacher] took it further in terms of these two girls."It was a special time for them. A lot of good things were happening to them and in the class at that point. Perhaps my own feelings about the group, and about the book, made a difference in the way I read it and in the way we discussed it. They felt good talking about that book, and good again as they reread it. And in discussing it, they understood it more."

This also reminded me of Leslie's [memo] and how she made *Charlotte's Web* her own.

One brief final thought. Isn't it too bad that kids can't have their own books to make theirs, even in a physical way—to mark, to underline, to outline the pictures, to turn down the pages of the best parts for rereading and sharing?

In this memo, Marcia Taft is just beginning to look for some categories that may be in her teaching journal. She is taking the time to ask herself,"What do my observations mean?"She includes in her memo her conversations with her fellow teacher-researchers as well, as she mulls over what she has learned, where she will go next, and possible teaching ramifications.

Patricia McLure, a first-grade teacher, was studying what happened when she instituted a new spelling program. After several months of recordkeeping and recording, her memo helped her sort out the categories that were emerging in the children's spelling patterns:

Spelling (5/15)

If you ask a group of first graders what they know how to spell, be prepared because they know a lot. The variety of words in their spelling vocabulary far exceeds any list we might assign to them.

In January, I started asking the children in my class to spell a word each day. It could be any word of their choice. We have this spelling lesson each morning sitting in a circle in the classroom meeting area. When I started, I thought of it as a positive way to reinforce the idea that there are conventional spellings for words. Well, it accomplishes that, but a lot more happens as well. Our spelling time has become a time to share experiences, affirm friendships, learn about geography and phonetic patterns, and hear about family members.

In looking back through our master list on which I record everyone's words, I see lots of names. Children have spelled names of people, cities, and countries, book titles, soccer teams, brands of sneakers, and names of pets. It becomes a public announcement of friendship when one child spells the name of a friend and the friend spells his or her name in return. The children share some news or an experience by spelling a name. Tara had a new cousin born recently and it took her three days to spell *Jacqueline*. Katherine spelled *Epcot Center* after her trip to Florida and Barry spelled *Ireland* and *Bunratty Castle* after his trip.

Some children have found word categories. Chris spelled a color word each day and Noa spelled a number word. Jill got interested in birds and practiced their names at home and at school. She spelled *robin* and *cardinal*, *goldfinch* and *blue-bird*. Then Chris became interested and she helped him learn some birds' names.

Many times the children's words lead us into a short phonics lesson. It's easy to look through the list and pick out some words with the short "a" sound, or one with a long vowel and silent "e." On one day, Nathan spelled *moving*, Bobby spelled *missing*, and Barry spelled *jumping*. That was the day we talked about adding the ending *-ing* to a word.

Long words were popular for a while. *Mississippi* was spelled by several children. Then Adrienne added *xylophone* to her list. Dwayne spelled *kangaroo*, Barry spelled *battleship*, and Kimberly learned *television*.

There seems to be no shortage of ideas. The list will continue to grow until the last day of school in June.

In our experience, memos are usually in narrative form, although they might be a visual representation of data, like the memo that describes how one first-grader's story later influenced other writers in the class (see Figure 4–8). This memo shows visually, in one page, how topics, themes, and genres spread through a class. This kind of memo can help a researcher work out relationships in a different way than narratives can and can be especially helpful when there is too much information or too many categories to present as text.

The Constant Comparison Method

The indexing and the categorizing described earlier are key methods of data analysis for building what is often called *grounded* theory, or constructing theory inductively from your fieldwork (Schatzman and Strauss 1973).

Glaser and Strauss (1967) list four steps in their method for data analysis, and these steps are called the *constant comparison method*. Here are the steps:

1. First, analyze your data in terms of categories and concepts. Look at the categories you have listed and ask yourself: What concepts are represented in these categories? How do these categories relate back to my original ques-

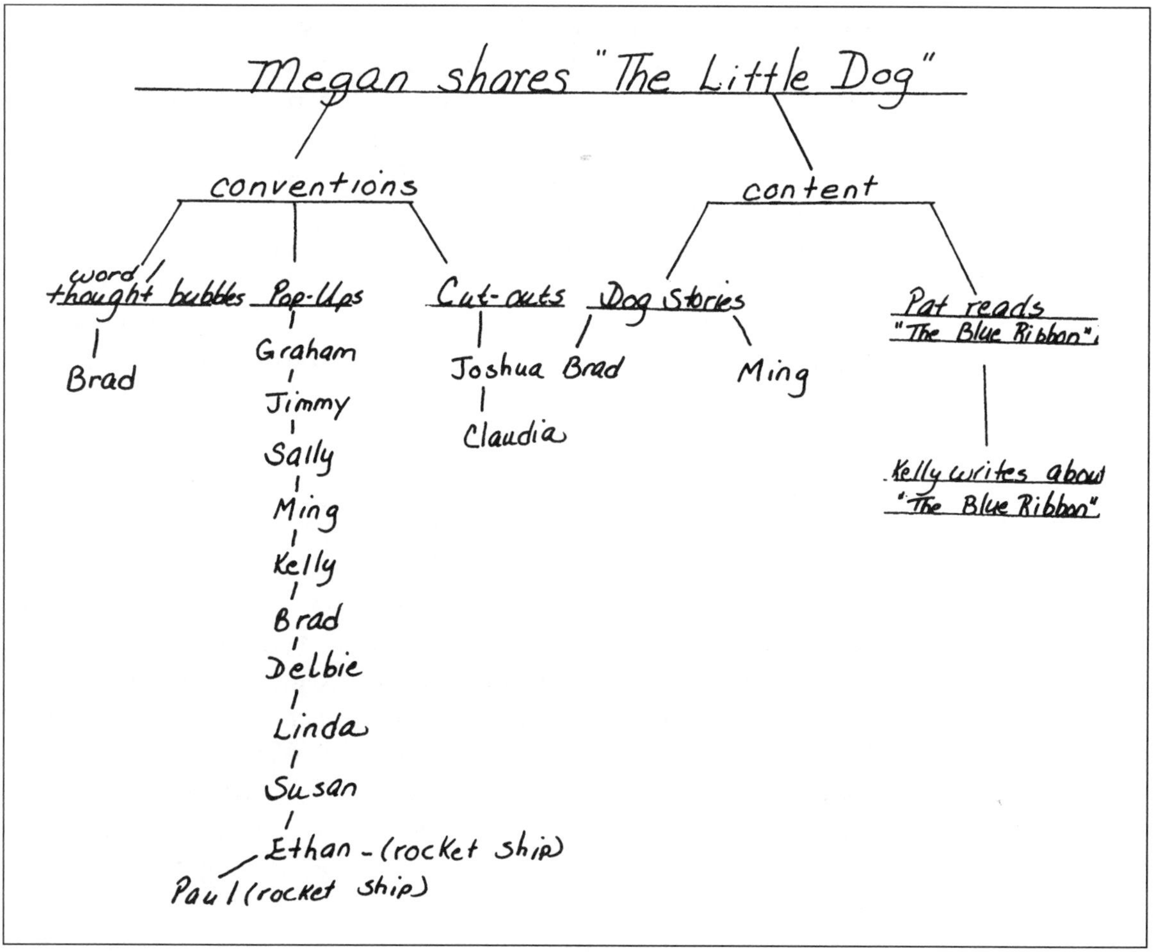

FIGURE 4–8. *Visual Memo*

tion? What new ideas have emerged based on my observations and other data? How can I define my categories?

As you collect more data, continue to code your notes and compare these with previously coded material in the same and other categories. This helps you to refine the properties of your categories, deciding just what elements constitute it.

2. Next, make the effort to *integrate* the conceptual categories and the properties of these categories. How are these categories and their properties related in some larger scheme or framework?

3. The third step comes later in your analysis, after you have collected most of your data. Here, you begin to define your emergent theory, or to make some theoretical claims about what you have learned. As you narrow your focus further, you will "test" it against the data. Does this category work to handle the new data as it emerges? How do these categories need to be further refined?

4. Now write up the theory by describing and summarizing it.

For more information about this strategy, see Glaser and Strauss (1967); see especially Chapter 5, "The Constant Comparison Method of Qualitative Analysis."

Data Analysis as Part of a Teaching Day

The constant comparison method is difficult to understand out of the context of a research study. To explain this and other data-analysis strategies, we have somewhat artificially separated them out from the daily classroom world. Before we go further in sharing ways to analyze your data, we would like to show you a teacher-researcher using data-collection techniques from her toolbox and several data-analysis strategies as a natural part of her teaching day.

Jenine Mayer explains how she collected her data, set up her recordkeeping for easier data analysis, transcribed her notes and tapes, wrote memos, and began to find and define her categories through constant comparison.

In her middle school writing workshop, she documented the growth of her students' self-directed learning. She decided to focus on miniconferences to find out what students knew so that she could respond to them. She developed a framework for her conferences and a data-gathering method that worked for her: keeping an anecdotal record. The following describes her miniconferences and the way she began to fit her data collection into the structure of her teaching day.

Components of Miniconference and Anecdotal Records

The miniconferences initially had four basic components—open-ended questions [OE], drawing-out questions [DO], paraphrasing [P], and summarizing [S].

1. I would begin with an *open-ended question*—"How's it going?" or "What's happening?"

2. Then I'd ask *drawing-out questions*—"What's going good?"—based on what the student said, to get more information.

3. When there was enough information, I'd *paraphrase* either the surface or implied content to see if I'd understood the meaning.
4. Sometimes, I'd paraphrase several things students said—in effect, *summarizing*—to clarify larger meanings.
5. As weeks went by, when I began to notice more about the student writing process, I also asked *drawing-out questions* based on what I noticed students *doing*.

My intent was to find out what students knew about writing. I tried to let their thinking be the focus of the conference first. Then I'd decide what I would add.

To gather data from the miniconferences, an anecdotal record seemed functional and workable. I had a chart with a dozen student names per page, and enough space to record about a week's worth of miniconferences and other notes. I expected to record the gist of what students said, with only a few phrases exactly as students stated them. I would decide what was significant as I conferenced. In addition, I'd add speculations as they occurred to me, then or later. I would read the anecdotal notes over once a week and write informal "memos" to myself about patterns I saw or questions I had.

I knew tape recording would provide verbatim data, but I'd heard horror stories about managing transcription. This way, the data would be processed by me as I was gathering it, rather than sitting in a cassette on my desk waiting to be typed.

Jenine has already made several important decisions about the ways she will collect data so that it will be manageable for her. In her description below, notice how Jenine's note-taking strategies are a part of her teaching day, incorporating anecdotal notes from her recordkeeping, "memory notes," and students' verbatim dialogue. Can you see where her wonderings are already beginning to narrow as she records data?

To make clear what I did when I miniconferenced and kept anecdotal records, I have recreated several miniconferences from a writing workshop session, labeling the components and showing my notes. This session happened several months into the year when writing workshop had gathered momentum. The dialogue is recreated from my anecdotal record, which has notes but only a few student comments verbatim, and from my memory. My notes are quoted beneath each miniconference, so one can see how I recreated the dialogue.

I was surprised by the efficiency of my memory. It had been sharpened by my concentration at the time of the conferences. My concentration was keen because I had a clear focus and knew I had to process information right then. Also, the very nature of the miniconferences aided my memory. To clarify what students said, I paraphrased and summarized their comments till I understood, in effect *rehearsing*, what they told me. I also processed the data again every time I looked over my anecdotal record. For this reason, much of the miniconferences are in my long-term memory.

In addition to the miniconference dialogue and anecdotal-record examples, I have tried to recreate a typical beginning of writing workshop—so that the miniconferences have a context.

The students form a typical heterogeneous group: a two-class team of sixty students with about eight gifted, eighteen learning disabled (instead of "lows"), and thirty-two average. One class at a time attended writing workshop.

A Typical Writing Workshop: Beginning and Miniconferences

"We're workin' on the computer together today, okay? Okay?? Pleeeze?" David and Nils pant as they bounce up and down before me.

"Okay. . . ." I say doubtfully. To the class, I announce, "One more minute till writing workshop begins." I hurry Jake along: "You're supposed to get the writing binders for your table group."

"Aww, you had number threes get binders yesterday," he complains on his way to the shelf.

"Will you talk to me today?" asks Joanne.

"Can I read my story in group share?" asks Britta.

"Yes, after Theresa and Kelly," and "We're not having group share today," I answer as I help Paul find a program disk that works.

The sixth graders gradually clear desks, open binders, sharpen pencils, load computer disks, and settle in to write. Ben stares at the wall, seemingly thinking. Tamara and Jackie write quickly, absorbed in their stories. Sean draws detailed, medieval/space weaponry. Nils and David confer fairly quietly at the computer, then Nils keyboards. I eyeball, as always, Paul, Mat, and Gus, who seem to be on-task, then with clipboard and pencil in hand I bend close to Theresa and quietly begin a miniconference:

ME: How's it going? [OE]
THERESA: Fine.
ME: What's going fine? [DE]
THERESA: This story.

ME: What's your story? [DO]

THERESA: Well, it's my story from before, but it's a play . . .

ME: What made you think of doing that? [DO]

THERESA: Well, I got so tired of writing he said, she said. This way I don't have to . . .

ME: Oh, interesting. So, you had a lot of dialogue, and it's going to be better now that you don't have to say that over and over . . . [PI]

THERESA: Yeah . . . it is . . . that was boring. I like it because it's easier . . . and I've never written a play . . . and Jason's writing a play.

ME: So you got the idea from being bored with he said, she said, and you've never tried a play before . . . [P/S]

THERESA: I like to try new things in writing . . . and Jason's trying one, too . . .

ME: Well, I'll be interested in what you think about writing a play instead of a story. Let me know how this goes.

I try to record the gist of this on my anecdotal record on my clipboard, getting a few phrases verbatim. I'm interested in how important dialogue is for Theresa, and how she likes to try new things in writing—and the social connection to Jason.

My notes read:"story->play/lot of dialogue/tired he said/she said/boring over & over /Jason's B-plays/always risk new, Jason??"

I move to Kelly, who I observe is unusually involved in writing today:

ME: How's it going? [OE]

KELLY: Good!

ME: Great! What's going good? [DO]

KELLY: Well, I've got a new topic that I think's going to make a really long story. It's about a girl who's blind and how it happens and how she lives with it. . . .

ME: I've noticed your stories are mostly shorter so far, but this one's going to be really long? [DO] How do you know? [DO]

KELLY: I have lots of ideas for it. It's not my usual boring story.

ME: What gave you the idea of writing about a blind girl? [DO]

KELLY: It's like the book I'm reading—*Deenie*—it helps me with ideas. I might want to find out some more things about blindness.

ME: So, you got the idea from your reading and you're going to maybe do some more research? [PI] I thought *Deenie* told a lot about scoliosis. [P] How does it feel to be writing on a really good topic instead of a boring one?

KELLY: Lots of ideas come while I write. It's not . . . boring; it's fun.

Again, I try to note the gist of this on my anecdotal record. I'm curious about her writing/reading connection, and about her dramatic topic choice. I wonder if she knows how much she would need to know to write a story like *Deenie*. I wonder if this student will finally come to life—school hasn't turned her on so far this year. My notes read: "long story/blind girl coping/lots of ideas!/from *Deenie*/research in lib/*a lot* needed/dramatic story/*excited!*/will this work?"

I then move on to Joanne, who, as usual, is writing with concentration:

ME: How's it going? [OE]

JOANNE: I'm almost done with my story.

ME: The one about your trip? [DO]

JOANNE: It's not really my trip—I mean, it is, but I changed it a lot—I'm the main character, but I go by myself to Hawaii . . . and other places.

ME: So, no parents, huh? [P] And you're almost done? [P]

JOANNE: Yeah . . . and I never even got to my second stop . . . it got resolved in the first place I went!

ME: How'd that happen? [DO]

JOANNE: Well, I thought of characters, me and another girl—she's really mean—and I thought of what might happen, what they'd say and do, and it worked out!

ME: So, it turned out different than you planned? [P] Why not just follow your plan? [DO]

JOANNE: Well, I didn't plan everything, I . . .

ME: So, you don't know everything before you write? [P] What do you know before? [DO]

JOANNE: Yeah . . . I planned the beginning and the journey and places, but I didn't like the middle so I changed and changed it till it turned out like this.

ME: You sound like you enjoy solving problems till they're better. [P]

JOANNE: Yes! I often stop in the middle on something. I didn't want to do that here. I wanted to finish this one, so I just stopped and thought and found a way to finish it.

ME: What made you finish this one? [DO]

JOANNE: I really liked it and it was fun writing it.

Again, I attempt to get the gist of this on my anecdotal record, recording some phrases from both of us verbatim. My notes (lengthy on this one) read: "trip->alone/= main character/story turned out different than planned/

journey but main Cs met in HI and solved problem *there*/ how much plan of story?/ planned beg and journey, places/didn't like middle so changed & changed/turned out like this, better/ seemed to like problem solving when didn't work/said yes/I often stop in the middle of something—I didn't want to do that here, I wanted to finish this one (she liked it) so I just stopped and thought & found a way to finish it/like it/fun writing." In the margin: "Do students only plan enough to preserve discovery or cannot plan well or are lazy? J a gifted problem solver."

At the end of a week or so, my anecdotal record for the class looked like this [see Figure 4–9].

Jenine's wonderings have spurred further questions for her. Now she begins to look at the patterns that are evident in her data and to flesh out the categories that have emerged.

Emerging Patterns

As my anecdotal record grew, I began to see patterns in student writing process—sometimes individual patterns, sometimes group patterns. To briefly summarize, in the initial stages I discovered *quality talk, evidence of problem solving done before students talked to me,* and *definite opinions in diverse areas.* To describe these discoveries in more detail, I noticed the students did not talk in a perfunctory or lifeless manner when I began miniconferencing. This was quality talk: interesting, flowing, energetic, and animated. We both enjoyed it. I was struck by how different it was from common classroom conversation. There's something important here, I thought.

Next, I noticed that students seemed to have already done most of their thinking *before* they talked to me. If I paraphrased incorrectly, students stopped to think about the difference between my statement and their idea. They were careful to restate their idea and listen to my subsequent paraphrasing until I understood. They seemed to care that I got their ideas right.

ME: So you don't like to put endings on your stories? [P]
KATIE: No, it's that I hate stories where the ending is wrong. It just ruins the whole story.
ME: So you want to end your stories, but you're afraid you'll ruin them?
KATIE: Yeah! I've tried several times to end "After You're Asleep," but I don't like any of them. I'm just not a good writer of endings.

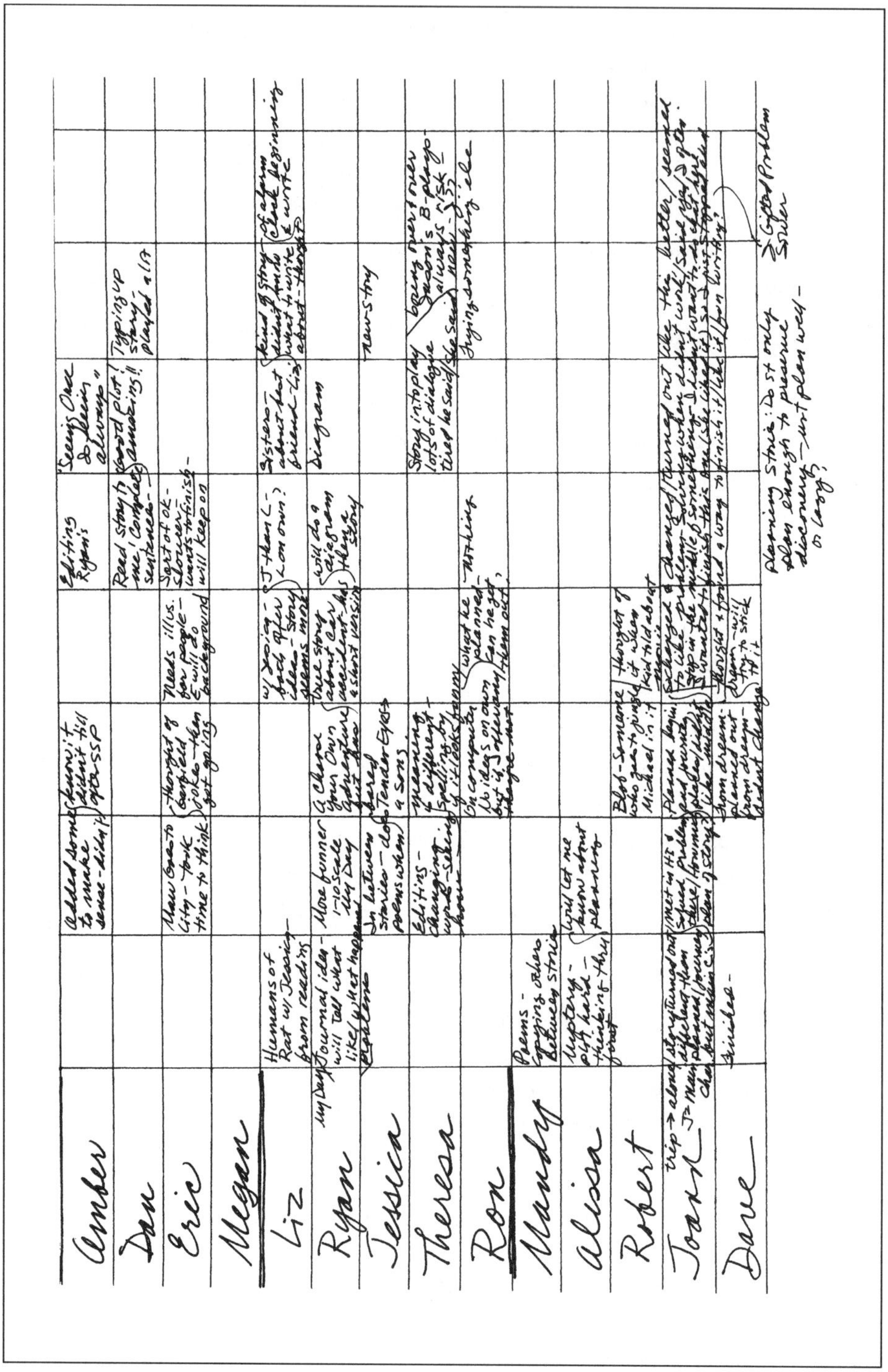

FIGURE 4–9. *Mayer's Anecdotal Record*

THE ART OF CLASSROOM INQUIRY, REVISED EDITION

Second, my drawing-out question often elicited a definite opinion: one phrase that popped up again and again was, "Well, the way I do it is . . ."

KELLY: Well, the way I write my rough drafts is to just go fast and not bother with my punctuation. Then when I type it on the computer, I add commas, periods and caps, and change words if I want.

JACKIE: When I plan a new story the first thing I do is make the characters. What they are like and their characteristics, what's their problem, and then an interesting lead.

I began to smile the fifth time I heard, "Well, *I* . . ."

My third impression, which took a little more time to develop, was that these students were figuring out so much on their own. More energy and ownership than I'd anticipated—and in diverse areas. As my anecdotal record grew, I began to see patterns in student writing process—some individual patterns, some group patterns. Logically, I began to ask questions in miniconferences about these patterns, as I described before.

In her quest to further refine her categories, Jenine enlists the aid of her students, taking her questions back to the whole class for the input they can provide.

Subsequent Discoveries: Group Problem Solving

After discovering that there was exciting problem solving about writing going on, and that there were patterns or themes to the problem solving, I naturally wondered how widespread a theme it was—and what further complexities it had. So, I took my data back to the whole group. From my anecdotal record, I read, for example, all the student comments about how to plan a story to the entire class, asking: "What are your opinions on this?" . . . Because I often couldn't keep up with my note taking during discussions, and because I wanted to know more about what each student thought, I logically asked students to do some writing—a letter or a questionnaire. . . . I not only enjoyed the student responses for their quality—the quantity enriched my data bank. And these were *verbatim comments*.

Data Gathering: Another Step

From the anecdotal record, my notes during discussion, the letters, and the questionnaires, I began to amass a large amount of data. I guess it was a burden, but it was so interesting. I followed the basic procedure I'd planned originally:

social desirability factor: do they say to please you

① Observation notes
who are my reluctant writers

② journals/logs

③ survey - completed

rereading data each week, highlighting the interesting parts, and writing memos to myself about what patterns I saw. I did a helpful interim step. It didn't take much time, but I'm a fast keyboarder: I stacked up the letters, questionnaires, and the anecdotal record and keyboarded the interesting statements, then I went back and organized the statements by patterns or theme. Then, I'd look at the now more organized data on the printouts. The data was less confusing this way. I wrote memos to myself on what I'd noticed. Here is a sample of a print-out and memo to myself [see Figure 4–10].

Jenine continued her research for the entire school year, redefining her role in her students' writing workshop and discovering what they were able to accomplish when their writing was more self-directed. One of her most critical findings was a redefinition of what it means to trust your students: "It means you trust them even when their learning behavior doesn't seem to justify that. It means trust includes time to struggle and fail."

Triangulation

multiple sources to consider it

Jenine's story of the data she collected and analyzed in the context of her classroom points out another important factor inherent to drawing conclusions: the use of multiple sources to support findings. In qualitative research, this is called *triangulation.* Webb and colleagues (1965) are credited with the term. In triangulation, a finding is supported "by showing that independent measures of it agree with it or, at least, don't contradict it" (Miles and Huberman 1984, 234). As the initial findings from Jenine's data—anecdotal records, whole-class interviews, and student writing samples—began to support each other, the picture of her students' learning became more distinct. She was reseeing the importance of their self-initiation and its impact on her classroom structure from several data sources.

When you use multiple sources to support your findings, you can build a compelling case for what you have discovered. Two examples of how teacher-researchers used different data sources for triangulation follow.

You may recall that sociograms were discussed in the data-collection chapter. Sociograms do not stand alone in explaining a finding, but they can support your findings. Grace Hoffman was doing a case study of a talented writer, Mickey, who did not seem to fit in with the rest of the class. Her research

STRATEGIES WHEN STUCK

When get tired of one story move to another--keep as many as three going
at once

Work through the tough parts of a story--the character has to tell how he
feels--wanted to get it just right--How did you know it was right?
Kept thinking like a reader--I'd to back and forth between what a
reader'd think and writing--it was hard and slow.

To not get stuck on names, make lists of them and a description of what
they're like to use when you need it

Harder to get going on a new topic at the beginning of ww easier if you're
continuing on something

Fastwrite

Bubble what you could do

Think, be patient

Make a drawing

Make a topics list, try a new story

B knows parts but can't get from part to part--tries fastwriting with little
success--I interview him about part--B writing about subject that
makes him a little uncomfortable--marrying his girlfriend

Talk over what will happen

Teacher-student interview--drawing out questions only

Think about what your character is like so you'll know what they'll do

Try a different kind of story: a play, then you don't have to write he said,
she said all the time

Think and think, and be patient, an idea can come days later

Teacher support: writing is hard, takes thinking and patience, you're
experiencing a common writing problem

When I get stuck on a story I go on to a new one and by the time I get stuck
on it, I have figured out something new to write on the other one.

It helps to just daydream for a while then write--or tell a story on a tape,
and write it down and make changes later.

If you get stuck ask your group, brainstorm, or SSP with someone.

If you get bored of writing something, write something else for a while.

Never think your writing is bad, because everything has a chance. If you get
stuck, go on to a new story.

If you can't write stories, than don't. Sometimes you should just sit and
think.

If you don't like a story that you've started, save it for later and start a
new story.

If you get stuck, just put everything down and think. Make a bubble of your
story.

[Handwritten marginal notes:]

- Summarize; Keep several pieces going at once
- Think of a reader's perspective: go back & forth bet. what a reader'd think & writing
- Be aware that some things are hard
- Beginning new topic harder than cont. on old
- Fastwrite
- Bubble
- Brainstorm
- Be patient
- Draw
- Have teacher interview w/ drawing out questions
- Talk over what happens
- Take time; think; be patient
- Get feedback from someone, group
- Don't be too negative
- Don't finish every piece

[Handwritten note at bottom:] Variety of strategies. I like student's awareness of hard problems in writing. They don't expect writing to be easy—they expect to have problems and they expect to be able to solve them. I like their grit and perseverance—they seem willing to struggle and problem solve—the payoff must be worth it. The section on importance of writing backs this up

FIGURE 4–10. *Mayer's Memo Printed Out*

question was, *What strategies can I develop to help children like Mickey, who face social challenges?* By doing a sociogram of the class, she discovered that only one classmate would choose to work with Mickey, and this was a mutual choice.

Grace also analyzed Mickey's writing and found that he rarely moved beyond wonderful leads in his pieces. In three months, he never finished a story. She also taperecorded and transcribed Mickey's interactions in small groups. Mickey had trouble focusing on the task at hand, but his classmates were quick to try to get him back on-task.

After analyzing all the data, one of Grace's findings was that Mickey worked best in small groups with peers, particularly with the peer who was his mutual choice on the sociogram. Her support for this finding, or triangulation, can be visualized like this:

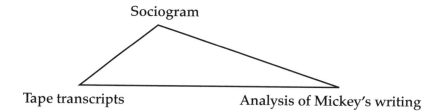

Sociogram

Tape transcripts   Analysis of Mickey's writing

Another finding from the same dataset could just as easily be triangulated this way:

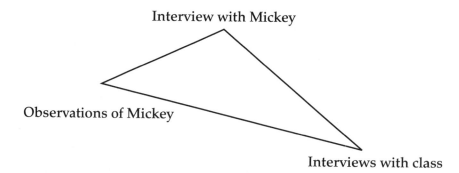

Interview with Mickey

Observations of Mickey

Interviews with class

The richer your database, the more possibilities you have for triangulation. Triangulation does not occur only within a dataset, either. Different researchers can also serve as triangulation points. Many teachers choose to look for patterns in student work, and then they also have students look for patterns. Triangulation in this instance might look like this:

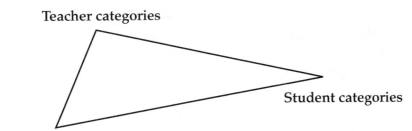

Teacher categories

Student categories

Transcriptions of class discussions

Just as Kinsey Milhone and Hercule Poirot pull together bits of evidence to solve their clients' cases in mystery novels, teacher-researchers search for clues to discover underlying patterns that will solve their own learning mysteries. The evidence doesn't fall into a neat pattern all on its own—we need to give ourselves space and time for the creative leaps that data analysis requires.

Crystallization

An intriguing method for data analysis that has emerged in recent years is _crystallization_. This is a three-dimensional version of triangulation. The method, as detailed by Richardson (2000), uses crystals as a metaphor to describe the data-analysis process:

> [Crystallization] combines symmetry and substance with an infinite variety of shapes, substances, transmutations, multidimensionalities, and angles of approach. Crystals grow, change and alter, but are not amorphous. . . . Crystallization provides us with a deepened, complex, thoroughly partial understanding of the topic. Paradoxically, we know more and doubt what we know. (522)

Valerie Janesick (2000) has used this method extensively in her work with researchers. The idea is that you use other disciplines to help understand your findings. Janesick has researchers write haikus to describe their findings or make collages from print materials. We like to set out a series of black-and-white photographs of everything, from abstract art to still-life bowls of fruit to landscapes. We ask teacher-researchers to choose a photograph and use it as a metaphor to describe their findings.

Jill Ostrow (2003) writes of the value of painting a watercolor as a starting point for describing her findings. The lines in a watercolor are necessarily blurry, and they help her think about ways of crossing boundaries in describing what she is seeing in the classroom.

Jill created a crystal to help visualize the ways she will embrace crystalization as part of her data analysis (see Figure 4–11). She writes:

> The idea of crystallization resonated with me so strongly, that I began to change the way in which I collected data for my research. Instead of a flat two-dimensional method of triangulating data through interviews, observations, document analysis, etc., I took Richardson and Janesick's advice and looked at my research through the lens of a crystal. In this way, my data becomes richer—three-dimensional—allowing me to dig deeper into my data through many facets. (2003)

With crystallization, you find ways to incorporate art or philosophy or history or diverse writing into your analysis. In doing so, you will be forced to view your work in a new way. By trying to come up with a poem, or doing a quick role-play with peers based on a critical incident in your project, you will see new

FIGURE 4–11. *Ostrow's Crystallization Figure*

THE ART OF CLASSROOM INQUIRY, REVISED EDITION

dimensions in the work. The findings will also shift and change before your eyes, even though your data will remain the same.

When Pam Kimball and Heather Smith reached the data-analysis phase of their research project on fifth-grader's math comprehension skills, they chose to crystallize their findings by presenting their work in progress to different audiences. Having to explain their discoveries to parents, fifth-grade students, the school board, and novice teachers gave them four different perspectives on the work, and deepened their awareness of its implications.

Teacher educator Brynna Hurwitz (1996) helped her preservice teachers empathize with their case studies through movement, role-plays, artwork, and writing:

> When asked to write what she was feeling while being her case study, Jaime scrawled in the following and then crumpled up the paper and threw it across the room. [Fortunately, she retrieved it later.]
>
> *I feel carefree I am in my own world. No one is here. I don't care about anything. I just want to be outside with the wind I want to . . . [illegible]. I don't need this. I feel out of control. I have no focus. I want to be myself . . . can't focus. O I hate this. I want to play. I can't concentrate.*
>
> This free-write captures the child's response to conforming. Jaime chose to focus on a child whom she describes as Van Gogh, an artistically talended six-year-old who was misunderstood and inappropriately treated in a "community-oriented" environment of which she never felt a part.
>
> . . . This exercise allowed the students to understand their case studies in a new way. As their bodies took on the physical characteristics of another, the feelings of this persona came through as well. (118–119)

We can also use crystallization to help us understand our students through intentional use of metaphor. One kindergarten teacher we know, Andie Cunningham, has set a goal for herself to write brief, metaphorical descriptions of one child per week to aid her in understanding the complexities of that unique soul in her care. She believes she will show through her actions the special understandings she is gaining.

Kristy Karsten looked at her student Malia through fresh eyes with the help of metaphor as well. Her first description of Malia was in typical educationese:

> Malia is a sixth-grade deaf student with a severe to profound hearing loss who wears bilateral hearing aids. Malia expressively communicates using sign language

and spoken English, however, both communication systems tend to break down when expressing multi-syllabic and complex ideas. Receptively, Malia relies on sign language and visual support (drawing, words in print). Malia has improved greatly in her reading skills, however, continues to struggle with main ideas, supporting details, and retelling/synethesis.

Notice the difference when Kristy reaches for a metaphor to describe Maila's learning:

Malia is like the toy machine in the grocery store: the kind where you put in $.50, take the controllers, and move the big claw to get just the toy you want. This is how Malia is. She moves that claw around her brain, trying and trying to grasp the perfect answer so she can "win," yet time after time she comes up with the ones that aren't quite what she meant, not quite the perfect toy, a letdown, frustration.

Through her metaphor, Kristy was able to crawl into Malia's mind and see her student more from an empathetic point of view, understanding the courage, determination, and the daily frustration that made up Malia's struggle to learn.

Making Room for Creative Leaps

After periods during which one has actively tried to solve a problem, but has not succeeded, the sudden right orientation of the situation, and with it the solution, tend to occur at moments of extreme mental passivity. . . . A well-known physicist in Scotland once told me that this kind of thing is generally recognized by physicists in Britain. "We often talk about the Three Bs," he said, "the Bus, the Bath, and the Bed. That's where the great discoveries are made in our science." (Wolfgang Kohler in Nachmanovitch 1990)

Have you ever made a long-distance drive and found yourself composing engaging mental letters you have been intending to write but didn't know just how to put your thoughts into words? Just the right turns of phrase, witty anecdotes, heartfelt messages come to mind to fill the spaces of your car. Or in that twilight interval between waking and sleep, does your mind hit on solutions to classroom dilemmas or just the right extension to build on classroom learning?

These insights and creative leaps seem to occur when we take a break from intense involvement. Artists, teachers, and researchers—and not just physicists—

rely on the breathing spaces that occur when they take a break from the problems with which they have been wrestling.

Our advice is to play with your data—as did Jill Ostrow, Gary Lynch, Kristy Karsten, and Jenine Mayer. We've shown you a number of methods for analyzing data, but in the end, there is no sure path to discovery. You might as well have fun along the way. Don't be afraid to take the risks that go along with playing with data.

K. C. Cole (1988) notes that playfulness is lacking in much research; too much carefulness prohibits real discovery:

> Foundations and federal agencies have become so careful (with a few notable exceptions) that researchers must submit lengthy, detailed descriptions of the expected outcomes of the experiments or projects they wish to pursue. Ironically, this precludes the discovery of anything unexpected, which in effect, precludes discovery itself. "Discovering" something you already know is there is like "discovering" the eggs that the bunny hid on Easter morning. Nature, unfortunately, isn't so cooperative and may hide treasures in the most peculiar places. She may even decide to hide toothbrushes instead of eggs, perhaps in a fifth (or tenth) dimension. (36)

If you want to be productive as a researcher, you also have to allow yourself unproductive time. Discovery comes from that think time on the bus or in the bathtub. There is no substitute for the quiet doing-nothing reflection time that leads to many leaps.

Trust, too, that your brain will be analyzing and sorting through your data even when you are not aware of that process. Poet Mekeel McBride (1985) believes that creative endeavors involve coming to know what is already known somewhere inside of us. Her words about poets and artists are also true for teacher-researchers:

> I think there's some part of a writer's brain or an artist's brain that is always working on the poem or the painting. You might not have access to it because there are big phone bills to pay and there's hurricane Gloria and classes to be taught and sick pets and so on. But I envision this part of my brain that's like a giant Hollywood prop set where everything exists. Where I could find, if I needed to, Cleopatra's shoe size. I could find out how the wolverine feels about snowmobiles. I think that everything is occurring in this part of my brain. I think that the minute I get inspiration for a poem, the prop people get it all figured out and set up and

it's there. The business of sitting down to write, and going through draft after draft, is a way of getting to that vision that's already complete somewhere in my brain. And even if that isn't a true vision, it's really comforting.

The business of getting to the true vision of what you have found in your research involves sifting through data, seeing, and seeing again, the truths underlying the busy-ness of classroom life.

Extensions

1. In your journal, freewrite for ten minutes about your thoughts and concerns regarding data analysis. Use your journal to "speak bitterness"; then, share your journal with two or three colleagues. Brainstorm ways to support each other to get past these concerns.

2. One of the best tools for beginning your analysis of data is a graphic organizer. In Appendix B, we've provided three of these organizers, which we've designed over the past few years, that have been most helpful in our own work with teacher-researchers.

3. Practice data analysis by taking a *cold* look at someone else's notes and experimenting with beginning categories. In Appendix C, we've included a set of field notes taken by a student intern in a high school class. Make copies of these notes for yourself and for a partner or a group of three or four. As you read through the notes, mark down beginning categories that strike you. Then share the results with a partner, noting both similarities and differences.

4. After you have about thirty pages of field notes, entries in your teaching journal, or tape transcripts, narrow your focus through the indexing exercise. When you have a list of categories on one page, set your timer for thirty minutes and write a few paragraphs about any emerging themes and possible ways to narrow your focus. A helpful next step is to meet with a research colleague and swap the indexes only, then do a free-write on what you have noticed in one another's categories. Set aside an hour or so to talk through these categories, setting goals for what your next steps may be.

5. Review your recordkeeping strategies. Choose one area to keep track of what you could incorporate into data collection. Plan a time each week that you can review this set of data as part of your teaching day. For example, do you have conference notes that could be incorporated? What kinds of anecdotal records do you keep that might be revised?

6. Memos:
   a. Try to use class time to write some of your memos. Every other week, as students work on projects or writing, write about a particular finding or muse about connections you are beginning to see. Sharing these with your students will provide useful feedback for your writing and help them be aware of what you are noticing within the classroom learning environment.
   b. Set up a schedule whereby you will meet a colleague on a regular basis, perhaps every other week, to share your memos by reading them aloud to each other. If you are not able to meet in person, use email or telephone calls.
7. Play with metaphors in terms of your research:
   a. Like Andie Cunningham and Kristy Karsten, reach for a metaphor to describe a student in your class. After writing your metaphor, share it with a colleague to see if she can help you flesh it out further. You can also extend your learning by following up with a quickwrite of how your perceptions have changed.
   b. Use visual metaphors to help you see your data in a new light. For a range of diverse images, you can use any book of posters or photographs. Collections from old calendars also work well. If you would like to order a set of 150 images with great variety, contact the Center for Creative Leadership (*palusc@leaders.ccl.org*); you can purchase their set called The Visual Explorer.
8. Read a mystery novel and look at the ways the detective has triangulated her data. This is also a wonderful way to make creative space for yourself by doing something enjoyable. There are lots of wonderful mystery writers; for example, Sue Grafton, Sara Paretsky, and Robert Parker have written books about clever detectives who are skillful data analyzers.

5

The Legacy of Distant Teachers
Creative Review of Literature

Review of Relevant Literature: Of course. I love to, all of the time
—excerpt from early draft of Research Proposal.
—Harry Matrone

M any researchers face the task of a literature review with the kind of anticipation reflected in Harry's tongue-in-cheek comment. It is often viewed as the necessary evil, separate from our real research agenda; an activity that takes us out of the classroom and into dusty, dry tomes in subterranean chambers of libraries or into the confusing universe of search engines, websites, and chatrooms. Looking at the body of work that has relevance to your research not only serves several important functions but can also be a creative and enjoyable enterprise.

Locating the Research in a Theoretical Framework

All of us learn, and continue to learn, from our colleagues, our experiences, and from our *distant teachers*—those separated from us not only by geographic distance but by time. In her study of the processes of creative individuals, Vera John-Steiner (1985) found that a range of artists and scientists learned from what she called "the legacy of their distant teachers." She explains:

> In their need to discover their own teachers from the past, there is a recognition of the importance of an intense and personal kinship that results when the work

of another evokes a special resonance in them. Once such a bond is established, the learner explores those valued works with an absorption which is the hallmark of creative individuals. In this way, they stretch, deepen, and refresh their craft and nourish their intelligence, not only during their early years of apprenticeship, but repeatedly throughout the many cycles of their work-lives. (54)

Who are your distant teachers? For us, it brings to mind people like Deborah Meier, Parker Palmer, John Dewey, Glenda Bissex, and Donald Murray. Our new ideas are often sparked by creative individuals as diverse as Zora Neale Hurston and Marge Piercy.

A favorite activity of ours is to imagine a dinner party for twelve where we can invite anyone we want, living or dead. The catch, of course, is that these twelve folks are going to discuss our research project. Whom would you want at that table? If a conversation among Jane Austen, John Dewey, Paulo Freire, and Linda Rief about collaborative learning strikes your fancy, you have discovered a few of your diverse distant teachers.

Creating an inventory of important theoretical influences that have helped to shape your thinking and your practice can help you fulfill one of the major reasons for a review of literature: *to locate your research in a theoretical framework*. Whether your review of literature is for a small audience that may offer support for your work, such as a research proposal board, or for a larger audience who will be reading your final research report, the first step is to conceptualize your research question in a larger tradition. Regarding your classroom practice, what authors have influenced your underlying theoretical framework? Try cataloguing the writers, artists, and theorists who have stretched and deepened your thinking.

Melissa Timm is a bilingual teacher who stepped out of her comfort zone to teach a two-way immersion class. Her review of literature clearly locates her research in a theoretical framework. Her classroom research focuses on the following initial question and surrounding questions:

In my two-way bilingual class, what happens when writing in the target language is used across the curriculum? How will the uses of writing across the curriculum influence language acquisition? Vocabulary learning in the target language? Comprehension in the content areas? How does student writing change? How do student's feelings about writing change throughout the year?

When Melissa describes the writing workshop that she conducts in her bilingual classroom, she cites Linda Rief's *Seeking Diversity* as the basis for the program. She then describes her theoretical basis for second-language acquisition as being dependent on Stephen Krashen's and Jim Cummins's writings. In the following bibliography, Melissa has mapped out the scholarly community of which she sees himself a member:

Cloud, Nancy. 2000. *Dual Language Instruction: A Handbook for Enriched Instruction.* New York: Heinle & Heinle.

Cummins, Jim. 1997. Metalinguistic Development of Children in Bilingual Education Programs. In *The Fourth Locus Forum 1997,* edited by M. Paradis. Columbia, SC: Hornbeam Press.

Freeman, David, and Yvonne Freeman. 1996. *Between Worlds.* Portsmouth, NH: Heinemann.

Hurley, Judith. 1999. *The Foundations of Dual Language Instruction.* New York: Addison-Wesley.

Krashen, Stephen. 1982. *Principles and Practices in Second Language Acquisition.* Oxford, UK: Penguin.

Rief, Linda. 1992. *Seeking Diversity: Language Arts with Adolescents.* Portsmouth, NH: Heinemann.

Bridgett Harkins situates herself in a different community of scholars in her research. In her work with middle school students with autism, she had concerns about their abilities to socialize with a larger group of peers:

As a behavior intervention teacher, I have been concerned about the lack of social interactions high-functioning students with autism display once they move to the middle school setting. I am curious about their need for social skills training and if that may play a part in the lack of social interactions I see them take part in. I hope that through setting up a socialization lab and researching what happens, I can discover more of what they need to be successful in socializing with one another. I also hope that these behaviors generalize to other settings and other peers within the school.

Because Bridget is looking at the particular needs of students with autism, she looks to leaders in that field, authors such as Janice Adams who explores creative ways to work with both children and adults with autism. Bridget seeks out classic texts in the field like *Social Skills for Students with Autism* by Richard Simpson, Brenda Myles, Gary Sasso, and Debra Kamps (1991). She also turns to people who have lived the experience: Temple Grandin (1996), an adult with autism who has written her autobiography, can share insights that few have been able to put into words. Grandin will prove to be a valuable distant teacher as Melissa's research progresses.

Janelle McCracken's concerns about how to bridge the gap between home and school led her to investigate the critical role that families play in the life and learning of each child. Her teacher-researcher question led her to set up "family nights" to build those home–school connections. In countering the conventional wisdom about parent involvement, Janelle (1994) locates her work in a larger theoretical tradition:

> I have been told by teachers that parents simply don't care anymore and that most don't have any desire to become actively involved in their child's education. They fear that many parents' involvement, particularly from minority and poor parents, might be detrimental to the child. I have found this to simply not be true. All of the families I have worked with, including those that had little education and literacy abilities themselves, were very eager to participate in programs such as Family Night. Furthermore, their involvement was crucial to the success of their children in school and to their children's self-perception as learners. Other studies support my findings. They conclude that most parents of minority students have high aspirations for their children, value education highly, and want to be involved in their academic progress (Delgado-Gaitan 1992; Wong-Fillmore 1983).
>
> Projects like the Haringey project in Britain (Tizard, Schofield, and Hewison, 1982) demonstrates that collaboration with families is an effective and powerful method of helping students achieve success in schools. Children involved in the family program showed increased interest in school learning and were better behaved. Nearly all parents, even those who were nonliterate and non-English speaking, welcomed the project and willingly participated in it. Based on his research, Goldenberg (1989) found that in reality, "Neither language-minority, low-economic, nor low-education status were obstacles to parents' ability or willingness to help their children learn to read (63)." (174–75)

Janelle, Melissa, and Bridget all relied on the larger community—a wider base of knowledge that already exists. It can be a relief to realize that we don't need to rediscover everything. Other researchers may have investigated the same area, and their work can often aid our investigations. This leads to another important aspect of a review of literature: to learn more about the field you have chosen to study.

Learning More About the Field

For most research questions, you will want to see who else has wondered similar things. What have they discovered? How have they approached this task? Because of his interest in his boys' writing, Michael Anderson (2003) began to look closely at the "culture of violence" in contemporary media as well as recent research on the ways boys in U.S. culture show friendship, use language, and create bonds within larger groups. Choosing one student who was typical of his young male students who chose to write most often on violent topics, Michael did an in-depth case study of "Jason":

> To better understand boys' writing, I explored these questions as they pertained to Jason, a fifth-grade boy in my room, who, when given a choice of topics, creates this kind of violent writing. Based on what I know about Jason, this writing, though violent, is not pathological. He doesn't get into fights. In fact, he is gentle and kind and is a vegetarian because he can't stand the idea of eating animals. I wondered what was so compelling for Jason about this kind of writing, and whether there was any real value in what appears, at least on the surface, to be little better than mindless drivel. Furthermore, I wanted to explore what I should do as a teacher with this kind of writing. (Anderson 2003, 224)

Through his discussions and interviews with Jason about his writing, Michael learned that much of Jason's inspiration came from television and videogames. This led Michael to look at the work of researchers who were exploring the effects of violent images in the media. His review of literature led him to magazines like *Newsweek* as well as contemporary researchers such as Sommers (2000), *The War Against Boys*; Pollack (1998), *Real Boys: Rescuing Our Sons from the Myths of Boyhood*; and Newkirk (2002), *Misreading Masculinity*.

Julie Ford's research questions led her to investigate what others have discovered about the effects of ability grouping (see Appendix A for her complete design). She wanted to place her findings within a broader national context. Like many other researchers, Julie decided to use the library service called Education Resources Information Center (ERIC) Search to obtain a list of books and articles from a data-based computer bank.

The ERIC database is an enormously helpful resource for education researchers. It contains almost all the books and journal articles published by educators in recent decades, as well as many unpublished papers from national and regional conferences. This database, now available and searchable online, gives you access to a wealth of documents. It is even possible to have many ERIC documents sent to users in printed or electronic versions relatively inexpensively. The main ERIC site is located at *www.aspensys.com/eric/index.html*.

Information is accessed in the ERIC system in a variety of ways, including searching for specific authors, titles, or topics. Topics are searched through keywords or phrases, known as *descriptors*. Finding the right descriptors for your search is the key to success with ERIC.

Julie initially chose two descriptors for her search: *tracking* and *ability grouping.* "I was amazed," Julie recalls. "There were tons of titles coming up on the computer, and as I looked at some of the titles under 'tracking,' I realized the articles didn't all deal with *my* definition of tracking in terms of ability grouping in the elementary school. I decided to add another descriptor to narrow down the list to what I could use, and added 'elementary.' "

Realizing that there were still far too many titles, Julie read through the short annotations.

> I scanned the titles and the brief descriptions and chose the ones that definitely pertained to my study, then ran a second annotated bibliography that gives just a little more information about each article. I was happy to find that two magazines had run theme issues on ability grouping. I knew those were issues I needed to read!

As she read these articles, Julie noted certain authors, for example Jeannie Oakes, who were cited often. After discovering "landmark" authors, it may be helpful to search ERIC for works by them.

AskEric is a more user-friendly version of the ERIC system (http://ericir.syr.edu). It describes itself as "a personalized Internet-based service providing educational information to teachers, librarians, counselors, administrators, parents." There are several parts to the AskEric service. The Question and Answer Service, for example, allows you to submit a specific request for information and receive an email response within forty-eight hours. The Virtual Reference Desk (*www.vrd.org*) is also linked to the AskEric site. Here, you have access to reference services that can answer almost anything, including ways to Ask a Scientist or Ask an Author.

Exploring New Territory

Although it helps to see what others have learned that relates to your field of study, it is not always clear at the outset of your research just what those fields of study may be. We have purposely placed this chapter *after* data analysis for that very reason. Most teacher research involves *grounded theory*, which is built from the patterns that emerge from the data. Since you do not know your categories prior to your research, you cannot know where your research may take you. An ERIC search at the beginning of a study, as in Julie's case, may not be appropriate. But as your categories emerge and you begin to define them, you may need to turn to *distant teachers* from fields other than educational research. Literature from other traditions can help you gain insights about your new grounded theory. It can be exciting to explore your work with the fresh eyes that other traditions can brir.g.

In Anne Hass Dyson's most recent classroom research, she wanted to understand "the landscape of contemporary childhood and how this landscape influences children's entry into school literacy" (2003, 4). Her emerging categories from interviews with the children led her to investigate the role of music in the cultural landscape of her young informants, particularly hip-hop. She turned to Davey D. Cook's *The History of Hip Hop* (1985) (available online at *www.daveyd.com/whatiship.html*) and *Hip Hop America* (George 1998). She also turned to disc jockeys in order to interview them about local hip-hop groups and the demographics of young children listening to their stations. Surely, when Anne was designing her research, she had no idea that her work in an urban first grade would lead her to the world of contemporary hip-hop culture!

The bibliographies of teacher-researchers are rich with titles from a range of fields that these teachers have explored as part of their quests. In their elementary school study of young children's conceptions of aging, Yvonne Mersereau and Mary Glover (1990) looked to fields as different as Margaret Mead's anthropological work and Donald McTavish's study of gerontology. Lisia Farley's (1990) investigation of cooperative learning situations led her to compare the successful student groups to aspects of both successful Native American tribal systems and business time management systems. Julia Crowl's (1991) case studies of how parents' literacy influenced their children led her to examine federal and volunteer programs that promote home literacy development. In her recent article describing her self-study of her planning framework, Betty Shockley Bisplinghoff (2002) has references from research on teacher planning to the philosophical writings of Parker Palmer to novels such as Jane Hamilton's *A Map of the World* (1994) and Julia Alvarez's *Iyo!* (1997).

Betty's use of a range of genres to inform her research is a strategy that is closely aligned with the notions of crystallization, which we discussed in Chapter 4. Poems, short stories, drawings, and the like can help us see our data through new lenses. Kimberly Campbell used the novel *Speak* (1999) to inform her inquiry into understanding adolescent readers. This novel is set in a high school and narrated by a ninth-grade girl. Readers see the world through her eyes as she details the cliques, the culture of the school, the teachers, as well as ups and downs with family and friends. Reading and discussing the novel with adolescents yielded rich insights into teenage culture because these young men and women could use the book as a foil to explore the ways their world was similar to and different from world of the protagonists.

The strategy of crystallization also encourages the use of metaphor. We have found it helpful to deepen these metaphors by searching out pertinent literature, which on the surface may have no connection to the research topic. For example, Ruth Hubbard and Andie Cunningham were searching for a fitting metaphor for the complex world of kindergarten. Framing kindergarten as a tidepool sent them off on a web search for information and photos to understand this ecosystem. They found that

> Kindergartens, like tidepools, are a meeting place of two systems. The land and the sea meet at tidepools and organisms in tidepools must adapt to adjust to the drastic changes in environment that come with the changing of the tides each day. This reminds us of the way that children must adjust to the very different environments of home and school at this cultural meeting place (Cunningham and Hubbard 2003, 1).

A closer look at this ecosystem, the daily patterns, the needs of its varied inhabitants, and the long- and short-term effects of different aspects of the environment helped Andie and Ruth see the kindergarten culture with fresh eyes.

As your categories emerge, keep yourself open to investigating areas outside of typical educational research to broaden your perspective as well as your knowledgebase, as these teachers have done. Like other aspects of the research process, your review of literature should be a *creative* enterprise. "Creativity exists in the searching even more than in the finding or being found" (Nachmanovitch 1990, 45). Be open to serendipity; we've found that we stumble across interesting references that beckon to be explored in surprising places—from reviews and editorials in newspapers to discussions on the current alternative music scene with neo-Bohemian adolescents. As your study progresses, you will begin to read the world with a researcher's eye, looking everywhere for roots and connections to your work.

Another helpful strategy as you review literature is to become a critical reader of the reference pages and the bibliographies of the books and articles you read. Although some of the journals or sources cited may be unfamiliar, they can lead you to rich resources you would have missed otherwise. One researcher we know even wrote in her teaching journal, "You really know you're conducting research when . . . you turn to the references at the end of article first."

It also helps to talk with others about what you are exploring. One of the best strategies for getting started in your bibliographic review is to start with a live expert. If your study involves students with autism, talk to colleagues and find out which teachers in your town or state are already immersed in exploring this issue. Chances are that these teachers will have some articles or books to get you started. They can let you know some of the landmark studies or researchers in the field before you confront the mountain of books and articles at the library.

It is time to open the curtains and let some light into the old dark, underground images of reviews of literature. The following extensions provide further suggestions for making your literature review a meaningful and creative enterprise.

Extensions

1. In your teaching journal, take some time to reflect on your distant teachers. Over the course of a week or two, create an inventory of the important theoretical influences that have helped shape your thinking and your practice. Plan to share and talk through this inventory with at least one other person. If you have a support group, you might bring your journal entries to share at one meeting. Hearing others' inventories may spark recollections of distant teachers you have not included in your list. On the other hand, it may also interest you in the writings of theorists who are new to you, but whose work could be useful to you.

2. Let others know the patterns that you see emerging in your data and the categories that you are forming. Plan brainstorming sessions with a partner or with your support group into your meetings so that others can tell you

about interesting sources and references they have encountered. Be on the lookout for intriguing references for your colleagues as well.

3. Choose several articles by teacher-researchers and take a close look at their references. What is the community of scholars in which they place themselves? What do you notice about the fields of study to which they refer? What can you learn from these references, and what suggestions would you offer to the authors?

4. Make a date to sit at your computer for a two-hour block of time and try a search that is not education-based. A search engine such as Google will lead you to a wealth of new sources if you type in a few keywords or phrases. Allow yourself the luxury of following new leads and exploring sites you would not have considered.

5. Rummage through your bookshelf and file cabinet to start a computer file of articles and books you have read, making brief annotations if you have time. Having a master list of references can save you time and energy down the road as your study of research multiplies.

6. Envision that dinner party of twelve folks, living or dead, discussing your research question. Whom would you invite? Why? What would these people argue about? Make a list and imagine directions the conversation might take. This can be fun to do with a group of teacher-researcher friends—creating the menus and guest lists and sharing imagined conversations.

chapter 6

Perishable Art
Writing Up Research

The classroom is like perishable art. It has an evanescence that makes it, for me at least, energizing and joyful, but also bittersweet, because the events are impossible to hold in time as a complete entity. Being a teacher-researcher, however, has given me some capacity to grab onto fragments of the life that is streaming by me.
—*Karen Gallas*

This is the chapter in a research handbook that should begin with words like, "so now you're ready to write." The words imply that the writing begins after the data is collected and analyzed and that you have come up with some big, wonderful, unique, "this will change the world" ideas about how learning works in classrooms.

But writing, like every other part of the research process, is not a neat, discrete step somewhere far down the road of exploring your question. Like data analysis, writing up research begins as soon as you consider possible research questions. Plus, as soon as you start to collect data, you also begin to draft and revise what it is you have to say about what you are seeing.

Why write? Only you can find the answer to that question. In this chapter, we'll encourage you to write for a range of folks, from the teacher next door to the scholar on the other side of the world. But perhaps Karen Gallas has the best answer for many of us—the most incredible and bittersweet moments in our teaching are always perishable art, and writing may be the only way to preserve them in our memories years from now.

We've accepted that writing up research and finding audiences for our work is much like the process Carolyn Chute (Murray 1990) describes when she writes:

> [The writing process] is sort of like when you've got no electricity and you've gotten up in the middle of the night to find the bathroom, feeling your way along in the dark. I can't hardly tell you what I do because I really don't know. (44)

We are hesitant to issue any edicts about what will or will not work in your writing. And we do not want to establish too many parameters for how you should write, what final audiences for your work are appropriate, or what is acceptable as research writing.

We are convinced that all potential audiences for teacher research—colleagues, editors of journals, parents, administrators, and even policymakers—want to hear fresh voices and insights. The standard templates for writing up research need to be tested, stretched, perhaps even broken and reinvented to reflect how teachers come to new knowledge in their classrooms.

We hope you will find new ways to present your findings and accept our insights for what they are. We are two authors whose work is rejected by reviewers as often as it is accepted, and we have much to learn about what makes writing successful. What we can tell you about writing up research comes from our own stumblings in the dark, trying to learn the workings of audiences and editors. In the end, you may have an entirely different writing process than the ones we and other teacher-researchers we know have developed.

Writing is hard work, but in the right environment it can be what Murray (1990) describes as "hard fun." We sincerely thank Donald Murray for his life's work. Most ideas in this chapter can be attributed directly to his teaching and writing. Those few ideas that are not direct descendants of his work were born from the care he showed in helping us understand ourselves and others as writers.

There is nothing more exhilarating or challenging than finding others who are interested in what you have discovered in your classroom. What follows are some simple principles for writing research that have endured in our work and have helped us and the teacher-researchers we work with to have healthy attitudes toward presenting research to wider audiences.

The Importance of Routine and Deadlines

Every step in the research process involves the editing, rehearsal, and revising of the final product. In fact, researchers who are successful in writing up their work and presenting it to diverse audiences follow the principles and routines established in successful writing workshops. Consistency in routine enables teachers to complete their writing projects.

One of the daunting aspects of teacher research is the ever-growing mountain of information. Student work, field notes, tapes, and transcriptions—the database becomes bulky fast. The process of writing up research becomes a process of containing and exerting some control over the mountain. Pulitzer Prize–winning writer Annie Dillard (1989) compares work in progress to a wild beast:

> A work in progress quickly becomes feral. It reverts to a wild state overnight. It is barely domesticated, a mustang on which you one day fastened a halter, but which now you can't catch. It is a lion you cage in your study. As the work grows, it gets harder to control; it is a lion growing in strength. You must visit it every day and reassert your mastery over it. If you skip a day, you are, quite rightly, afraid to open the door to its room. You enter its room with bravura, holding a chair at the thing and shouting, "Simba!" (71)

Writing and thinking a little bit each day about the research is the teacher's way of saying "Simba!" regularly and whipping the inquiry into shape. You can never feel truly in control of all the information and possible findings at your fingertips. But daily writing will at least make you feel as though you are managing the task.

Perhaps the most important aspect of learning to write up your research is to do it often. Researchers need to practice the craft of writing even while they are in the midst of collecting and analyzing data. Daily thinking and writing will occur only if it is integrated naturally into your teaching day. The writing has to start with the oral and written responses you already exchange with students and colleagues.

In previous chapters, we have shown how blurred the lines between teaching and research should be. Data collection and analysis can build on record-keeping strategies you already use as part of your teaching day. Writing up research can also build on the natural audiences for your work within your school.

There are many ways to get this daily practice with an audience. One of the best ways to foster writing daily for us has been to write to our students. Writing to students helps us clarify our ideas and budget our writing time. We've never been able to understand how some researchers are able to set aside a few hours on Saturday or two months in the summertime to do their writing.

If we didn't have the routine of daily response to students and colleagues, we would lose most of our insights and findings in the long stretch between doing the research and writing it up. We find we need immediate, sympathetic audiences for our work in order to refine ideas and findings continually.

Researchers also need to follow William Stafford's advice to "lower their standards." Unrealistic standards breed procrastination. You may have already identified procrastination as one of the hurdles to overcome in writing up your research. You are not alone; almost everyone procrastinates. Many researchers aren't lazy—they are just unrealistic. What is in your head will always be more eloquent than what lands on the page. The frustration of producing words on the page that are not up to the quality of the words in our heads makes many researchers avoid producing work. It also fosters last-minute work. Both of us have procrastinated right up until a deadline. Days or minutes before the deadline, a draft is finally blurted out; we hold our noses and close our eyes, and the piece is shot out at its audience. These writing experiences are not pleasant memories, and lowering our standards helps us to produce work well before deadlines.

The daily practice of responding to students forces teachers to lower their standards and accept the uneven quality of their own work. The drive for perfectly formed ideas and responses is overridden by the knowledge that students need regular responses. In the same way, regular practice in writing up research helps teacher-researchers overcome the too-high standards we all carry in our heads, standards that often keep us from searching hard for an audience or the best way to present what we know.

The concept of lowering standards to write is a paradox. If you don't lower your standards, nothing will land on the page. If you do not write, you will not improve. By lowering your standards, you do get a draft, however ill-formed, on the page. You then have something to revise, and revise again. The process of improving writing cannot begin until *something* lands on the page.

We also find that our students are wonderful resources for testing out research findings. They will present blunt challenges to our assumptions about how the classroom works. When preliminary findings are shared on a daily basis, in hastily scrawled form, a teacher-researcher feels less wedded to them. We find that it is easier to make revisions in our findings and write-ups when we share them in the midst of trying to make sense of them.

The issues around sharing research-in-progress are similar to those faced by a teacher in a writing workshop. During a daily workshop, some teachers wait for students to come to their desks for a writing conference. In our experience, these conferences with student authors often fail in getting students to revise work. Students usually wait to approach the teacher's desk until they feel they have finished a piece; since they believe the piece is finished, they often become hurt or frustrated by revision suggestions.

The same is true when teacher-researchers present drafts of articles only in final stages. At that point, it is painful to accept criticism of the ideas and suggestions for major revision. It is far easier to revise an idea that is scrawled on a sticky note you have attached to a student's work, a memo that is read to the class, or a theory in fragmented sentences that is exchanged with a colleague weekly in a dialogue journal.

Some writers believe that *all* writing is a form of revision. Every sticky note, journal notation, letter sent across the country to a friend—all are pieces of drafts. When you write regularly to students and colleagues, weaving your findings and theories naturally into your correspondence with them, you will have produced hundreds of drafts of these ideas by the time you attempt to write an article for publication.

One of the worst things that you can do is to hoard your research writing time, cutting down the writing you do for colleagues and students. Do not try to segregate research writing from the daily writing that is a natural part of your teaching day. In the data-collection chapter, we showed how teachers adapted or developed note-taking tools that informed both teaching and research. Fluency and confidence in your writing comes from practice. The more you rehearse your ideas in daily recordkeeping, the better the final drafts and presentations of your research will be.

Finally, the critical element in establishing a routine is to build deadlines into your work. Some of these deadlines may turn out to be imposed for you—a date when a conference proposal is due, the evening when you must present your research to colleagues, or the month when submissions for a themed issue of a journal are due.

You will have more success meeting big deadlines if you impose and meet smaller deadlines for your work. Set a date to send a research memo to a friend, or to present a rough sketch of findings to colleagues over lunch, and stick to it.

In Chapter 4, we showed how different teachers used memo exchanges to experiment with presenting findings. Brief narratives like those of Pat McLure or Marcia Taft are a good way of testing out how to present a finding and can eventually evolve into longer texts. Self-imposed deadlines for brief narratives or memos provide small points of closure throughout a project and help researchers see the larger deadlines as more manageable.

Know What You Want to Say

You will not be able to include everything you want in your research writing. You will not even be able to include most of what you want to say. After months of collecting and analyzing data, the monumental task becomes distilling all that you have learned into a twenty-minute presentation for colleagues, a ten-page article, or a five-minute conference with parents. The hardest part of writing up research, and the one that leads many researchers to avoid this part of the research process, is deciding what to leave in and what to leave out of their drafts. Writer Annie Dillard (1987) believes this sorting is essential if you want to avoid losing your audience; she writes:

> The writer of any work, and particularly any nonfiction work, must decide two crucial points: What to put in and what to leave out. . . . You have to take pains in a memoir not to hang on the reader's arm, like a drunk, and say, "And then I did this it was so interesting." (53)

Research reports that present a chronological account of what happened in the classroom are not engaging to readers. Reading a lengthy and lightly edited chronological research account is akin to sitting through four carousels of slides from someone else's vacation. If you want to avoid slurring the ideas of your text together and losing your audience, you have to slog through the data first and narrow your findings down to essentials. Once you know what your finding or findings are, follow the old writing axiom of "showing, not telling." The best way to show findings is to look for those critical incidents in your data, the "aha" or "oh no" moments, when you had a breakthrough in answering your research question. If it was a moment of vivid insight for you, it may well be a breakthrough for your audience too.

The challenge after you identify the moment is to recreate the significant, concrete details around the event that can make it jump off the page for your readers. Details are not enough—you need to pick and choose what Ken Macrorie (1987) calls the telling details.

One of our favorite "aha" and "oh no" moments is in writer Raymond Carver's essay "Fires" (1983), an eloquent analysis of what influenced his decision to be a writer specializing in short fiction rather than in longer novels. In his essay, he shows his readers the enormous role his children played in this decision. His moment of truth came not in front of a typewriter but in a laundromat:

In the mid 1960s I was in a busy laundromat in Iowa City trying to do five or six loads of clothes, kids' clothes, for the most part, but some of our own clothing, of course, my wife's and mine. My wife was working as a waitress for the University Athletic Club that Saturday afternoon. I was doing chores and being responsible for the kids. They were with some other kids that afternoon, a birthday party maybe. Something. But right then I was doing the laundry. I'd already had sharp words with an old harridan over the number of washers I'd had to use. Now I was waiting for the next round with her, or someone else like her. I was nervously keeping an eye on the dryers that were in operation in the crowded laundromat. When and if one of the dryers ever stopped, I planned to rush over to it with my shopping basket of damp clothes. Understand, I'd been hanging around in the laundromat for thirty minutes or so with this basketful of damp clothes. I'd already missed out on a couple of dryers—somebody'd gotten there first. I was getting frantic. As I say, I'm not sure where our kids were that afternoon. Maybe I had to pick them up from someplace, and it was getting late, and that contributed to my state of mind. I did know that even if I could get my clothes into a dryer it would still be another hour or more before the clothes would dry, and I could sack them up and go home with them, back to our apartment in married-student housing. Finally a dryer came to a stop. And I was right there when it did. The clothes inside quit tumbling and lay still. In thirty seconds or so, if no one showed up to claim them, I planned to get rid of the clothes and replace them with my own. That's the law of the laundromat. But at that minute a woman came over to the dryer and opened the door. I stood there waiting. This woman put her hand into the machine and took hold of some items of clothing. But they weren't dry enough, she decided. She closed the door and put two more dimes into the machine. In a daze I moved away with my shopping cart and went back to waiting. But I remember thinking at that moment, amid the feelings of helpless frustration that had me close to tears, that nothing—and brother, I mean nothing—that ever happened to me on this earth could come anywhere close, could possibly be as important to me, could make as much difference, as the fact that I had two children. And that I would always have them and always find myself in this position of unrelieved responsibility and permanent distraction. (23–24)

In this "aha" moment, Carver recreates an experience that may be universal. Not all of us have waited for a dryer in a busy Laundromat; but those feelings of momentary, frantic helplessness are probably universal. We all have spent surreal minutes when strangers ahead of us in a line, in a doctor's waiting room, or at the local motor vehicle registry have forced us to rearrange our plans for the rest of the day or week. That heavy weight of responsibility, of running but never quite catching up to all that needs to be done for others, is probably also universal (at least for teachers!). The incident Carver relates is interesting, and it would be hard for anyone to not make some connection to it.

But the power in Carver's writing comes from his ability to move us to *his* connection, his moment of truth. Showing a moment of truth in your classroom needs to build on that paradox. The more concrete and specific your presentation of the "aha" and "oh no" moments is, the more likely you are to find some universal connection with your readers. Notice how Kelly Chandler (1999) draws readers in with this "aha" moment from her write-up of the Mapleton, Maine, teacher inquiry group study of spelling:

Last spring, Gail Gibson (the Mapleton Elementary School Principal) did a workshop on spelling at a conference for reading specialists, aides, and administrators. In a folder of handouts she prepared ahead of time, she included paper of various sizes, kinds, and colors. Her opening activity was to administer a brief list of tricky words, which she intended to use as a starting point for discussion about the strategies participants used as spellers. The most interesting aspect of the exercise, however, turned out to be the way the fifty members of the audience approached the task, not the strategies they used to figure out the words.

"When I told them I was going to give them a spelling test," Gail remembers, "everyone in the room automatically took the half-sheet of white lined paper out of their folders and started numbering to twenty, without my telling them to do it. I stood back and watched. I smiled when I realized what they were doing. It was so telling about how ingrained our ideas about spelling are. It was an artifact of their past instruction." (77)

For Lyn Wilkinson (1989), a moment of truth came early in the year as he tried to deal with the contradictory behavior of Chadd:

Chadd was five years old when he first started school in my class. He stood out in a class of children who were generally conformist and anxious to do the "right thing." I noticed him on his first day at school when I asked the kids to come to the mat. He stood at the back of the room and said, "No." But this was not open defiance. Rather, because he said it with a big smile on his face, it was a teasing invitation to play—"Come on, how will you make me?" Because he had attracted my attention particularly, I noticed other things about him: that he found it very hard to sit still and that he frequently hit, punched, or annoyed other children; that he didn't appear to be interested in listening to stories (even to the pop-up books that intrigued the others); that he often didn't come in to class after recess or lunch (I'd find him ten minutes after the bell playing in the sand or climbing trees at the back of the oval). And, most frustratingly, he would begin asking about 9:30 A.M., "Is it time to go home yet?" These behaviors surprised me, because he is the youngest of five children and I thought that he would have known a lot more about what was expected at school, and what the school day would be like.

At first, I was intrigued because he seemed so different from the other children. I had frequently worked alongside teachers in junior primary classrooms and had never come across a child as uninterested in stories as Chadd. During storytime he would constantly interrupt with loud comments like, "I hate this. It's boring," and "When's this gonna be finished?" or "I hate reading stories." And yet at the least opportune moment (as in the middle of a book), he would ask with a puzzled look on his face, "How do you do that (read)?" But would he listen to an explanation? No! No matter how brief or simple I tried to make it. His curiosity seemed to last only as long as he was asking the question. Nor did he listen when I got him to ask other children. I was faced with an apparent contradiction: he hated reading, but he wanted to know how to do it. (749–55)

Lyn Wilkinson shows this moment of truth through a series of "aha" and "oh no" moments. We see Chadd sitting at storytime and playing in the sand at recess. Through specific images and words from Chadd, we see patterns that build to Lyn's moment of truth about Chadd's contradictory nature.

Lyn's writing also brings us back full circle to the issue of tension. In the chapter on finding a research question, we emphasized that a good question starts with a point of tension in your teaching. Good writing also has tension. The reader should feel the contradictions and tensions you felt as you developed your question and research project.

Every research project has moments of truth that the researcher knows are important, that mark points of tension in trying to answer the research question. Recreating them in the final text is the first step in building a strong research presentation. The next critical step is finding the thread that ties these moments together, the finding or findings woven throughout the moments of insight.

Finding the Shape

The challenge in writing up research is to make it coherent—to make seemingly disparate elements fit into the whole. Your piece will have punch if you build in those "aha" and "oh no" moments. But it will only work if these moments are somehow tied together. When deciding what to leave in and what to leave out, you might want to begin by thinking about the shape of your piece.

Pulitzer Prize–winning nonfiction writer John McPhee believes that every piece of writing has a shape to it. He is famous for taking copious notes during any research project, filling volumes and volumes of notebooks, and then distilling the notebooks down to an essay or book. His process of finding the shape of a piece is recounted by Norman Sims (1984):

> John McPhee reached up to his bookshelf and pulled down a large, hardbound book. . . . "This is a hefty one," he said. These typewritten pages represented his passage from reporting to writing, from the field to the typewriter. Hidden inside those detailed notes, like a statue inside a block of granite, lies a structure that can animate the story for his readers.
>
> "The piece of writing has a structure inside it," he said. "It begins, goes along somewhere, and ends in a manner that is thought out beforehand. I always know the last line of a story before I've written the first one. Going through all that creates the form and the shape of the thing. It also relieves the writer, once you know the structure, to concentrate each day on one thing. You know right where it fits." (21)

McPhee then describes his process of finding the shape of one of his essays, "Travels in Georgia":

> McPhee rummaged around in a file cabinet for a moment and came up with a diagram of the structure in "Travels in Georgia." It looked like a lowercase "e."
>
> "It's a simple structure, a reassembled chronology," McPhee explained. "I went there to write about a woman who, among other things, picks up dead animals off the road and eats them. There's an immediate problem when you begin to consider such material. The editor of *The New Yorker* is practically a vegetarian. I knew I was going to be presenting this story to William Shawn and that it would be pretty difficult to do so. That served a purpose, pondering what a general reader's reaction would be. When people think of animals killed on the road, there's an immediate putrid whiff that goes by them. The image is pretty automatic—smelly and repulsive. They had not been mangled up. They were not bloody. They'd been freshly killed. So I had to get this story off the ground without offending the sensibilities of the reader and the editor.
>
> McPhee and his friends ate several animals during the journey, such as a weasel, a muskrat, and somewhere well along into the trip, a snapping turtle. But the piece *begins* with the snapping turtle. Turtle soup offends less than roasted weasel. (31)

The Lead Is Critical

The most critical element in the shape of the piece is the lead. Frequently, it is also the most neglected element in the presentation of teacher research. There is nothing harder than facing the blank page. Writers will often stumble for a few paragraphs before hitting a writing rhythm, or finding a way to say what they really want to say. By the time they are into the rhythm, the "good stuff" of the piece, they've forgotten how awkward that initial lead is. One of the most important aspects of writing up research is to return to the lead again and again, crafting and honing it.

For McPhee, the lead needs to avoid offending readers in a way that stops them from continuing through the piece. As teacher-researchers consider their leads, they need to think about the kinds of language or images that, in one whiff, can turn off the reader.

We could write an entire chapter that just tackles different ways of crafting leads. But we'll settle for examples of three different leads that teacher-researchers use often.

The Circular Lead/Close

Once a first draft is completed, a circular lead/close is easy to create. You just need to look at the start of your writing, and see if there is a way to bring the same image or incident back in the close of the piece. Barry Lane (1996) used this technique in his essay about his experiences as a teaching aide, working with a teenager with autism:

> His arms would stiffen like two-by-fours at his side. His face would distort into a grotesque mask as if he were being poked with hot irons. His eyes would close tight in horror. "She's comin' back!" he'd shout, patting his chest like a penitent as his whole body recoiled in terror. "It's all right, Greg," another voice inside him would reply. "She's gone, Greg." Greg was about to tie his shoe, and each time I tried to teach him he turned into a B-movie monster. (3)

By the end of the essay, when Barry returns to the image of Greg strapping up the self-stick fasteners of his shoes, we know much more about Greg, autism, and where his anguish comes from (as well as why ties on his shoes are not appropriate). Teacher research is often complex, with no easy answers by the time a research study is completed. The circular lead and close provides a tidiness and a way of ending the writing when you as a writer may feel there is still much to be learned.

The Dialogue Lead

Who can forget E. B. White's classic lead from *Charlotte's Web?* "'Where's Papa going with that axe?' said Fern to her mother as they were setting the table for breakfast." To write a strong dialogue lead, just scan your rough drafts or teaching journals until you come to a strong incident of talk. In her essay linking memoir to her teacher research, Karen Hankins (1998) takes us into her elementary classroom and sets the scene for the words from one of her students:

> The room was filled with the chatter of writing workshop. Nat puzzled over two crayons in his hand, one of them blue, "Mrs. Hankins, ain't you had you a blue bicycle when you was a little-girl-teacher?" Nate had a way of naming me for what I was, always a teacher—or is it always a little girl? I answer his *now* question, remembering my *past* blue bicycle and a childhood story I had shared with the children recently. Perhaps it was one of those tell-me-about-when-you-were-little moments that brought memoir to the forefront of my teaching journal. (13)

Think of how much weaker this lead would be if the quote from the student was something like, "Mrs. Hankins, didn't you have a blue bicycle when you were a little girl?" By capturing the real words of the child, in authentic dialect, we can feel vividly Karen's immediate rush of recognition. We can't stress the importance too much of getting accurate dialogue from students, rather than translating it into our teacher dialects.

The Climactic Lead

Writer Becky Rule says it's a good idea to pick up your readers by the scruff of their necks and drop them into the heart of a conflict. For example, who wouldn't want to read writer Mary Comstock's holiday story after this opener? "The remains of Thanksgiving dinner sat like an abandoned wreck on the dining room table: she had eaten it all and the guests hadn't even arrived yet. This would have to stop." Mary's words promise humor and pathos. But it's that "abandoned wreck," the climax of the story, that gives the lead immediate energy.

Every research project has a climax, which doesn't always come at the very end of the study. Finding the point of greatest tension in your research, and writing up that moment as the lead, will grab readers and hold their attention.

Karen Gallas (1998) achieves a similar mix of humor and pathos when she writes the lead to a chapter about dealing with troublesome young boys in her first-grade classroom:

> One spring morning a few years ago, I asked myself a question that oddly, after more than twenty years of teaching, had just occurred to me: "Why had I chosen to spend so many years of my life in a classroom sequestered for most of the day with young children, half of whom often seemed like aliens?" The aliens I speak of were the little boys in my class of first and second graders, and what had suddenly become clear to me was my realization that the very essence of their beings was a mystery to me. At that particular moment in school time, my little boys had temporarily taken over the classroom, staging a sort of minor coup. This was a routine event that usually happened several times each day and was always accompanied by noise (something I really hate), milling around, flailing of arms, and other forms of anarchy. (25)

Karen uses the aside of "something I really hate" and the image of those aliens to help teachers chuckle in agreement. At the same time, it opens readers up to Karen's provocative challenges to the status quo in dealing with young boys. We can feel ourselves in her classroom at that climatic moment when the boys are in charge, and like her, we realize we need a few new strategies for dealing with similar students in our own classrooms.

The concept of finding strong shapes and leads for writing also gets back to the ideas in the data-collection and analyses sections about the power of images. Breaking away from words for a time can be helpful if you are stumped about representing what you see. We encourage students to draw webs of what it is they want to say or to draw a picture of their findings. A visual representation of the whole can help where words fail.

For example, Ruth asked her student-teaching interns to form a mental picture of what it was like to student teach. One student's mental image was of himself on a seesaw with Orson Welles. He said, "Needless to say, I spent most of my time up in the air. But every so often without telling me, Orson would decide to take a hike! And then I would crash-land!" We think this student's image works better than more prosaic language in capturing the overwhelming responsibilities and feelings of inexperience that are an inherent part of student teaching.

Our students draw images of themselves standing on bridges, walking on tightropes, and nurturing babies as they picture themselves as teachers and researchers. Finding a visual metaphor is a way to break through barriers when you are trying to write; visual images can lead to metaphors that may help you frame your writing.

Caryl Hurtig (1996) uses a metaphor to lead into her study of diversity, which is sometimes a challenge for teachers:

> As I was driving to Powell's Bookstore in downtown Portland, Oregon, a white van cut in front of me. Emblazoned on its side in clean blue letters were the words "ODS Health Care: Trust Us With Your Health." Leaning forward with squinted eyes to identify the driver, this representative of my health's future, I caught a glimpse of a guy as he gunned the van through a yellow light; he was smoking. Laughing out loud, I had a moment of identification. Students enroll in my classes not realizing that at times I'm the driver of this van, a bit out of control and smoking like a madwoman, dangerous to myself and all on board.
>
> In no area do I feel more like this smoking, speeding driver than when I approach diversity issues. So often in teaching, we place ourselves in expert positions when our knowing is superficial, gleaned from fragments of information picked up in books. As a skinny white woman raised in a segregated southern

California suburb, ethnic diversity is something I passionately want to understand but have had limited experience with. (63)

We are struck when we read compelling accounts by teacher researchers how often humor is used. A humorous metaphor, image, or self-deprecating remark is sometimes the best way to disarm a reader, and open her up to new ways of thinking about students and teaching.

Know Your Audience

Having a clear sense of what you need to say is only the start of saying it well. You cannot know the best way to present your findings unless you know your audience. Once you know who makes up your audience, you will experience more success with your writing if you try to speak their language. Knowing your audience will give your writing its voice:

> Voice is more than grammar. A credible, authoritative, authentic, and trustworthy voice engages the reader through rich description, thoughtful sequencing, appropriate use of quotes, and contextual clarity so that the reader joins the inquirer in the search for meaning. And there are choices of voice: the didactic voice of the teacher; the searching, logical voice of the sleuth; the narrator voice of the storyteller; the personal voice of the autoethnographer; the doubting voice of the skeptic; the intimacy of the insider's voice; the detachment of the outsider's voice; the searching voice of uncertainty; and the excited voice of discovery offer but a few examples. (Patton 2002, 64)

Tom Newkirk of the University of New Hampshire used to share a story from his summer writing and reading institutes. In the early days of the program, enough funds existed for Tom to visit teachers and administrators during the school year following their attendance at the program. These visits allowed Tom to assess the impact of the program on schools throughout the state.

One spring visit brought him to a school in a far corner of New Hampshire. Tom had scheduled this visit for the end of the school year. He suspected that the teachers and administrators who had participated in the summer program would have a problem implementing what they had learned in the conservative community where they worked. But he was wrong.

Tom was surprised at the number of classrooms in the school that had started writing workshops and developed literature-based reading programs.

The school proved to be one of the most successful in the state in implementing the principles learned in the summer program.

When Tom visited the principal at the end of the day, he asked how they had been able to make such sweeping changes in the conservative community; he replied:

> It really wasn't that tough. I met with parents at an orientation presentation early in the fall. I told them, "Look. We've tried all these newfangled reading and writing programs from publishers, and they aren't working. We've decided to go back to the basics. From now on, when it's time to write, we're going to put pencil and paper in front of our students and have them write. When it's time to read, we're going to put real books in front of them and have them read." Parents have been very supportive of this back-to-basics program. (Newkirk 2002)

The principal was not being dishonest—he had reframed the arguments for a literature-based literacy program. The school's program is a back-to-basics program in the true sense of the word. Basals are a fairly recent invention in the reading instruction scheme—they are only decades old. Using trade books is a return to earlier instructional methods.

The principal could have chosen the language of the summer institute to plead his case to parents. He could have presented the curriculum the school wanted to try as an innovative, progressive child-based literacy curriculum that the staff was exposed to at a university more than a hundred miles from this town. Using this language in the principal's presentation would have been the equivalent of the one "putrid whiff of roadkill" in the McPhee piece. The language most likely would have dredged up long-held negative convictions about newfangled university methods. We doubt his presentation would have been nearly as successful.

There are all kinds of ways to learn the language of your potential audiences. If you are going to present your research to peers at a staff meeting, listen closely to their concerns at meetings preceding your presentation. If you frame your findings within the context of what they value, they are more likely to see value in your work.

Teacher-researcher Terri Austin (1991) created a wheel to show the way she approaches the issue of audience. She begins at the center with the author's first audience—self. Then she spirals outward to fellow teacher-researchers, to professional audiences, and to an often-neglected audience—the outside world—through newspapers and magazines for general audiences (see Figure 6–1). By beginning with *yourself* as the important first audience as Terri suggests,

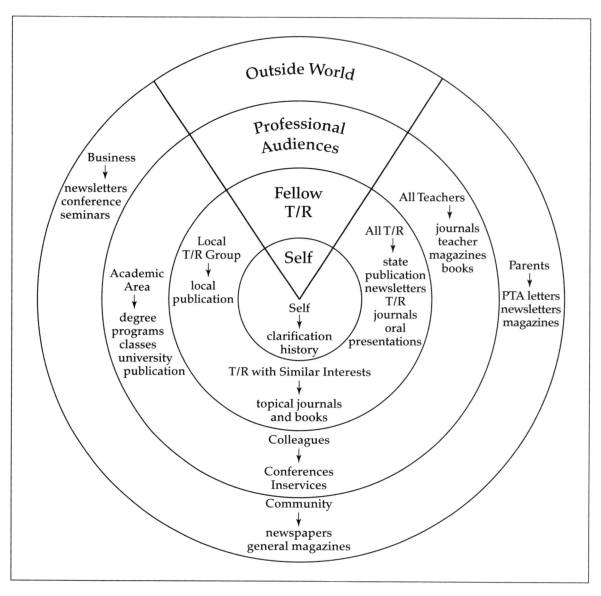

FIGURE 6–1. *Austin's Audience Wheel*

you will rediscover how writing can be a tool for learning, helping you clarify your thoughts, identify points that need further clarification, and make new leaps in your thinking.

Terri's second audience ring identifies *fellow teacher-researchers* who can help you by responding to your drafts and aiding with further revision. They will also be part of the audience for final publication, if you choose to share your work in local or regional publications. Some forms of publication are not written, as Terri notes by including the audience of oral presentations.

Presentations to colleagues at conferences and inservice workshops are also an important component of the third ring of the audience wheel, if you choose to share your work with *professional audiences*. To share your work with larger audiences, you will need to submit it for publication in books, teacher magazines, and/or journals. One of the biggest complaints of editors at professional journals is that contributors do not read their journals before submitting work. Most journals will provide sample issues and guidelines to potential contributors. By reading samples of publications, you will get a sense of potential audiences and begin to learn their language.

One of our early mistakes in considering audiences for our work was limiting our submissions to a few journals. *Language Arts, The Reading Teacher*, and *English Journal* are three fine journals that regularly publish work by teacher-researchers; but there are dozens of other journals that also publish teacher-researchers' efforts. Because many of the smaller journals do not deal with the volume of submissions found at the largest ones, they can respond to work much more quickly. The smaller journals often provide more extensive feedback on submissions and allow for more interaction between editors and authors.

In the past few years, we have found the web to be an invaluable resource for finding the newest journals. Start with a search on a national organization for teacher or administrators you admire, such as the National Council of Teachers of English or the Association of Supervision and Curriculum Development. Their home page should list regional and state organization contact information. From there, you can find out if one of these regional organizations has a regular publication. (For a list of Resources for Publication, see Appendix E.)

We urge you to have the courage to send your work out for publication. We and so many other teacher-researchers around the world need to know what you have discovered in your classroom. Teachers by profession also have an obligation to share what they have learned with others—it is our stock in trade.

We've learned to identify at least three potential audiences for every piece of research we write. Donald Murray advises writers to prepare the envelope for the *next* submission of the piece at the same time as they first send it out. If the piece comes back rejected, they can just slip it into the new envelope. We do not make revisions unless the piece has come back at least twice from editors, and we follow editors' suggestions for revision only when we agree with them.

If your work is not accepted at first, keep at it. In the next chapter, we provide some principles for developing a support community. Support is critical if you want to see your work in print. Almost all teacher-researchers face rejection from journals at some time. Most editors are fair and supportive in their rejections; however, every researcher we know has also received at least one or two vicious reviews.

Your responsibility is to make sure your article fits the format and audience of a journal. If you have done this and still receive a mean-tempered response, take the time to let the journal editor know the ways the review was not helpful to you. Editors need to know they are dealing not only with research but also with researchers in the process of getting better at their craft. Teacher-researchers need to remind editors of this when their reviews are inhumane or unfair.

We hope reviewers of teacher research are also individuals who attempt to publish research. It is almost impossible to be vicious in response to writing if you have been through the review process yourself. If you want an insider's view of the publication process, consider putting out a small collection of teacher research for your school or district at the end of the year. Analyzing, responding to, and compiling the work of your colleagues is exciting. With desktop publishing, your publication can look professional at little expense.

Don't neglect the wider community as an important audience for your work either. As Terri shows in her outermost ring, the *outside world*, a range of publications exist that can show the public what we are learning about students' knowledge and abilities. Being proactive in sharing the results of your research through parent–teacher organizations' publications and through magazines for parents can lead to important new understandings.

Newspapers can be another outlet for sharing aspects of our work with the world at large. Responses to editorials and other letters to the editor are often too brief to share more than one important finding—or to refute one. But writing editorials yourself can give you the space you need to present a well-crafted argument. Opposite Editorial (Op-Ed) pieces appear in most newspapers and in many national magazines.

Mark Oldani, a teacher-researcher in Portland, Oregon, wrote a compelling Op-Ed piece, which was published in *The Oregonian*, based on findings from his research. Mark conducted a careful, yearlong study of his students' abilities in reading/writing workshops and compared these findings with the results of the Portland Area Levels Test. He also explored cultural bias in the wording of the test examples and found numerous instances where his students' many

Suggestions for Writing Op-Eds

1. Have a local angle. The Op-Ed is much more likely to be published if your points are directly connected to local concerns. Write up a brief draft of your piece. Then look daily for letters to the editor or feature stories published that can be connected in some way to your inquiry. We've seen teachers publish essays on their studies of authentic assessment in their classrooms right after statewide standardized test scores were published. And early September is always a good time for sending in Op-Eds—newspapers are looking for back-to-school grist as soon as the leaves start to change.

2. Email, fax, and use regular mail to submit your work. It's hard to know which form of communication is used most readily by your local editor, so use all three. Many Op-Ed editors especially like email submissions, because they then have the essay in electronic form. But they will need a hard copy of a signed letter from you explaining that the piece has not been published elsewhere.

3. Fact-check, and provide fact-checking references. An Op-Ed is more likely to be accepted if you include some facts to back up your points—a few statistical references are particularly appealing to editors in backing up your opinion. But make sure you do your own fact-checking. Rather than just referencing a professional journal, it's best to include the name and phone number of the researcher in the article. The same goes for facts from national organizations—include a name and phone number that is accurate. Many media organizations have recently been criticized for poor fact-checking. They will appreciate the accuracy of your work if you include names and phone numbers for cross-referencing. A bonus from good fact-checking—often editors will use the names listed for interviews for a future feature about the issue you are tackling in your inquiry.

4. Don't worry about providing statistical support if your inquiry is qualitative. There is always a fact or number out there somewhere to buttress what you are saying. For example, if you are writing about understanding diversity in your classroom, you can cite evidence from teacher-advocacy groups that this is an area where teachers most often request support or curricular materials. If you are writing about some aspect of teaching that is discouraging, cite the high numbers of teachers who are leaving the profession.

5. Keep it short. Most Op-Eds are limited to a range of 500 to 800 words. It's important to stick to the limit. If you go over it by much, your work will not even be considered. And if a longer Op-Ed is accepted, you run the risk of the editor making cuts that muddle the points you are trying to make.

strengths and abilities were not tapped by these tests. Mark made his full research article available to the Portland test makers, the school board, and the superintendent of schools. Through his brief Op-Ed piece, written for a more general public, he was able to reach a wider audience.

Writer's Block

We want to close by considering writer's block, the all-encompassing malady that stops some teacher-researchers cold. Is there really such a thing? We do not believe in it. Nor do we see any blocks that absolutely stop researchers from writing—only hurdles that need to be crossed.

Every teacher-researcher has both psychological and pragmatic constraints in getting the work done. The psychological constraints include the "devils on your shoulder" who try to convince you that you have little to say and that you will not be able to say it well anyway. Ignore them. The pragmatic constraints include the clothes that have to be washed, the kids that have to be carpooled, the garden that needs tending. There are times, particularly at the end of a research project, when closure is needed. This requires a shift in priorities. Once again, Annie Dillard (1987) has good advice for occasionally ignoring practical routines so that the writing can get done:

> I don't do housework. Life is too short and I'm too much of a Puritan. If you want to take a year off to write a book, you have to *take* that year, or the year will take you by the hair and pull you toward the grave. *Let* the grass die. I almost let all of my indoor plants die from neglect while I was writing the book. There are all kinds of ways to live. You can take your choice. You can keep a tidy house, and when St. Peter asks you what you did with your life, you can say, I kept a tidy house. I made my own cheeseballs.

Anyone who knows how to put pen to paper can write. The problem in producing work is those high standards that keep writers from producing. The advice about procrastination given earlier applies here: Keep lowering your standards until you can produce something on the page. Don't expect your first draft to be any good—it rarely is for even the best writers, as Anne Lamott (1994) notes:

> All good writers write shitty first drafts. . . . This is how they end up with good second drafts and terrific third drafts. People tend to look at successful writers, writers who are getting their books published and maybe even doing well finan-

cially, and think that they sit down at their desks every morning feeling like a million dollars, feeling great about who they are and how much talent they have and what a great story they have to tell; that they take in a few deep breaths, push back their sleeves, roll their necks a few times to get all the cricks out, and dive in, typing fully formed passages as fast as a court reporter. But this is just the fantasy of the uninitiated. I know some very great writers, writers you love who write beautifully and have made a great deal of money, and not *one* of them sits down routinely feeling wildly enthusiastic and confident. Not one of them writes elegant first drafts. All right, one of them does, but we do not like her very much. (21–22)

When the two of us try to write, our most important audience is each other. We have collaborated for a long time over many research projects. Many drafts of articles begin as conversations with each other or as friendly letters sent via email. You need at least one friend who is supportive of your work. If you get stuck when you try to write an article for an anonymous group of reviewers, start again. Write a letter to a supportive friend describing what you have discovered in your classroom. You may have a solid first draft of an article after the letter is completed!

If you can't begin with even a letter, try starting with a word (see Appendix D). We like Richard Rhodes' (1996) advice about getting down to the essentials in writing:

If writing a book is impossible, write a chapter.
If writing a chapter is impossible, write a page.
If writing a page is impossible, write a paragraph.
If writing a paragraph is impossible, write a sentence.
If writing a sentence is impossible, write a word and teach yourself everything there is to know about that word and then write another, connected word and see where the connection leads.

Go through your notebooks, sticky notes, or any data-analysis material; find three individual words that appear numerous times and that are critical for understanding your findings. Freewrite about the importance of each one. We have found that writing about a word or two that appears often in our research can be the breakthrough to more writing and insight.

Finally, if you are having trouble writing up your research, look at young children and their enthusiasm for publishing. Children love to present their work to larger audiences. Once they learn something, they want others to share in that knowledge. We know that some of the most important discoveries about how children learn are being made by teacher-researchers even as we write this chapter. *We* want to read your research accounts so that we can share your knowledge with other teachers.

Some people believe that the benefits of teacher research and the knowledge gained from teachers' research are primarily for the teacher completing the research. We disagree. Teacher research can enrich your professional life immeasurably. But learning for yourself isn't enough. If you have discovered something that can help other teachers work with their students, you have an obligation as a professional to share it. Teachers are eager for this knowledge. If you start with the understanding that there are teachers who want to know what you have learned, it will be easier to face that blank page.

We write these words in troubling times for teacher-researchers, when their knowledge, autonomy, and purpose are being questioned every day in the media and throughout state and federal governments. In times like these, our own writing is an oasis—a way back to our core beliefs. The words of Alice Hoffman (2001) resonate for us. She describes the place of writing in her life when she was recovering from chemotherapy:

> I wrote to find beauty and purpose, to know that love is possible and lasting and real, to see daylilies and swimming pools, loyalty and devotion, even though my eyes were closed and all that surrounded me was a darkened room. I wrote because that was who I was at the core, and if I was too damaged to walk around the block, I was lucky all the same. Once I got to my desk, once I started writing, I still believed anything was possible. (98)

We hope your writing also takes you into the possibilities of your research—not just for your own transformation, but for teachers and students everywhere.

Extensions

1. Set aside ten minutes a day for freewriting—writing as quickly as possible about what you see in front of you. You might even set a timer so that you can write without thinking about the clock. If you get stuck, use a stem to get you going again—such as "I remember . . ." or "What I really want to write about . . ."—until you have something else to write. Keep your pen moving.

2. Free yourself from too-high standards by trying to produce the world's worst writing. Write an anecdotal lead that makes you cringe, a self-conscious "academic" lead that cites *everyone*, using all the jargon you can cram in, or a poem with every cliché in the book. If you know what bad writing is, you also know what makes writing good.

3. Examine your writing history. When has writing been hard for you? When has it been easy? What are your earliest memories of writing? It may help to "speak bitterness" about your experiences with writing, as suggested in Chapter 4.

4. Find a teacher-researcher article you like, then write to that person. Authors love responses to their work. You will also be clarifying what you value in good research writing for yourself.

5. Start a writing support group. Require each participant to write a one- or two-page memo each week about what they are seeing in their research, much like the memos by Marcia Taft and Patricia McLure in Chapter 4. Try some of the other suggestions listed here with your group or with a trusted partner.

6. Meet with a friend in a café or restaurant and bring some paper. While you wait for your meal to arrive, take out your pen or pencil and write. You might work on a part of your writing where you are stuck, on an alternate ending or two, or from a stem such as "My research is *really* about. . . ." Then, read your work to your partner and be a good listener and responder in return.

7. Try the "Starting with a Word" writing exercise in Appendix D.

8. Try the "Two or Three Things I Know for Sure" writing exercise in Appendix B.

9. Read through the "Favorite Quotes on Writing" in Appendix D with a colleague who is also doing research. Talk about what quotes connect with your own experience as a writer. Why do these quotes resonate for you? What are the differences in your processes as writers?

chapter 7

You Are Not Alone
Finding Support for Your Research

No writer needs more critics. She only needs support.
—Gertrude Stein

Researchers don't need more critics, either. Your ability to develop as a researcher depends on support. Sustaining a commitment to teacher research is difficult without support from colleagues. This support can take two forms. You will need a sympathetic ear, but it also helps to receive some material support for your work.

Most teacher-researchers we know do not receive thousands of dollars to support their work, and few belong to well-organized networks or support groups. A small amount of support, however, goes a long way. One colleague who listens or the money for a transcription machine can make all the difference when it comes to teacher research.

In this chapter, we explore possibilities for research funding. We also look at how other teacher-researchers have formed long-term relationships with colleagues based on their research projects. Research friends and research funding can provide critical boosts for your work and for your ego when you hit rough spots in your studies.

Fishing for Funds

If you are going to seek funding for research, you must be the proverbial patient fisher. Many lakes and rivers hold thousands of fish, but the fish cannot be seen from the surface, and different lures are needed to catch different fish. People who fish do not know what will work in advance; they cast again and again, testing out the surface and depths of the water, trying odd-sized and colored baits and lures until they find one that works. Any lucky day for one who fishes is balanced by hours and hours of patient casting.

We have worked with many teacher-researchers, and almost all who have sought funding have received some financial support for their work. The grants awarded are generally modest, often only enough to purchase some books or a tape recorder. Few researchers have received support the first time they applied; the application process requires the patience for trial and error.

Someone who fishes is well prepared for the sport. A teacher-researcher is prepared for the sport of fishing for funds when she has a rough draft of her research design in her computer. Having a draft done means that you are ready for any funding opportunities that may come your way. If your research plan is in electronic form, adapting it to the different formats and demands of funding audiences is relatively easy.

Before you begin to cast out your line for research funds, you also need to know what needs funding. Think about what is most difficult and time-consuming in your research and then envision ways that funding could ease that burden. Many teacher-researchers request some release time to analyze data, photocopy machines for their rooms, tape transcribers, tape recorders, or videocameras.

How do you even begin to find sources for funds? You ask questions and read journals. You make phone calls. Teacher-researchers have baffled bureaucrats at local and national levels when they have called and asked about grant competitions for this strange new movement called teacher research, but they have also discovered some little-known funding sources.

The weekly periodicals, *The Chronicle of Higher Education* and *Education Week*, both have sections that list grants by topic and deadline. You might inquire whether your principal would be willing to pay for a school subscription to *Education Week*. It also has frequent articles about teacher research.

The Reading Teacher, Language Arts, The New Advocate, and *English Journal* periodically list grant competitions for teacher-researchers. These grants are national and are very competitive, but it never hurts to submit a proposal.

Teacher-researchers we have worked with have had the most success at state and local levels. Many states set aside money for competitions among teachers. Some of these competitions are not specifically for teacher-researchers; more often, the funds are earmarked for innovations in education. But it is relatively easy for most teacher-researchers to frame their needs in terms of innovations for their classrooms.

Teachers can also look to businesses in their region. Many companies regularly discard computers, printers, transcribers, or other supplies that might support your research. Businesses are also looking for low-cost ways to help local schools. A brief letter outlining your needs is often all that is necessary to receive funding or equipment from businesses.

In the past year, teachers we have worked with have received teacher-research grants from their principals, district offices, local parent–teacher organizations, community businesses, and state and national literacy organizations. The following sections describe three types of awards.

Teacher-Researcher Awards

Teacher-researcher competitions are offered more and more frequently by state and national teacher organizations. The National Council of Teachers of English (NCTE), for example, offers several teacher-researcher grants of $1,500 each year. In their proposal form, they request the following:

- *A discussion of the purpose and significance of the study,* including the research question(s) itself and why this is an important teaching question
- *A short exploration of the topic,* such as relevant readings or previous research activities
- *A methods section,* which explains what data will be collected and how it will be analyzed
- *The feasibility,* including a timeline of activities
- *A dissemination plan,* that is, what do you intend to do with the results of this study
- *A budget with justification*
- *Letters of support*

For application forms and more information, contact the NCTE Research Foundation (Attn: Project Assistant, 1111 Kenyon Road, Urbana, IL 61801).

While other proposal forms may differ, the general format will require similar information. The main intent in writing a proposal is to convince your audience that you have a reasonable research design and are capable of carrying it out. You will usually be required to specify your design as well as some review of the literature and a proposed budget. The budget criteria are generally listed, and you need to pay careful attention to them. NCTE grants, for example, do not cover such items as travel, release time, or permanent equipment.

One of the most innovative and thoughtful grant programs for teacher-researchers over the past decade has been the Spencer Foundation's Practitioner Research Communication and Mentoring grant program. These grants do give money for travel for teachers, permanent equipment, and many other items crucial to teacher-researchers, which are rarely funded in traditional grant programs. The Spencer Foundation has also made a commitment to funding more teacher-research studies in all of its small- and large-scale grant programs. These programs' grant recipients are routinely invited to meet with other novice and veteran researchers at retreats. We don't know any other foundation that listens to teacher-researchers carefully and targets funds accordingly. For more information, go to the Foundation's website at *www.spencer.org*.

Curricular-Improvement Grants

These grants are given by local districts, businesses, and government agencies that want to see tangible proof of improvement in schools. Improvement grants can be specific—funding changes in science programs or promotion of cultural diversity; they also can be open-ended, with any curricular changes eligible for consideration.

Recognition Awards

There are many grant programs to support good work that has already been completed. You can apply for one of these awards and then use the funds to support your research.

Writing a Successful Proposal

There is no *perfect* proposal that will fit any situation; the proposals you write will be as varied as your research and the agencies to which you apply. The proposal may be a fairly straightforward listing of your design with a literature review and a budget, or it may be more in the form of an essay. David Bucknell, for example, applied for and received funding for the Reflective Teaching Scholarship and Study Award through Teachers College at Columbia University in New York. In his proposal, on page 172, he makes clear his intent to study students' development as readers and writers as well as his commitment to learning and teaching.

Application for Reflective Teaching Scholarship Study Award

When we regard our students as unique and fascinating, when they become case study subjects even while they are students, then the children become our teachers, showing us how to learn. (Calkins, Lessons from a Child, *1983, 6–7)*

"Ladies and Gentlemen, I present to you Miss Daria Fortune." Ned O'Gorman's big smile followed his announcement into my Harlem classroom at The Children's Storefront and there, beneath his great frame and big hands, was ten-year-old Daria. She shook my hand when I offered it but said not a word and sat down in the chair I showed her.

I wondered at the difference between Daria described and Daria sitting in my classroom. My imagination had created a picture of a street urchin during the two weeks of school we waited for her to appear. Beverly, her mother, I had been told, jumped out of a second-story window last year in a pathetic suicide attempt—pregnant. Baby and mother survived to perpetuate a hard life for a family of twelve. Daria missed school often after that. I wondered if this meek little girl, who smiled faintly when she recognized her old friends in the room, could be the one of whom I'd heard.

Her silence was disturbing. During writing, she sat stoically and refused to put pen to paper. "I don't have nothin' to write about." I worked with her to find a topic. She had gone South over the summer, but that wasn't interesting because she'd done it before. I grew nervous. How could I get her over the first hump? She watched other students try freewriting, but made no sign that she wanted to participate.

I asked her the next day to search her memory like a photo album. Who, what jumped up on the page? Write it down. Make a list. Choose one to start with. Daria just sat. I tried showing her how to web ideas and she sat some more. Nothing grabbed her. Finally, I left her alone. Despair.

Yet all that proved was my impatience. When she appeared the next morning, she had a page filled with a list of names.

"Who are these people?" I asked.

"My family," she said.

"Do you know what you're going to write first?"

She nodded and for the next two classes, she didn't stop. When I finally got to ask her some questions, her answers thrilled me. She had not written one, but two stories and knew which one was good and which wasn't. She could also tell me why she thought so. "I like the way it sounds and it says everything I want it to."

When I noticed her reading the good one over and changing punctuation, I asked her what she was reading to find.

"I looked for mistakes."

"Like what?"

"Letters I put wrong or when I put 'me' for 'mine.'"

"And what do you do about it?"

"If I write it and it's got something that I don't like, I change it."

Daria and the other students in my class are ten-year-old illiterates according to tests. It is true, they "walk on words," as Paolo Freire calls it when a reader does not "read the world" beneath the symbols (*Language Arts*, Vol. 62, No. 1, 1985). But literacy has everything to do with making meaning out of written language. If learners are given authority over their language as authors, then they are likely to develop an authentic being-in-the-world with language—they will learn to see writing as truth-telling.

I am applying for the Reflective Teaching Award to study how these children develop as readers and writers. Is the path the same one followed by children studied by Shirley Brice Heath? Do they use the same thinking strategies as the younger children studied by Ruth Hubbard? I intend to document their progress by note taking and tape recording from daily writing and writing conversations and to review data for findings at year's end.

But there is another reason for my application—to improve my teaching. Ever since I began thinking of applying, my teaching has changed. My listening has improved and I find nearly everything the children say fascinating. I enjoy the new attitude and the students benefit from a responsive teacher. As Lucy Calkins (1986) writes, "The goal of the case report is not only to learn but also to teach" ("Forming Research Communities Among Naturalistic Researchers," 98). That's my goal, too.

David demonstrates clear knowledge of audience and form in this proposal. His anecdotal lead is striking—it draws reviewers in immediately. His study of thinking strategies is clearly linked to other researchers' work. Finally, David shows how his research will ultimately make him a better teacher.

Fishing Suggestions

Here is a list of some procedures to follow when entering a competition for funding:

Talk to the grant coordinator or contact person.   It is usually better to pick up the phone and talk to the contact person rather than to write a letter. A conversation with the grant coordinator can give you a better sense of whether your proposal will interest the group. Often the annual call for submissions in grant competitions is vague, but the committee may still have specific areas of interest designated for funding that year, which aren't mentioned in advertisements for the program.

Get a list of previous winners.   Most people who have won awards are happy to explain their success. By gaining a sense of what was funded in the past, you'll have a good idea of the best ways to present your proposal.

Anticipate the competitions from year to year.   Announcements often appear only shortly before proposals are due. Keep a contact person's name handy after a competition and call them the following year when you think advertisements for the competition might soon appear.

Always follow-up when a grant is rejected to find out what worked and what didn't.   Learning how to get funding is a process, like research. There are no real mistakes in the process, only experiences from which to learn. Also, contacting the grant agency lets them know you will be applying again. We know of one state competition that has an unwritten rule: Any applicant who appears before the review board to discuss a rejected application will receive some financial support from the board for the project.

Prioritize your wish list.   Often teacher-researchers think they need a video-recorder for their research. But many schools already may have a recorder that is rarely used. Check with your principal before requesting expensive equipment. On the other hand, tape transcribers and good tape recorders can save teachers hundreds of hours of time when they begin to transcribe and analyze data.

Besides these procedures, we have discovered some *general funding principles* that help teachers become more successful in getting support. The first principle was partially explained in the last chapter on writing up your work (Chapter 6). You need to know the language of the funding agency: What are the key concerns, pet peeves, or phrases that appear again and again in its literature? Do not rely just on the literature provided to determine this language. Always talk to someone from the agency about the grant competition before beginning work on your proposal. Sometimes the most important rules of the game are not written down. The call for funding proposals may remain the same year after year, but each year many agencies target specific areas to receive special consideration.

One teacher we work with wanted more books to continue to expand and develop her literature-based reading program and to look at literacy changes in her fourth-grade students. But she had received funding the previous year for books for the program during the local grant contest. She wrote a proposal detailing how she would develop a program using multicultural literature to promote racial understanding and target at-risk students. To be sure, this teacher *is concerned* about multicultural understanding and at-risk students. She had also sat through numerous staff meetings with district officials where the terms *multicultural* and *at-risk* were uttered over and over again by administrators. It took her less than two hours to rewrite the grant proposal, emphasizing the benefits of the grant for multicultural education of at-risk students. In the end, she received what she needed—more than one thousand dollars worth of new books.

The second funding principle is that funding agencies support program development and research plans, not proposals for materials to improve the classroom environment. A class of teacher-researchers we worked with read a proposal written by Marie Greve of Wilmington, Delaware, to obtain funding for a large saltwater aquarium (see Appendix F). Marie was developing a science-writing program in her class. One of the teachers in the group began to whine: "Well, it must be nice to have an aquarium in your class. I've wanted one for years."

Now, the sight of anyone whining is not appealing. One of us resolutely walked over to talk to her at break time. "No one just gave Marie that aquarium," she was told. "It is part of a systematic, developed plan. Who have you asked for funding for your aquarium?" "No one," she replied. "My district would never fund anything like that." "Well, you don't know till you ask. And before you ask, you need to know how it will be used in your classroom. Will you try to develop a scientific literacy program with it, like Marie?" she was asked. "Oh no," the teacher replied. "My students are third-grade special ed. They can't *do* anything."

There was a pause then, as there often is when you have to avoid blurting out the first raw comment that pops into your head. The teacher was finally told, "You need to figure out how an aquarium will be part of your curriculum, whatever that curriculum is. Then you can ask your district for funds. Many local groups, like the Lions Club, are also interested in improving schools. But it's up to you to take some steps to get an aquarium in your room."

This was not a positive, hopeful exchange. Yet one week later, this same teacher returned to class, excited and smiling. "You're not going to believe this!" that teacher exclaimed and continued:

> I wrote up a plan to have my students take on responsibility for caring for class-room pets as a way of building their self-esteem. We already have a hamster, but I thought adding fish to the room would be a way to develop the program. I called the president of the local Lions Club, and he told me that the club would love to fund the project. All I needed to do was write a letter. I was so excited I marched right down to tell my principal. He was excited too, and he told me that I didn't need that funding. There was a large, old aquarium in a storage room at the school, which no one had used in three years. If I cleaned it up, he would supply all the fish, filters, and food.

When we tried to congratulate her, she held up her hand.

> No wait, this gets better. I called the Lions Club back to tell them I was all set. They said they still wanted to help me because it sounded like such a good program. Could they fund other materials or animals for the program? Would I accept volunteers to help? So now I will have a wonderful menagerie, and adults to help while I collect data.

If you don't ask for funds, you will never receive them. Perhaps this is the most important funding principle of all. As we work with teacher-researchers, we are also reminded of a key aspect of their work. Doing research really does make you a better teacher. That third-grade special education teacher began to taperecord her students' interactions with the animals, and she also analyzed her own interactions with the children. By the end of the year, she made a discovery that startled her. She realized that her way of talking to her students and dealing with them made the students totally dependent on her. They didn't take on much responsibility in the classroom because she did not allow it. Having the aquarium improved that environment; however, what this teacher learned about how her teaching needed to change improved the environment even more. The teacher transformed both her view of her students and the ways she talked to them.

Forming a Teacher-Researcher Support Group

The importance of having a community of colleagues who are teacher-researchers cannot be overemphasized. This community may be as local as your own school or as far-flung as a few key teacher-researchers you find in journals and texts. But you do need someone, somewhere, who can help you develop ideas. You need to have people you trust to read or to listen to your research proposals, to critique your design and budget plans, and to encourage you to try and try again when a proposal is rejected. We end the book with images of teacher-researchers supporting each other, because this mutual support among teacher-researchers is what keeps the movement growing.

If you have tried any of the activities or extensions suggested in this handbook, you have already realized the importance of having a research colleague. We envision a day years from now when there will be release time in schools for teacher research, many in-school grants to promote research, and teams of teachers poring over data with the support of administrators. That day is not here yet. But we have hope, because we have seen the promising beginnings of this scenario in "pockets" of teacher-researchers throughout the country.

Being part of a group discussing inquiry goes far beyond having a sympathetic audience. We work in a profession that has a deeply rooted cultural belief in the myth of the superteacher—the idea that teachers working alone with little assistance can and should change the world. Teacher-researcher Tim Gillespie (2000) explains why this myth is so dangerous:

> There's a narrative of teaching in our culture that holds some dangers, and that's what I call the narrative of heroism. The bestseller shelves and movie screens have been filled for the whole of my teaching career with this heroic narrative whose storyline is basically, "How I went into a rotten school with venal administrators and predatory students and by the application of my special skills and insights and heroic commitment—all by myself of course, supported by no one or no community of fellow teachers or parents—turned things around and then saved the world . . . oh, and then got fired." Name 'em: *To Sir with Love, Stand and Deliver, Lean on Me, Dead Poets' Society, Mr. Holland's Opus, Dangerous Minds,* and on and on. Certainly we need inspirational stories, stories of hope and success. But what they convey to the general public is that educational success is more a matter of the dedicated individual teacher rather than the community's commitment of time and talent and money to the common endeavor of schooling our children.

Worse is the effect on us, because these romanticized tales of "superteachers" diminish and oversimplify our work. They offer miracle cures in place of the real work of the classroom. (3)

When we sit with our peers and discuss the real work of the classroom through our inquiry, we make connections that just aren't possible without this talk. And, we realize our colleagues are struggling with many of the same issues and concerns even with all of our "surface" differences when we teach.

The Mapleton Elementary School in Maine has a typically diverse corps of teachers: Some are early in their careers, juggling babies and full-time work. Others are veterans who may have empty nests but elderly parents who need support. Still others are ready to commit evenings and weekends to any endeavor that improves their teaching, including participation in an inquiry group. Mapleton has a tremendous number of teachers who participate in inquiry groups because the groups are open-ended—teachers can participate for a short period of time whenever they can. Time for inquiry is naturally built into ongoing professional development at the school. There is a sense that inquiry is a choice—and because of this, it's a choice many teachers at the school make.

Mary Moreau and Paula Moore decided to form a teacher-researcher support group at their school in Old Town, Maine, but their group was different from others. They did not want to meet on their own time as most research support groups do, unsanctioned and unsupported by their administration. Instead, they asked the district to allow them to meet during the regular district inservice days. They submitted a yearlong plan of action for developing professionally through teacher research, including a time frame for their work and a list of various guests who would talk to the group.

If you have a few teachers interested in research in your district, you might consider asking administrators to allow you to develop an inservice research support group. Like Mary and Paula, you will have to present a clear plan of action, with timelines and goals.

Some districts have sabbatical leave programs to help teachers grow personally and professionally. But one district in southern Maine has taken the sabbatical leave program one step further, developing a program to promote growth of all teachers in local schools. Each year, a teacher is designated as the "Teacher–Scholar-in-Residence." The teacher is released from teaching responsibilities for one year. She pursues a learning agenda that is negotiated with other teachers at the school. For example, if the teachers are interested in learning about integrated themes, the teacher–scholar reads, writes, talks to experts,

Tips From Mapleton Teachers on Forming School Inquiry Groups Adapted from Chandler (1999).

If you are meeting after school:

◆ Choose a location that most teachers will pass: the teachers' lounge, the cafeteria if it's on the way to the parking lot, a room near the office.

◆ Set the date well in advance so people can arrange for rides, child care, and so on. Then remind people with a poster or email message a day or two before the meeting.

◆ Schedule the meeting as a continuation of another one that's required. You might compress the faculty meeting agenda so that there will be a contractually guaranteed time left for research-group talk.

◆ Set a definite ending time so that people know how much time they need to commit. End early, rather than late, and some folks may come back to continue an unfinished conversation.

◆ Order pizza—food is a great draw, and the smell may attract people who will decide to stay.

◆ Don't limit your invitees to full-time, onsite faculty; welcome instructional aides, student interns, and itinerant teachers.

◆ Appoint a facilitator with enough influence to nudge the group beyond negativity if the discussion edges there.

◆ Leave your charts up or post your minutes in a public place to intrigue those who missed the session—maybe they'll be curious enough to join you next time.

If you are meeting during the school day:

◆ Meet with the school board and relevant administrators first. As much as possible, link the goals of the inquiry group with whole school and districtwide goals.

◆ Everyone who participates should be involved in an inquiry. This includes university faculty and district administrators who are supporting or facilitating the inquiry group.

◆ Early meetings should focus on research design and data collection. Allow everyone to develop flexible time frames for their studies. Some might want very short-term inquiries; others will design projects that will continue for more than a year.

◆ Data analysis is particularly challenging for many novice researchers. Bring in datasets to look at collectively, and provide plenty of time for practice with coding and audit checks.

◆ Accept that attendance will not be as high as attendance at regularly scheduled university courses. Emergencies are a part of the daily life of schools, and teachers need to keep their students' needs in mind first.

◆ Provide opportunities for teachers to share their research with other audiences. District newsletters, university courses, and regularly scheduled inservice events are a terrific way to build in discussion, collaboration, and closure.

and develops a program of support to help her peers learn about this topic. The teacher–scholar grows professionally, but this growth is earmarked to support the professional needs of her peers.

Universities can be a great resource for onsite inquiry groups, especially if your school has an ongoing partnership with local colleges involving teacher preparation. We have participated in many of these partnerships, and have found placing a cluster of student teachers at one school site can be a useful way to free up teachers during the day for periodic inquiry discussions. Student teachers are often amazing research partners too, lending a second set of eyes to data or assistance in transforming a set of data into a snazzy graphic with their computer skills.

Teacher-researchers are also making use of new technology. Alaska has the Alaska Teacher Researcher Network (ATRN), a far-flung and diverse group of teachers throughout the state who meet a few times during the year. But they also plan to carry out much of their communication online. If you decide to form some kind of support group, you will need to start by agreeing on a structure. Support groups work best when there are clear goals and required tasks for members. In addition, Marge Piercy's rules for support groups also help you develop a structure that supports all voices being heard (1991, 15–16). Piercy emphasizes respect, equal time, participation by everyone, copies of work for each participant, rules for who talks, support in work habits, and an attitude of we try to help. You may want to discuss Piercy's goals at a first support group meeting, as a way of deciding how you can structure your meetings with rules to foster a helpful atmosphere.

It also helps to periodically take stock of what is going well and what should change in your support group meetings. The ATRN members noticed after two years of meetings that some of them rarely spoke and that a few members dominated meetings. They decided to try an activity to balance contributions. Each discussion group member was given three poker chips. Every time a member said something, he or she had to throw a chip into a center pile.

"We told the talkers they couldn't wave that chip for ten minutes and have it count as one contribution," explained Terri Austin, an ATRN member. "There were many long silences, too, waiting for those who rarely talked to contribute," added Shirley Kaltenbach, another member. "But we made a rule that all chips had to be used, and we stuck with it. After we finished, everyone said they had learned something through having our talk patterns broken. We heard new voices, and some of our chattiest members said they had never listened as closely before to others."

Creative Scheduling 101: Developing an Inquiry Program with Preservice Interns Covering Classes

1. Work with a local university to place a large block of student teachers at your school for field placements. Both university and public school faculty tend to underestimate how many student teachers a school can comfortably host.

2. Reserve a communal space (preferably the library) for a set time throughout the year for inquiry meetings.

3. Don't require teachers to participate. Time, energy, and resources are precious, and they are used up rapidly on veteran teachers who only attend under duress.

4. Arrange for student teachers individually or in teams to have a "home" classroom for inquiry meeting days. Student teachers should always be armed with a couple great read-aloud books, just in case instructional plans are missing.

5. Don't schedule the first inquiry meeting until the student teachers have become comfortable in the classrooms—this usually takes a couple weeks of full-time work, six weeks if interns are only in classrooms two days a week.

6. As much as possible, involve the student teaching interns in the research process. Student teachers may develop their own inquiry projects, but many chose to be full collaborators with mentor teachers.

It is hard to make a commitment to stay with a support group and juggle the responsibilities of being a support group member with all the other responsibilities we have as professionals. But that collaboration sustains research efforts, as Terri Austin (1995) writes:

> I've been thinking about how I compared teacher research to climbing a mountain with valleys and peaks. I've thought about this idea of support and it's not like climbing a mountain at all. Doing teacher research is much harder and more exhausting. It's like crossing a desert. It's the daily toil of trying to reach the watering hole (which is the support group). It takes a great deal of inner strength to continue the walk when even nature (sun and sand) works against you. But the desire to be a part of the group is so great, I keep going. My group helps me keep the inner passion alive and that passion sustains me for my next walk to the watering hole.
>
> This sounds really grim, but there are so many things working against teacher-researchers—time, energy levels, administrative directives. . . . Without that inner passion to inquire or the enveloping support of colleagues, I could not possibly continue researching.

Terri's honest reflections highlight the barriers to teacher research. At times, teacher-researchers are overwhelmed with the responsibilities of research and the lack of structures in place at institutions to support this important work.

But there is a also a feeling among teacher-researchers that we are in at the start of something big. We are all making this up as we go along, and this is as exciting as it is daunting. Shirley Kaltenbach, Terri's research buddy, recognizes the newness of the teacher-researcher movement and wonders where we are headed:

> This movement called *teacher research* reminds me of my early days with the writing process. This was a time when we spent hours developing fluency activities and we got kids to do what they already could!
>
> Now here we are in our teacher research fluency period where we are beginning to see and hear projects and attempts. Some may be too long or ill-thought out but no matter—they will *be*. Continual refinement will follow, and think of what lies ahead five years from now. Imagine whole schools of teachers sitting together at the end of a tiring day celebrating what they saw or learned or heard in their classes that day. Hurray, hurray, let the wild rumpus begin! (1995)

Teacher-researcher support doesn't begin with computer networks or in-service meetings or even a grant that provides funding for work. Teacher research begins and is sustained over time when you have one fine friend who is willing to listen and to work with you. That is the simple story of support we have uncovered over and over again as we talk to both long-term teacher-researchers and the newest members of the research club.

Cyndy Fish and Lynne Young made a commitment to do research after completing a graduate course in research. They work together at the same school; Cyndy is a resource room specialist and Lynne is a first-grade teacher.

"We knew we couldn't do the research unless it fit into a larger plan of working together to help students and change our curriculum," Cyndy explained. "We started with a learning agenda, mapping out how teacher research fit into a larger frame of developing a math program" (see Figure 7–1).

"We're eight months into the project, and we are just about ready to find our research question," said Lynne with a laugh. "There's just so much worth exploring! We could look at how the children's language changes as they do more math. We're going to make math bags with home activities; we could research what happens with math in the home. And we're also changing so much. Maybe we should document our own changes?" she mused.

Cyndy and Lynne began with weeks at the library and daily talks with peers, trying to figure out the most theoretically sound ways of presenting math. "We could never have done this without each other," Cyndy emphasized. "It is so discouraging to spend an hour trying to track down an article at the library, only to discover someone has torn it out of the issue. But when we're together, we just laugh about it!"

They also surveyed parents and students and gathered many materials. As Edward Albee writes, sometimes you have to travel a long road to come back a short distance. Cyndy and Lynne have traveled all the way back to the beginning—they are now ready to find and frame a research question.

This point in Cyndy's and Lynne's evolution as teacher-researchers brings us back to our initial chapter about finding questions. Teacher research is a series of circles. Ultimately, it may take you all the way back to your first year of teaching, as Cyndy writes:

I remember my first year of teaching, when I would spend so much time reflecting on what was happening in my classroom. I would drive to and from school, thinking and thinking some more about what I was learning through my students. I've lost that conscious reflection slowly in the years since. Maybe it's all there in

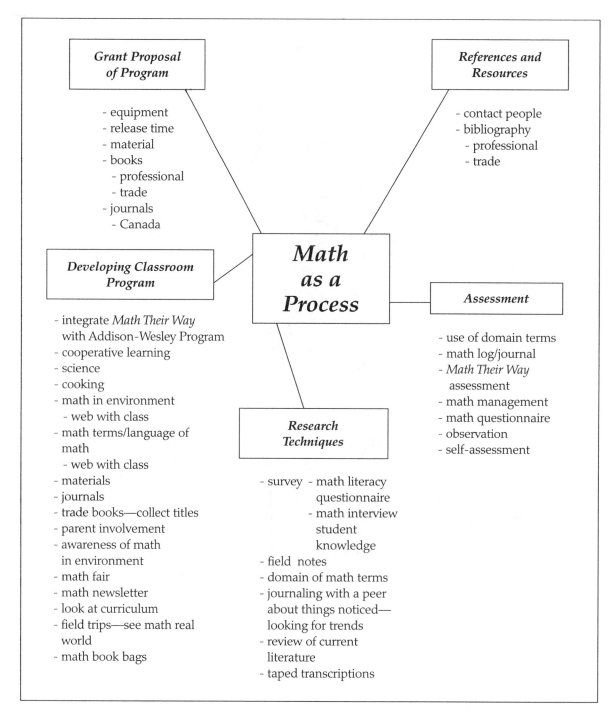

Grant Proposal of Program

- equipment
- release time
- material
- books
  - professional
  - trade
- journals
  - Canada

References and Resources

- contact people
- bibliography
  - professional
  - trade

Developing Classroom Program

- integrate *Math Their Way* with Addison-Wesley Program
- cooperative learning
- science
- cooking
- math in environment
  - web with class
- math terms/language of math
  - web with class
- materials
- journals
- trade books—collect titles
- parent involvement
- awareness of math in environment
- math fair
- math newsletter
- look at curriculum
- field trips—see math real world
- math book bags

Math as a Process

Assessment

- use of domain terms
- math log/journal
- *Math Their Way* assessment
- math management
- math questionnaire
- observation
- self-assessment

Research Techniques

- survey
  - math literacy questionnaire
  - math interview student knowledge
- field notes
- domain of math terms
- journaling with a peer about things noticed—looking for trends
- review of current literature
- taped transcriptions

FIGURE 7–1. *Learning Agenda*

my unconscious, but teacher research is bringing me back to the days when I spent all kinds of time reflecting on my students.

We hope this book is a beginning for you. It should raise as many questions about research processes as it answers. The next teacher-researcher text that matters for you is the one you will begin to write as research becomes a part of your life—through your research explorations in your school, the audiences with whom you share your wonderings, the new support networks you form.

By now you've realized that the research process is not an easy one for many teachers. And it's possible with all the pressures, constraints, and demands on your time that one more challenge—becoming a teacher-researcher—is not possible right now in your life. But we hope the enthusiasm of the teacher-researchers represented in this book leaps off the page. The challenge of inquiry has been valuable for many of them, as these researchers write:

> Struggle is not necessarily a negative phenomenon. It can be the creative process of moving outside the rigidity of the boxes we inhabit to create new identities for ourselves and new practices that may be useful to others. Like snakes we outgrow our skin, struggling to free ourselves of it, to become what might be, in the ongoing challenge of life. (Byrne-Armstrong, Higgs, and Horsfall 2001, 10)

If there is any profession that has been put in a rigid box in recent years, it is teaching. Teacher research isn't something you must do; we refuse to write that it's something you should do. We're weary of living in an education world that places ever-more demands on teachers to conform to outside standards, that presents half-baked theories and policies as edicts that must be followed. What we wish for you is what we've found for ourselves through our research—the joy in learning about ourselves and our students, which provides fuel for new dreams and possibilities. Throughout our teaching careers, inquiry has been *oxygen* for us; and we hope, at its root, your research can be a source of similar joy:

> There is pleasure in finding a voice; pleasure in writing and creativity; pleasure in the solitary nature of the writing process; pleasure in the rites of passage to greater understandings; pleasure in creating and recreating direction; pleasure in finally getting one's head around theory; pleasure at reinventing ourselves as competent researchers; pleasure in setting our own high standards and reaching them; pleasure because research provides, in many examples, a cliff edge at which

to test ourselves to see what we are capable of, and to wonder what will happen if. . . ? (Byrne-Armstrong, Higgs, and Horsfall 2001, 10)

This book is an invitation to learn more about yourselves and your students, to move from what is to *what-if?* in your classroom. May your inquiry questions lead you back to the pleasures in learning that brought you to teaching in the first place.

Research Designs

Research Design: Sharon Curtis Early

Origins of Your Question

I will have a gifted child who is also autistic in my sixth-grade class next year. I know that I will be doing a lot of reading and thinking about autistic children and about this student in particular in order to better understand him.

Question

How does a cooperative classroom influence an autistic/gifted child?

◆ During focused small-group work, what are the social interaction patterns of this child? Of other students?
◆ How does this student's writing change?
◆ How do his attitudes toward school and his behavior at home change?
◆ How is my teaching style affected?

Data Collection

I will videotape this student during small-group work at the beginning, middle, and end of the school year.

I'd like to have audiotapes of conferences with his mother and ideally, if she is willing, I'd like to have his mother journal about her son's behavior and how it reflects his attitude toward school. Perhaps the student himself will be able to journal and will be taped during conferences.

I will be journaling about my perceptions of the student and his social interactions—what I observe and what I learn.

Copies of his writings will be collected during the school year.

Reflecting

◆ I will analyze the type and frequency of interaction patterns as reflected on the videotapes.

◆ I will review my journal entries at least biweekly, looking for and reflecting on patterns I find.

◆ I will compare the journal entries of his mother with my observations at school.

Readings

I will be reviewing the literature on autism in general and autistic behavior in the classroom.

Research Design: Scott Christian

I. Purpose

My purpose in conducting this research is to determine the value of response logs as a tool for evaluating progress in a variety of areas. Since I will be making substantial changes in the format of the logs this year, I want to see if this change will enhance my understanding of the process that the students are engaged in.

II. Questions

How do response logs reflect students' progress as readers and writers? What conclusions can I draw from analyzing the progression of the responses over the school year?

These are the central questions which are the impetus for the study. However, I want to use the logs themselves to determine the specific question that I will look at for a given period of time. For instance, one of the following more specific questions may be selected during the year:

1. What are the levels of responses to literature (assigned or student-selected) that are occurring? How can I move the responses toward the analytical and away from plot summaries?
2. How do students select books to read?
3. How do they select topics for writing?
4. What is the most difficult aspect of the writing process for the students?
5. To what extent are the reasons for making changes during revision internalized? How dependent are they on response? Is response valuable?

6. What patterns are developing in terms of the sophistication or the risk-taking of the responses?
7. What kinds of dialogue develop between the teacher and the student in the log and why?

III. Method

I teach three seventh-grade Language Arts classes. Each class will turn in their logs on a different day during the week. I will focus each evening on two or three logs from the class which strike me as particularly revealing or insightful. I will be keeping a log and will record excerpts from the logs, will reflect on them and generalize on the process and form until I see something specific to evaluate. I want to focus on one specific question each semester. In other words, the data will provide the question.

As the year progressed last year, I found myself trying different techniques, dialogue entries with other students, modeling on the overhead, varying the time between when they were collected, altering my response, positive notes/calls, and so on, to parents in order to alter the nature of response. I want to be more analytic in that process this year to determine what is happening, what I should do, and how effective my actions are in regard to the specific question. Once the specific question in regard to the logs is determined (within the first two weeks of the quarter), I will also collect some very limited alternative data (i.e., brief questionnaires, comments from parents, comments from conferences and interviews, etc.). These will not be terribly involved but will mainly serve as a way to lend weight to my conclusions as they develop.

In terms of support, I will be meeting regularly with one of the members of my regional support group, as well as communicating with other workshop teachers. It is possible that the specific questions could arise from one of the other researchers as well as from the logs.

IV. Research

The program which is in place in my classroom is based on research regarding the areas of teaching reading and writing. Among the authors that were most influential are Nancie Atwell, James Moffet, and an article called "A Synthesis of Research on Teaching Writing," which validates several of the techniques that are used. Also, Bob Tierney originally inspired me to begin learning logs several years ago. I've experimented with different formats and structures and this year will be the application of what I've learned so far.

V. Calendar

Weeks 1–10
Get permissions. Formulate specific question #1. Keep teacher log, initial survey record.

Weeks 11–20
Consider form and begin draft 1 of phase 1. By the end of the quarter, have draft 1 complete. Discuss with other researchers.

Weeks 11–15
Select question #2. Revise draft 1. Begin writing draft 1 of phase 2. Have phase 1 readable, understandable before the meeting.

Weeks 16–20
Draw conclusions about process. Do final survey. Edit/revise both pieces. Final deadline for both pieces will be July 1.

Research Design: Carolyn Bowden

Research Purpose

In 1968, each of my second-grade students spoke English as a first language—with the exception of Andrew, a native Navajo student. Andrew understood a great deal, but spoke only a few words in English; he was forced into silence in a strange world far removed from his home and extended family in Arizona.

As I return to a teaching career, my goal is to teach to the strengths and needs of each child in my classroom or group. As I observed and volunteered in classrooms during the past year, I realized I would need to begin to study Spanish and earn an English for Speakers of Other Languages (ESOL) Endorsement if I hoped to meet the needs of all students in today's multicultural classrooms. The experience of learning a second language has taught me much more about the process of language acquisition, speaking, reading, and writing than any graduate course. I will never be truly bilingual, but I intend to continue studying Spanish. Linda Rief (1992, 14) wrote, "Most importantly, I must model my own process as a learner."—thus my question.

Research Question

How will a teacher modeling second language learning impact ESOL learners' English acquisition and literacy?

Subquestions

◆ Will modeling serve as a bridge to learn more about ESOL students, their background, and their interests?

- Will English-speaking students develop an interest in learning Spanish language and culture?
- How will the classroom as a multicultural learning community be affected?
- How will be make-up of the peer study groups be affected? Will they be more diverse?
- How will my best efforts in language learning impact parent–teacher communication?
- Will modeling my process encourage "fearful" ESOL students to speak?

I have no doubt that these questions will produce new questions that may be more relevant and important to our teaching and learning classroom.

Data Collection
- I will keep a teacher journal of anecdotal notes and involve students as teacher-researchers.
- I will tape student writing table conversations every eight weeks.
- I will survey students in September and in May. Possible questions include:
    - Do you ask other people at your writing/reading table questions?
    - Who do you ask for help?
    - What have you learned from other students in the classroom?
    - Who have you learned from?
    - Have you helped Mrs. Bowden speak/read Spanish? If so, tell me about the time.
- I will do sociograms in the fall and spring.
- I will videotape student groups at work on publishing projects.
- I will work to develop a parent survey after I research the questions, format, timing, translation, and cultural appropriateness, and so on.

Data Analysis
- I will review my teaching journal each week, noting significant learning events, social interactions.
- I will listen to the writing table discussion tape each quarter and note peer discussions in my teaching journal.
- I will review videotapes to see if other data patterns hold true here or offer different insights.
- I will analyze student surveys for trends and/or patterns.

Tentative Timeline

SEPTEMBER
- Talk to principal
- Send permission slips home
- Discuss plan with students and emphasize the importance of learning from one another
- Taperecord during the first week
- Start teaching journal first week

OCTOBER
- Review teaching journal and consider possible data coding

NOVEMBER
- Share research process with parents during conferences

MAY–JUNE
- Review and compile data.
- Reflect on process and application for next academic year
- Second student survey

SUMMER
- Reflect/revise/evaluate/plan

Reflections Before Beginning

In Annie Dillard's words (1989, 87), "A plan is a net for catching days." The frenetic pace of each school day can easily overwhelm any teacher's good intentions for keeping a journal, documenting, highlighting, recording student interactions and questions, and so on. I think this research plan is doable and will no doubt be the key to documenting my first year as a returning teacher.

Resources

CARY, STEPHEN. 2000. *Working with Second Language Learners: Answers to Teachers' Top Ten Questions*. Portsmouth, NH: Heinemann.

HUBBARD, RUTH, AND BRENDA POWER. 1999. *Living the Questions*. York, ME: Stenhouse.

IGOA, CHRISTINA. 1995. *The Inner Life of the Immigrant Child*. Mahwah, NJ: Lawrence Erlbaum.

RIEF, LINDA. 1992. *Seeking Diversity: Language Arts with Adolescents*. Portsmouth, NH: Heinemann.

Research Design: Julie Ford

Research Question

What impact does ability grouping have on academically low-level students, and what is the extent of the impact?

Discussion

My school district is currently dealing with the issue of gifted students and ways to meet their needs. With the upcoming state mandate related to this issue, the school board is wanting a districtwide policy on serving the gifted students in the classroom. Ability grouping is being considered as one of the best means of serving these kids. Although most of the school board members are in favor of such grouping, teachers have been speaking out for and against it. Those in favor of it often state that it is the most ideal way to meet the needs of all students. Those opposed to it often state that it provides unequal educational opportunities. Research related to this issue has yet to be conducted in the district though.

The teachers and school board are only part of the ability grouping equation. Students make up the final part of it. They are the ones most impacted by grouping decisions. On the basis of my observations, I know they also have feelings about it. When the students discover which groups they have been placed in, those in the average to high groups react more favorably than those in the lower groups.

In the grouping situations I have taught, students have made it a point to ask about the ability level of their placement. As a teacher, it has been far easier to tell a student placed in a higher group his or her level than it has been to tell a student placed in a lower group. I feel this way based on the student reaction I have encountered.

I wonder about the differences I've noticed in student's reactions to the information they receive. How is a student's self-concept affected by ability grouping? Are peer relations impacted in any way?

When I consider the teaching component of grouping, I recall faculty room chatter I've heard and the observations I've made. There have been teacher comments about the dropping of student expectations when the "lower-level" kids are taught. Those teaching the "higher levels," though, have instead shared exciting lessons about what's occurring in their classrooms. Comments about student behavior also crop up in a discussion on grouping. Many of the teachers of these "lower-level" students appear to be less eager to instruct them than those who teach the average to high groups. I wonder, How do teacher attitudes impact student performance levels, and how does grouping impact student behavior?

All teachers and students are impacted in some way when ability grouping occurs. Based on my own observations, though, it appears that the "lower-level" students are affected the most dramatically. Because of this, my intent is to focus on the "lower-level" students to find out exactly how they are affected and the extent to which grouping affects them. I then intend to present the results of my research to the school board to help them make a fully informed decision about grouping.

Methods of Data Collection

I feel that I am in a position to gather a variety of data. I have a sixth-grade homeroom classroom that is heterogeneously grouped for all students but reading and math. I am responsible for teaching a "high" reading group and a "low" math group. I am in a teaching situation that involves both mixed and ability groups.

I also teach in a rather large school. There are many teachers and students to interview, survey, and observe. The feelings on ability grouping vary, so data collected will not all sway to one point of view.

I intend to gather several kinds of data that will provide information on the social, emotional, and academic impacts of grouping. The methods for collecting this data are described next:

Surveys Surveys will be given to both homogeneous and heterogeneous groups, because I teach both. Surveys will also be given to teachers who instruct students in these groupings. The surveys will be anonymous to provide an element of safety when responding. The surveys will provide me with information about the students' and teachers' feelings about both homogeneous and heterogeneous classroom situations. Because the individuals from these two grouping methods are surveyed, social implications will be available to me.

Interviews To get more in-depth responses, I will conduct audiotaped interviews of both students and teachers. Again, I will gather information from the students in the various grouping situations and their teachers. The interviews will provide emotional (self-concept), social (peer relations and views of others), and academic (students' and teachers' attitudes and viewpoints about academic abilities) information.

Sociograms I will ask students of the varying grouping situations to list their individual choices for working partners and/or seating partners. I will ask students to first select choices within their classroom settings and then within the entire grade level. Information about peer relations will be the outcome of these sociograms.

Student Work I will look over students' papers for a variety of reasons including effort and quality. Papers from the various groupings will be collected so that comparisons can be made. Academic and emotional information will be provided through this data.

Student Records I will look at the attendance and behavior records of students from the different groupings.

Faculty Room Chatter I will take notes on the informal chatter about the different groups that I hear in the faculty room. In a stressless situation (unlike an interview), teachers may be more free in expressing their feelings about grouping.

Data Analysis

The results of *surveys and interviews* will be compiled and common responses will be looked for and listed.

For the *sociograms*, I will record student choice results onto circular diagrams. Arrows will denote student selections so that peer relations will be apparent. I will analyze the charts looking for specific choices between the differing groups. Do the students select in or out of their ability groups? Are there any trends?

As I took over the *student work*, I will record the results I find on a chart. I will took for different characteristics by group.

By ability group, I will list the findings from the *attendance and behavior records*. I will analyze the data I gather to see if similar information appears within each group. I will then compare the results across groupings.

I will record the *faculty room chatter* in columns related to whether they are positive or negative comments. I will then analyze the data to see if the comments made about the "lower-level" students tend to fall into positive or negative columns. I will also make special note of the academic expectations comments.

After gathering and analyzing these data, I will compile written "pictures" of the students in the various groupings. These written pictures will be compared so that the impact of ability grouping on "lower-level" students will be evident.

B

Data Collection Writing Strategies

Aha! Moments

Research Question

DATA POINT	WHY DOES IT STRIKE YOU?	REFLECTION ON WHAT IT MEANS

Two Things I Know for Sure

Inspired by Dorothy Allison's quote about her Aunt Dot:

"Lord, girl, there's only two or three things I know for sure." She put her head back, grinned, and made a small impatient noise. Her eyes glittered as bright as a sun reflecting off the scales of a cottonmouth's back. She spat once and shrugged. "Only two or three things. That's right," she said. "Of course it's never the same things, and I'm never as sure as I'd like to be." (Allison 1995, 5)

One finding I'm certain of in my research is . . .

What data led you to this conclusion?

What new data could make you change your mind?

One finding I'm certain of in my research is . . .

What data led you to this conclusion?

What new data could make you change your mind?

Data Collection and Analysis Mid-Point Check

Inquiry Question

Emerging Themes or Patterns

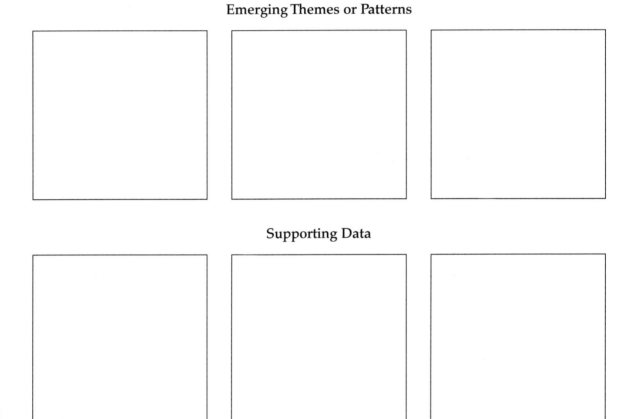

Supporting Data

What data sources are you using most of the time for your evidence?

What data sources are you rarely using?

What does this mean for how you might change your data collection and/or analysis in the next phase of your work?

Sample Field Notes

Field Notes #1—10:25–11:00 A.M.

These notes were taken during a World Lit class. The current material is African folktales, and the teacher, Lisa Arch (LA), has assigned the students to interpret or otherwise dramatize the tales in groups of 3–4, students being grouped by a 1–4 "count off" method which prevents buddying-up. There is wide latitude given for ways tales can be retold and some groups are devising visual props. Today is "rehearsal" day.

I choose to approach one group because they exude a boisterous, "macho" quality and I am interested to see how this will affect the process of interpreting a folktale, particularly because they've chosen to do a dramatic interpretation. I explain my task and they are quite affable about being observed. It soon becomes evident that their affect is greatly a result of lots of physical energy which they can use in this activity.

As a first-time ethnographer, I probably couldn't have picked a more difficult activity to follow. Rarely are any less than two students speaking at one time and sometimes all four! I soon postpone my attempts at verbatim transcribing until a more settled day and try to focus on movement and interaction.

The students in this group are:

Nabil (N)—a short, intense, and mature-seeming boy who is a new student this year from Lebanon. His English speech is excellent and contains very little accent. He is the narrator and briefly plays the farmer's son.
Tim (T)—a burly, cheerful, blond (longish hair), white male. He plays the lion.

Sean (S)—A tall white male whose long, somewhat sleepy features may at first belie his restless intensity. His deep voice has a way of commanding attention when he speaks out, which is often. He plays the farmer, the principal role.

David (D)—A tall (6′4″), black senior athlete. Also very affable and mild, he tends to hang in the background and these traits can mask the fact that he's quite attuned to what's going on. He has minor roles as the lion's son and a neighbor farmer.

Sean is also a senior and my guess is that Nabil and Tim are as well—though they may be juniors. Nabil has the most "preppy," clean-cut look. Sean and David are characteristically dressed in caps and T-shirts, Sean wearing jeans and David his usual sweats and high-tops. Tim wears a plaid wool shirt and jeans.

This group has been assigned a tale which recounts the original friendship between a farmer and a lion and their separation over a period of years which results in the farmer killing the lion when he fails to recognize his old friend. This is said to be the reason Man and Lion now avoid each other.

David provides an initial direction.

D: Let's go out in the hall. It's too noisy in here.
They straggle outside, milling around, arms flapping. They're waiting for Nabil who's clarifying something with LA.
T: How does he say his name . . . Nabl . . . Nabel?
LA: He knows your names, I think you can try to know his.
N: It's Nabil (pronounced Na-beel).
T, D and S are lined up now, backs to the lockers, as if waiting for something. N takes charge.
N: Do you all know what you're doing?
At this point almost nonstop cross talk begins. T goes over some of the physical mechanics of his performance. S acts out his entrance: "I'll do this . . . I'll do this."
T: No, I go over here when S goes back to his house.

Things are on the verge of becoming listless and unfocused. Nabil, who is "on-task" in an impressively persistent, yet not pushy, manner (is this why he's got the narrator role?) quickly steps into the vacuum. He talks quite a bit to Tim who, though rather passive, is available and compliant, and through him Nabil actually begins to direct the process. He does this without being bossy or officious. He simply keeps talking and bringing the group back to the "script." T and D follow this lead, while S is willing to attend to his part when it's time, but otherwise roams off, his arms and torso swinging around loosely and restlessly.

D, because he has a minor part, lingers at the edges. But he manages to follow the process fairly closely, maintaining his pleasant, dreamy expression. After a sketchy runthrough, it is D who suggests they go through the whole thing again.

N: I walk on first.

S: No, say "the hunter is leaving . . ."

N: The hunter leaves . . . T crosses to "go to sleep" on the hunter's doorstep. S discovers him.

T: This is my land too!
They shake and become friends.

S: You do the hunting, I'll do the farming.
N at this point questions how the two will show fatigue with their roles. N is doing a lot of focusing for the group at this point, clarifying problems and gently offering suggestions. Sean starts talking with a student who's poked his head outside the room.

T/N *(in unison)*: Why don't you guys *(sic)* listen?

S: I'm getting tired and I want to . . .
He looks awkward and embarrassed as JoAnne, a quite self-possessed senior, comes up to her locker.

J: No, that's really cool, I was listening.

The rehearsal settles down at this point, S and T acting out their principal roles, D watching, N filling in narration and supplying low-key impetus with his attentiveness and clarity. He seems intelligent and verbally competent. I wonder if reading or writing are problems for him.

An aide strides up with a box of papers.

AIDE: Can you open the door?

S *(joking)*: Don't interrupt me!
A crucial scene—S shoots T, the lion.

D: You need a drama class!
D, who up to now has only a silent role as a neighboring farmer, gets his big moment as the lion's cub.

D: Father, father, what have they done?

His statement and kneeling gesture are so emotive and convincing that we are all momentarily stunned. We've just seen a bit of real acting! N sums up the "moral" of the story. They (and I) clap. S says, "We'll be too nervous." They mill around, looking through the window of the door.

D: How are we going to use the room? Where will we set up?

They go into the room and return to their corner where they mill around quietly for awhile, N and T try to get S, who's acting more distractible, going again. They decide to move to the front of the classroom and I remain in back where I can't really hear, but can watch. N is still the hub, he and T doing most of the work. S continues to space out, twice initiating conversations with students from other groups, the second time pulling his whole group in. T, N, and D return to business, but S continues to chat with his friend Matt and soon they are chasing each other with marking pens. There is brief tension as Matt appears on the verge of anger. Possibly because of this, S suggests they go back into the hall.

After going into the hall, David suggests they move to the outside landing. I follow and volunteer to stop writing and critique a full runthrough. With only a few diversions—usually due to S's self-conscious "straying" after a line or action—they act out their parts efficiently, using the space well. I compliment them on this and suggest they be clear about their minor characters. They seem satisfied by what they've achieved and I wonder how it will go in front of the class.

Observations/Conclusions

No other group (even though another is doing a dramatic interpretation) puts anywhere near the amount of physical activity into their analysis/rehearsal. My group spends the entire period on their feet, leaving the room twice to practice in the halls and outside the building. They also attempt to use the front of the room.

The Nabil/Tim axis, and their ability to keep the distractive and energetic Sean and his major role "on-task," is the key here. Sean, Tim, and David all exhibit, at times, a shyness or self-deprecating attitude which probably stems in part from past academic difficulties. Nabil, on the other hand, is the most impressive in the mature and consistent low-key way he holds things together. Sean actually takes over briefly at times—as much, I sense, to get hold of himself as anything—and Nabil is always willing to let this happen. I suspect he takes the lead because no one else will and he just wants to get the job done.

They are all aware that they're getting a group grade and of LA's admonition that they can fail by their weakest link; this is a strategy on her part to encourage groups to integrate all members. Nabil seems the most consistently aware of this condition. Because he's a "new kid," and possibly because he's a "foreigner," his management role must walk a line between direction and taking over. Were he not so adroit at backing off his role when others assert themselves, he might spark friction and rejection.

A certain, possibly unspoken (I was not in on their initial sorting-out meeting) balance has been struck here and it works. This can be seen by the fact that on a number of key occasions it is David who makes pivotal suggestions which all agree to! What's impressive overall though is that these four low achievers have had the discipline and caring to put themselves through three different rehearsals, improving each time. I deliberately remained in the back of the room later in the period to see if their coherence would dissipate out of range of my scrutiny. But after Sean's escapade with Matt, they pulled themselves together and found a new site for their final successful try. Up to this point, I don't think they were at all confident about pulling it off. I see Nabil's influence as pivotal but I think it's merely a kind of prompting the other three needed (which they possibly recognized by letting Nabil organize them) to begin to produce and feel competent—something which, whether or not they know it, they want to do!

Writing—Starting with a Word and Writing Quotes

Writing—Starting with a Word

If writing a book is impossible, write a chapter.

If writing a chapter is impossible, write a page.

If writing a page is impossible, write a paragraph.

If writing a paragraph is impossible, write a sentence.

If writing a sentence is impossible, write a word and teach yourself everything there is to know about that word and then write another, connected word and see where the connection leads.

—Richard Rhodes

Go through your notebooks, sticky notes, or any data-analysis material and find three individual words that appear numerous times, and that you think are critical for understanding your findings. Freewrite about the importance of each one.

WORD 1:

WORD 2:

WORD 3:

Favorite Quotes on Writing

The beautiful part of writing is that you don't have to get it right the first time, unlike, say, a brain surgeon.
—Robert Cormier

Close the door. Write with no one looking over your shoulder. Don't try to figure out what other people want to hear from you; figure out what you have to say. It's the one and only thing you have to offer.
—Barbara Kingsolver

I learned that you should feel when writing, not like Lord Byron on a mountain top, but like a child stringing beads in kindergarten—happy, absorbed and quietly putting one bead on after another.
—Brenda Ueland

I am irritated by my own writing. I am like a violinist whose ear is true, but whose fingers refuse to reproduce precisely the sound he hears within.
—Gustave Flaubert

If the doctor told me I had six minutes to live, I'd type a little faster.
—Isaac Asimov

I find that the harder I work, the more luck I seem to have.
—Thomas Jefferson

It is good to have an end to journey towards; but it is the journey that matters in the end.
—Ursula K. LeGuin

Only those who risk going too far can possibly find out how far one can go.
—T. S. Eliot

Writers seldom write the things they think. They simply write the things they think other folks think they think.
—Elbert Hubbard

All words are pegs to hang ideas on.
—Henry Ward Beecher

The faster I write the better my output. If I'm going slow I'm in trouble. It means I'm pushing the words instead of being pulled by them.
—Raymond Chandler

Read, read, read. Read everything—trash, classics, good and bad, and see how they do it. Just like a carpenter who works as an apprentice and studies the master. Read! You'll absorb it. Then write. If it's good, you'll find out. If it's not, throw it out of the window.
—William Faulkner

Why do people always expect authors to answer questions? I am an author because I want to ASK questions. If I had answers I'd be a politician.
—Eugene Ionesco

I'm astounded by people who take eighteen years to write something. That's how long it took that guy to write Madame Bovary, and was that ever on the best-seller list?
—Sylvester Stallone

A single word often betrays a great design.
—Jean Racine

Writing is the only thing that, when I do it, I don't feel I should be doing something else.
—Gloria Steinem

Half my life is an act of revision.
—John Irving

The only time I know that something is true is the moment I discover it in the act of writing.
—Jean Malaquais

A blank piece of paper is God's way of showing a writer how hard it is to be God.
— Joel Saltzman

I love deadlines. I love the whooshing sound they make as they fly by.
—Douglas Adams

Good writers do not litter their sentences with adverbial garbage. They do not hold up signs reading "laughter!" or "applause!" The content of dialogue ought to suggest the mood.
—James J. Kilpatrick

Remember that you should be able to identify each character by what he or she says. Each one must sound different from the others. And they should not all sound like you.
—Anne Lamott

Advice to aspiring writers: Fasten your seat belts—it's going to be a bumpy ride.
—Christopher Buckley

You will never be satisfied with what you do.
—Fay Weldon

If you want to write, you can. Fear stops most people from writing, not lack of talent, whatever that is. Who am I? What right have I to speak? Who will listen to me if I do? You're a human being, with a unique story to tell, and you have every right. If you speak with passion, many of us will listen. We need stories to live, all of us. We live by story. Yours enlarges the circle.
—Richard Rhodes

My own best advice to young writers is: follow your curiosity and passion. What fascinates you will probably fascinate others. But, even if it doesn't, you will have devoted your life to what you love. An important corollary is that it's no use trying to write like someone else. Discover what's uniquely yours.
—Diane Acherman

Put your notes away before you begin a draft. What you remember is probably what should be remembered; what you forget is probably what should be forgotten. No matter; you'll have a chance to go back to your notes after the draft is completed. What is important is to achieve a draft which allows the writing to flow.
—Donald M. Murray

Cut out all those exclamation marks. An exclamation mark is like laughing at your own joke.
—F. Scott Fitzgerald

Short paragraphs put air around what you write and make it look inviting, whereas one long chunk of type can discourage the reader from even starting to read.
—William Zinsser

Keep in mind that the person to write for is yourself. Tell the story that you most desperately want to read.
—Susan Isaacs

Don't get it right, get it written.
—James Thurber

The secret of good writing is to say an old thing in a new way or to say a new thing in an old way.
—Richard Harding Davis

Most people quit. If you don't quit, if you rewrite, if you keep publishing in fancier places, you will understand that "What's the secret?" is not *the question,* which is, Are you having fun?"
—Robert Lipsyt

Resources for Publication

We encourage you to start a file of potential publication resources for yourself and the teachers in your support group. There are many outlets for the writings of teacher-researchers. Consider local affiliates of national organizations for regional publications, for example. For a wider audience, we suggest more general educational journals. The following publications welcome diverse contributors. (For specific publishing guidelines, go to their homepages or write to the editors enclosing a stamped, self-addressed envelope.)

Networks: An Online Journal for Teacher Research
> The Managing Editor, *Networks*
> Department of Education
> University of California at Santa Cruz
> 1156 High Street
> Santa Cruz, CA 95064
> Email: gwells@cats.ucsc.edu
> *www.oise.utoronto.ca/~ctd/networks/*

Teaching and Learning: The Journal of Natural Inquiry and Reflective Practice
> Box 7819
> University of North Dakota
> Grand Forks, ND 58202-7189
> Email: jeanette_bropy@und.nodak.edu
> *www.und.nodak.edu/dept/ehd/journal/center.html*

Rethinking Schools
  1001 E. Keefe Avenue
  Milwaukee, WI 53212
  www.rethinkingschools.org

Curriculum Inquiry
  The Ontario Institute for Studies in Education
  252 Bloor Street West
  Toronto, Ontario M5S IV6 Canada
  fcis.oise.utoronto.ca/~ci/

Anthropology and Education Quarterly
  University of Arizona
  Department of Language, Reading, and Culture
  College of Education Building, Room 512
  1430 East Second Street
  Tucson, AZ 85721-0069
  www.aaanet.org/cae/aeq/

QSE: International Journal of Qualitative Studies in Education
        Contact *www.tandf.co.uk/journals/*

The New Advocate
  Department of Reading, Language, and Culture
  512 College of Education
  PO Box 210069
  University of Arizona
  Tucson, AZ 85721-0069

Radical Teacher
        c/o Larry Hanley
        Department of English
        City College of New York
        135th and Convent Ave.
        New York, NY 10031
        www.wpunj.edu/radteach/

Incentive Education
Project Proposal Form

Applicant's Name: *Marie Grove*

1. **Project synopsis (50 words or less)**

   This project involves the establishment, maintenance, and study of a self-contained saltwater ecosystem in an aquarium. Using the saltwater aquarium as a catalyst, students will use an interdisciplinary approach to investigate the interrelationship and interdependence between the marine plants and animals in the ecosystem, to explore various issues relating to saltwater ecology, and to study Delaware's coastal saltwater areas and aquatic organisms native to our state.

2. **Equipment and/or materials needed for project**

   One 55-gallon aquarium tank, one wet/dry (filtering) system, a lighting system, one sterilizer, gravel, salt, one hydrometer, one heater, one thermometer, and one test kit (to test pH and nitrate levels).

   Money will also be needed to stock the aquarium (e.g., to buy invertebrates and plants to put in the tank, etc.).

3. **Indicate the educational significance of the project**

   a. **Problem or need to be addressed:**

   This project provides equipment, hands-on experiences, and a much-needed catalyst for marine aquatic instruction. Because of our school's location, students do not have access to the natural habitat of these marine plants and animals. By establishing a saltwater aquarium with marine plants and invertebrates, our students will have the opportunity to experience and study a marine ecosystem up close.

   Through the exploration of various issues relating to saltwater ecology (water pollution, etc.), students will develop an appreciation of water as a precious resource, and students will develop an awareness and knowledge that will hopefully result in informed decisions about environmental issues.

This project is also needed to help develop our students' observational skills and to help develop their techniques for gathering, recording, organizing, interpreting, and communicating scientific information.

b. Major activities:

The saltwater aquarium will be used as a catalyst for the study of many things. Using an interdisciplinary approach involving science, math, reading, English, and so on, students will do the following:

1. Identify and research a variety of saltwater aquatic plants and animals
2. Develop "biographies" of the aquatic organisms using school or public library sources and state and federal agency sources—have an aquatic poster contest using the research results
3. Study the life cycles of various saltwater animals from birth to adult stages and draw the changes that occur
4. Study the mating behavior of animals in the aquarium
5. Observe and describe any schooling behavior and territorialism (pecking orders) that may occur
6. Use taxonomy keys to classify organisms in the tank
7. Research aquatic environments as food sources (research the use of algae and seaweed derivatives)
8. Try some aquatic recipes in class (algae pudding)
9. Study the components of a habitat that are essential for most aquatic animals to survive; Examine and experiment with slight changes in temperature, salinity, pH, dissolved oxygen, and the presence of a pollutant
10. Study the effects of water quality on the organisms—identify and research the major sources of aquatic pollution (chemical, thermal, organic, etc.), describe the effects of a variety of pollutants by experimenting with them (raising the temperature, etc.)
11. Study and identify the range of conditions that each lifeform (plant and animal) can tolerate, including such things as deep versus shallow water, moving versus static water, etc.
12. Test, monitor, and graph pH levels and study the effect it has on the organisms

13. Study and diagram the carbon dioxide/oxygen cycle and the nitrogen cycle in the tank
14. Study how salinity affects the distribution of some aquatic animals
15. Describe and draw the way saltwater animals move
16. Describe how saltwater animals get their food and how they protect themselves from predators
17. Describe any adaptations the marine animals may have developed to survive in their habitat
18. Investigate if water pressure varies at different depths (do pressure ratings)
19. Take quantitative measurements of the lengths of the organisms
20. Test, chart, and graph the changes in dissolved oxygen levels as the water temperature increases—describe how animals respond to low-oxygen environments
21. Investigate the special structures that enable fish to stay up in the water and to move in the water—teacher possibly conducts a fish dissection demonstration
22. Study the surface of the water (surface tension)—have a contest to design a model organism that rides on surface tension
23. Investigate how tiny, drifting animals keep from sinking to the bottom—have a contest to design an organism that sinks the slowest
24. Investigate how fish swim—study the correlations between body shape, swimming technique, and speed
25. Study the relationship between light availability and photosynthesis in aquatic plants
26. Study parasitology
27. Use the tank to raise plant and animal species native to Delaware
28. Describe and draw the food web in the self-contained saltwater habitat—describe the interrelatedness of various aquatic plants and animals, including the roles of the producers (plants) and consumers (animals)

In addition, the teacher will arrange for a visit/presentation by a marine education specialist from the College of Marine Studies Sea Grant Office in Lewes, DE, to discuss marine ecology, marine organisms, and so on, OR arrange for a visit by state fish and wildlife agency personnel to discuss native fish and native marine organisms.

The teacher will arrange for a visit to the National Aquarium in Baltimore to explore the diversity of marine life.

The class will present a mini-program (learning exposition) to the entire school population about the marine plants and animals, the research reports, and experiment results (charts, graphs, drawings, etc.).

c. **Evaluation procedures:**

Observations of students' behavior and attitudes will be made to determine if students have developed an awareness and appreciation of water as a precious, life-sustaining resource. Observations will also be made to determine if students can explain the interrelationship and interdependence between marine plants and animals.

The quality of students' written reports, experiment results, drawings, graphs, charts, and so on, will be examined to determine whether students understood the scientific concepts involved in the project, whether they learned about marine life, and whether they were able to use observational skills and techniques of gathering, recording, organizing, interpreting, and communicating scientific information effectively.

4. **Indicate curricular objectives to be addressed by this project**

The following curricular objectives relate to this project: The student will be able to:

1. Build and maintain a terrarium and/or aquarium
2. Collect and record data (kinds of organisms, number of different organisms, food sources of organisms, space availability for organisms) about populations observed in a classroom aquarium
3. Test the water in an aquarium to see whether it has acid-base properties
4. State what environmental factors marine plants and animals need to grow and reproduce
5. Identify similarities and differences in marine animals on the basis of body parts
6. Identify a producer, a consumer, and a decomposer
7. Describe the behavioral and physical adaptations of aquatic plants and animals that allow them to live successfully in their environment
8. Describe food source relationships among populations
9. Construct a food chain to show producers and consumers
10. Order the stages in the life cycle of various marine animals

11. Discuss the effects of water, light, and food on plant growth
12. List reasons for protecting our water resources
13. Diagram an energy food web
14. Describe the water, oxygen, carbon, and nitrogen cycle
15. Develop techniques of gathering, recording, organizing, interpreting, and communicating scientific information
16. Develop the skill of observation

5. **Indicate the number of students to be served and the grade and/or subject**

Initially, the aquarium will be placed in one fourth-grade classroom of 29 students so that those students can use an interdisciplinary approach to closely observe the tank, conduct experiments, make observations, and so on. However, eventually the tank will be moved to a more central school location (lobby) for view of the entire school population of more than 500 students in grades 1–5.

In addition, all students in the school will be able to learn about marine ecology and marine life through our mini-program presented to the school.

6. **Indicate any plans for coordination and cooperation between grades and teams at the elementary level and subject areas at the secondary level**

The entire school population will be able to learn about marine ecology and marine life through our mini-program presented to the school.

The entire school population will be able to observe the tank when it is moved to a more central school location (the lobby).

7. **Indicate any plans to integrate the equipment and/or materials requested in this project with others that presently exist**

Participation in many of the aquarium activities previously outlined, including the taking of quantitative measurements and the charting and graphing of oxygen and pH levels, will enable the students to use and practice many of the math skills taught in the Holt Mathematics series currently being used. In addition, as part of our grade level's study of state history, the tank will be used as a catalyst to study Delaware's coastal saltwater areas and aquatic plants and animals native to our state. (The tank will be used to raise plant and animal species native to Delaware.)

8. **Total project cost:** $1,300.00
   Amount requested: $1,000.00

_____

Applicant's Signature

References

Allen, JoBeth, and Linda Labbo. 2001. "Giving It a Second Thought: Making Culturally Engaged Teaching Culturally Engaging." *Language Arts* 79 (1): 40–52.

Allison, Dorothy. 1995. *Two or Three Things I Know for Sure.* New York: Penguin.

Anderson, Michael. 2003. *"Reading Violence in Boys' Writing." Language Arts* 80 (3): 223–30.

Anderson, Laurie Halse. 1999. *Speak.* New York: Farrar, Strauss, and Giroux.

Atwell, Nancie. 1991. "Wonderings to Pursue." In *Literacy in Process,* edited by Brenda Miller Power and Ruth Hubbard 315–33. Portsmouth, NH: Heinemann.

Austin, Terry. 1991. Personal communication.

———. 1995. A Little Too Little and a Lot Too Much. Presentation at AERA, San Francisco, CA.

Bargar, R. R., and J. K. Duncan. 1982. "Cultivating Creative Endeavor in Doctoral Research." *Journal of Higher Education* 53 (1): 1–31.

Bisplinghoff, Betty Shockley. 2002. "Teacher Planning as Responsible Resistance. *Language Arts* 80 (2) 119–33.

Bissex, Glenda L. 1987. "What Is a Teacher-Researcher?" In *Seeing for Ourselves: Case-Study Research by Teachers of Writing,* edited by Glenda L. Bissex and Richard H. Bullock. Portsmouth, NH: Heinemann.

———. 1996. *Partial Truths.* Portsmouth, NH: Heinemann.

Boyatzis, Richard. 1998. *Transforming Qualitative Information: Thematic Analysis and Code Development.* Thousand Oaks, CA: Sage Publications.

Boyd, T. A. 1961. *Prophet of Progress: Selections from the Speeches of Charles F. Kettering.* New York: Dutton.

Bryne-Armstrong, Hilary, Joy Higgs, and Debbie Horsfall. 2001. *Critical Moments in Qualitative Research.* Woburn, MA: Butterworth-Heinemann.

Calkins, Lucy. 1983. *Lessons from a Child.* Portsmouth, NH: Heinemann.

————. 1986. "Forming Research Communities Among Naturalistic Researchers." In *Perspectives on Research and Scholarship in Composition,* edited by Ben McClelland and T. Donovan, 96–115. New York: Modern Language Association.

Carver, Raymond. 1983. *Fires.* Santa Barbara, CA: Capra Press.

Chandler, Kelly, and the Mapleton Teacher Researchers. 1999. *Spelling Inquiry.* York, ME: Stenhouse.

Cole, K. C. 1988. "Play, by Definition, Suspends the Rules." *New York Times,* 30 November, p. 36.

Corsaro, William. 1981. "Entering the Child's World: Research Strategies for Field Entry and Data Collection in a Preschool Setting." In *Ethnography and Language in Educational Settings,* edited by J. Green and C. Wallach, 77–89. Norwood, NJ: Ablex Publishing.

Crowl, Julia. 1991. Teacher Research: Principles, Practices, and Techniques. Paper presented at National Council of Teachers of English Fall Conference, November, Seattle, WA.

Cunningham, Andie, and Ruth Hubbard. 2003. Of Kindergartens and Tidepools. Unpublished NCTE proposal.

Dillard, Annie. 1987. "To Fashion a Text." In *Inventing the Truth,* edited by Howard Zinsser, 53–76. Boston: Houghton Mifflin.

————. 1989. *The Writing Life.* New York: Harper and Row.

Dyson, Anne Haas. 2003. *The Brothers and Sisters Learn to Write: Popular Literacies in Childhood and School Cultures.* New York: Teachers College Press.

Eisner, Elliot. 1991. *The Enlightened Eye: Qualitative Inquiry and the Enhancement of Educational Practice.* New York: Macmillan.

Farley, Lisia. 1990. Unpublished research proposal.

Fletcher, Ralph. 1996. *Breathing In, Breathing Out.* Portsmouth, NH: Heinemann.

Gallas, Karen. 1998. *Sometimes I Can Be Anything.* New York: Teachers College Press.

George, Nelson. 1998. *Hip Hop America.* New York: Viking.

Gillespie, Tim. 2000. Stories and the Teaching Life. Keynote address at Lewis & Clark College Teacher Research Symposium, May, Portland, OR.

Glaser, Barney. 1978. *Theoretical Sensitivity.* Mill Valley, CA: Sociology Press.

Glaser, Barney, and Anselm Strauss. 1967. *Discovery of Grounded Theory: Strategies for Qualitative Research.* Chicago: Aldine Publishing.

Glazier, Debbie. 1996. "Fast and Easy." *Teacher Research Journal* 4 (1): 113–15.

Glesne, Corrine. 1999. *Becoming Qualitative Researchers.* 2nd ed. New York: Longman.

Goldberg, Natalie. 1990. *Wild Mind: Living the Writer's Life.* New York: Bantam Books.

Grandin, Temple. 1996. *Thinking in Pictures and Other Reports from My Life with Autism.* New York: Vintage Books.

Hankins, Karen. 1998. "Cacophony to Symphony: Memoir in Teacher Research." In *Engaging Teachers,* edited by Betty Shockley Bisplinghoff and JoBeth Allen, 13–16. Portsmouth, NH: Heinemann.

Heard, Georgia. 1995. *Writing Toward Home: Tales and Lessons to Find Your Way.* Portsmouth, NH: Heinemann.

Heath, Shirley Brice. 1998. Keynote Address. Qualitative Research Special Interest Group at the American Educational Research Association Annual Meeting, Montreal, May.

Hellman, Lillian. 1973. *Pentimento.* New York: Plume Books.

Henry, Jeanne. 1995. *If Not Now.* Portsmouth, NH: Heinemann.

Hinchman, Hannah. 1997. *A Trail Through the Leaves: The Journal as a Path to Place.* New York: W. W. Norton.

Hoffman, Alice. 2001. "Sustaining by Fiction While Facing Life's Facts." In *Writers on Writing,* edited by John Darden, 75–98. New York: New York Times Books.

Hubbard, Ruth. 1988. "Unofficial Literacy in a Sixth-Grade Classroom." *Language Arts* 65 (2): 126–34.

Hurtig, Caryl. 1996. "One Long Line." In *Oops: What We Learn When Our Teaching Fails,* edited by Brenda Power and Ruth Hubbard, 63–67. York, ME: Stenhouse.

Hurwitz, Brynna. 1996. "Flowing with the Go." *Teacher Research Journal* 3 (2): 115–23.

Janesick, Valerie J. 2000. "The Choreography of Qualitative Research Design: Minuets, Improvisations, and Crystallization." In *Handbook of Qualitative Research,* edited by Denzin and Lincoln, 66–81. Thousand Oaks, CA: Sage Publications.

Johnson, George. 1991. *In the Palace of Memory: How We Build Worlds Inside Our Heads.* New York: Alfred A. Knopf.

John-Steiner, Vera. 1985. *Notebooks of the Mind.* Albuquerque: University of New Mexico Press.

Kaltenbach, Shirley. 1991. A Little Too Little and a Lot Too Much. Presentation at AERA, San Francisco, CA.

Koyritzin, Sandra. 1999. *Facets of First Language Lost.* Mahwah, NJ: Lawrence Erlbaum.

Lamott, Anne. 1994. *Bird by Bird: Some Instructions on Writing and Life.* New York: Doubleday.

Lane, Barry. 1996. "One, Two, Buy Velcro Shoes: What Greg Taught Me." In *Oops: What We Learn When Our Teaching Fails,* edited by Brenda Power and Ruth Hubbard, 3–6. York, ME: Stenhouse.

Le Corbusier. 1946. *Towards a New Architecture.* Translated by Frederick Etchells. London: The Architectural Press. (First published as *Vers une architecutre.* Paris: Editions Cres, 1923.)

Lévi-Strauss, Claude. 1968. *Structural Anthropology.* New York: Penguin.

Macrorie, Ken. 1987. "Research as Odyssey." In *Reclaiming the Classroom: Teacher Research as an Agency for Change,* edited by Dixie Goswami and Peter Stillman, 49–58. Portsmouth, NH: Boynton/Cook.

Marshall, Catherine, and Gretchen Rossman. 1989. *Designing Qualitative Research.* Thousand Oaks, CA: Sage Publications.

McBride, Mekeel. 1985. Poetry reading. Durham, NH.

McCracken, Janelle. 1994. "Family Nights: Building Strong Home and School Connections." *Teacher Research* 1 (2): 169–79.

Meier, Deborah. 1995. *The Power of Their Ideas.* New York: Beacon Press.

Mersereau, Yvonne, and Mary Glover. 1990. "Surrounded by Angels." *Language Arts* 67 (4): 354–61.

Miles, Matthew, and A. Michael Huberman. 1984. *Qualitative Data Analysis.* Thousand Oaks, CA: Sage Publications.

Miller, Debbie. 2002. *Reading with Meaning.* Portland, ME: Stenhouse.

Moreno, Jacob. 1953. *Who Shall Survive? Foundations of Sociometry, Group Psychotherapy, and Sociodrama.* New York: Beacon House.

Murray, Donald. 1990. *Shoptalk: Learning to Write with Writers.* Portsmouth, NH: Boynton/Cook.

Nachmanovitch, Stephen. 1990. *Free Play: Improvisation in Life and Art.* Los Angeles: Jeremy P. Tarcher.

Newkirk, Tom. 2002. *Misreading Masculinity.* Portsmouth, NH: Heinemann.

Oldani, Mark. 1991. "Biased Achievement Tests Not Most Crucial Yardstick" (Op-Ed article). *The Oregonian,* 26 February, Metro Section, D5.

Ostrow, Jill. 2003. Personal communication.

Patton, Michael. 2002. *Qualitative Research and Evaluation Methods.* 3rd ed. Thousand Oaks, CA: Sage Publications.

Piercy, Marge. 1991. "Starting Support Groups for Writers." In *Literacy in Process,* edited by Brenda Power and Ruth Hubbard, 15–16. Portsmouth, NH: Heinemann.

Pollack, William. 1998. *Real Boys: Rescuing Our Sons from the Myths of Boyhood.* New York: Henry Holt.

Proulx, Annie. 2001. "Inspiration? Head Down the Back Road and Stop for Yard Sales." In *Writers on Writing: Collected Essays from the New York Times,* edited by John Darnton, 185–99. New York: New York Times Press.

Reilly, Kathleen. 1995. "Making New Audiences: Moving Through Classroom Walls." *Teacher Research Journal* 2: 49–60.

Rhodes, Richard. 1996. *How to Write: Advice and Reflections.* New York: Quill.

Richardson, Laurel. 2000. "Writing: A Method of Inquiry." In *Handbook of Qualitative Research,* edited by N. K. Denzin and Y. S. Lincoln, 516–29. Thousand Oaks, CA: Sage Publications.

Ridington, Robin. 1990. *Little Bit Know Something: Stories in the Anthropology of Language.* Iowa City: University of Iowa Press.

Rief, Linda. 1992. *Seeking Diversity: Language Arts with Adolescents.* Portsmouth, NH: Heinemann.

Rilke, Rainer Maria. 1934. *Letters to a Young Poet. Letter Number 4.* Translated by D. Herter. New York: W. W. Norton.

Rubin, Herbert J., and Irene S. Rubin. 1995. *Qualitative Interviewing: The Art of Hearing Data.* Thousand Oaks, CA: Sage Publications.

Sax, G. 1989. *Principles of Educational and Psychological Measurement and Evaluation.* Belmont, CA: Beacon House.

Schatzman, L., and Anselm Strauss. 1973. *Field Research.* Englewood Cliffs, NJ: Prentice-Hall.

Simpson, Richard, Brenda Myles, Gary Sasso, and Debra Kamps. 1991. *Social Skills for Students with Autism.* Washington, DC: Council for Exceptional Children.

Sims, Norman. 1984. *The Literary Journalists.* New York: Ballantine Books.

Sommers, C. H. 2000. *The War Against Boys.* New York: Simon & Schuster.

Sullivan, Louis. [1924] 1956. *The Autobiography of an Idea.* New York: Dover.

Vygotsky, Lev. S. 1962. *Thought and Language.* Cambridge, MA: MIT Press.

Weaver, Constance. 1988. *Reading Process and Practice: From Socio-Psycholinguistics to Whole Language.* Portsmouth, NH: Heinemann.

Webb, E. J., D. T. Campbell, R. D. Schwartz, and L. Sechrest. 1965. *Unobstrusive Measures.* Chicago: Rand McNally.

Wilhelm, Jeffrey. 1996. "To Make Reading Visible." *Teacher Research* 4 (1): 52–62.

Wilkinson, Lyn. 1989. "When Teaching's as Exciting as Christmas!" *Language Arts* 66 (7): 749–55.

Willard, Charlotte. 1972. *Frank Lloyd Wright.* New York: Macmillan.

Wolcott, Harry. 1992. *The Art of Fieldwork.* London: Altamira Press.

Yin, Robert. 1989. *Case Study Research: Design and Methods.* Thousand Oaks, CA: Sage Publications.

Index